PHILIP CAPUTO HAS WRITTEN A TIME-
LESS TESTAMENT TO THE MEN WHO
LEAVE THEIR HOMES TO KILL AND DIE
IN STRANGE LANDS...AND OF THE
THINGS THAT GROW AND PERISH IN
THE DEEPEST PART OF THEMSELVES.

A RUMOR OF WAR

"UNFORGETTABLE...gripping, infuriating,
cruelly honest, forcefully written."
—*Chicago Daily News*

"POWERFUL, COMPELLING...A thoroughly
honest view of what the experience of Vietnam
meant to a young college graduate, a 'gung-
ho' lieutenant in the Marine Corps who enlisted for the 'heroic experience' of war...IT IS
THE MOST ELOQUENT STATEMENT YET ON
WHAT VIETNAM WAS FOR THE LOWER ECH-
ELONS WHO HAD TO DO THE DIRTY WORK."
—*Seattle Times*

(more)

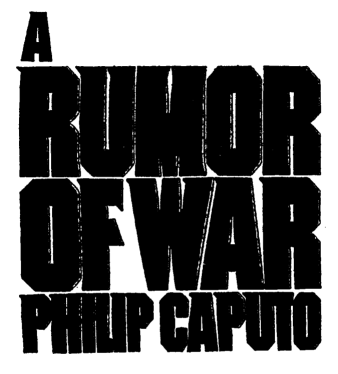

A RUMOR OF WAR

PHILIP CAPUTO

BALLANTINE BOOKS • NEW YORK

Copyright © 1977 by Philip Caputo

Grateful acknowledgment is made to Mr. G. T. Sassoon and to The Viking Press for permission to reprint lines from "The Effect," "Dreamers," and "Base Details" from *Collected Poems* by Siegfried Sassoon, Copyright 1918 by E. P. Dutton Co., 1946 by Siegfried Sasson; and for permission to reprint lines from "Elegy" and "Aftermath" from *Collected Poems* by Siegfried Sassoon, Copyright 1920 by E. P. Dutton Co., 1948 by Siegfried Sassoon.

Grateful acknowledgment is made to The Owen Estate, to Chatto & Windus Ltd., and to New Directions Publishing Corporation for permission to reprint lines from "Arms and the Boy" and "Apoloia Pro Poemate Meo" from *Collected Poems* by Wilfred Owen, edited by C. Day Lewis, Copyright Chatto & Windus Ltd., 1946, © 1963.

All rights reserved under International and Pan-American Copyright Conventions, including the right to reproduce this book or portions thereof. Published in the United States by Ballantine Books, a division of Random House, Inc., New York, and simultaneously in Canada by Random House of Canada Limited, Toronto.

Library of Congress Catalog Card Number: 76-29900

ISBN 0-345-33122-2

Manufactured in the United States of America

This edition published by arrangement with Holt, Rinehart and Winston

First Ballantine Books Edition: June 1978

47 46 45 44 43 42 41 40 39 38 37

AND YE SHALL HEAR OF WARS AND RUMORS OF WARS. SEE THAT YE BE NOT TROUBLED, FOR ALL THESE THINGS MUST COME TO PASS, BUT THE END IS NOT YET. . . . FOR NATION SHALL RISE AGAINST NATION AND KINGDOM AGAINST KINGDOM . . . THEN SHALL THEY DELIVER YOU UP TO BE AFFLICTED AND SHALL PUT YOU TO DEATH . . . BUT HE THAT SHALL ENDURE UNTO THE END, HE SHALL BE SAVED.

—MATTHEW 24:6–13

Contents

xi

Prologue

In thy faint slumbers I by thee have watch'd
And heard thee murmur tales of iron wars. . . .
—Shakespeare
Henry IV, Part I

This book does not pretend to be history. It has nothing to do with politics, power, strategy, influence, national interests, or foreign policy; nor is it an indictment of the great men who led us into Indochina and whose mistakes were paid for with the blood of some quite ordinary men. In a general sense, it is simply a story about war, about the things men do in war and the things war does to them. More strictly, it is a soldier's account of our longest conflict, the only one we have ever lost, as well as the record of a long and sometimes painful personal experience.

On March 8, 1965, as a young infantry officer, I landed at Danang with a battalion of the 9th Marine Expeditionary Brigade, the first U.S. combat unit sent to Indochina. I returned in April 1975 as a newspaper correspondent and covered the Communist offensive that ended with the fall of Saigon. Having been among the first Americans to fight in Vietnam, I was also among the last to be evacuated, only a few hours before the North Vietnamese Army entered the capital.

Although most of this book deals with the experiences of the marines I served with in 1965 and 1966, I have included an epilogue briefly describing the American exodus. Only ten years separated the two events, yet the humiliation of our exit from Vietnam, compared to the high confidence with which we had entered, made it seem as if a century lay between them.

For Americans who did not come of age in the early sixties, it may be hard to grasp what those years were like—the pride and overpowering self-assurance that prevailed. Most of the thirty-five hundred men in our brigade, born during or immediately after World War II, were shaped by that era, the age of Kennedy's Camelot. We went overseas full of illusions, for which the intoxicating atmosphere of those years was as much to blame as our youth.

War is always attractive to young men who know nothing about it, but we had also been seduced into uniform by Kennedy's challenge to "ask what you can do for your country" and by the missionary idealism he had awakened in us. America seemed omnipotent then: the country could still claim it had never lost a war, and we believed we were ordained to play cop to the Communists' robber and spread our own political faith around the world. Like the French soldiers of the late eighteenth century, we saw ourselves as the champions of "a cause that was destined to triumph." So, when we marched into the rice paddies on that damp March afternoon, we carried, along with our packs and rifles, the implicit convictions that the Viet Cong would be quickly beaten and that we were doing something altogether noble and good. We kept the packs and rifles; the convictions, we lost.

The discovery that the men we had scorned as peasant guerrillas were, in fact, a lethal, determined enemy and the casualty lists that lengthened each week with nothing to show for the blood being spilled broke our early confidence. By autumn, what had begun as an adventurous expedition had turned into an exhausting, indecisive war of attrition in which we fought for no cause other than our own survival.

Writing about this kind of warfare is not a simple task. Repeatedly, I have found myself wishing that I had been the veteran of a conventional war, with dramatic campaigns and historic battles for subject matter instead of a monotonous succession of ambushes and fire-fights. But there were no Normandies or Gettysburgs for us, no epic clashes that decided the fates of armies or nations. The war was mostly a matter of enduring weeks of expectant waiting and, at random intervals, of conducting vicious manhunts through jun-

gles and swamps where snipers harassed us constantly
and booby traps cut us down one by one.

The tedium was occasionally relieved by a large-
scale search-and-destroy operation, but the exhilaration of riding the lead helicopter into a landing zone
was usually followed by more of the same hot walking,
with the mud sucking at our boots and the sun thudding
against our helmets while an invisible enemy shot at
us from distant tree lines. The rare instances when the
VC chose to fight a set-piece battle provided the only
excitement; not ordinary excitement, but the manic
ecstasy of contact. Weeks of bottled-up tensions would
be released in a few minutes of orgiastic violence, men
screaming and shouting obscenities above the explosions of grenades and the rapid, rippling bursts of
automatic rifles.

Beyond adding a few more corpses to the weekly
body count, none of these encounters achieved anything; none will ever appear in military histories or be
studied by cadets at West Point. Still, they changed us
and taught us, the men who fought in them; in those
obscure skirmishes we learned the old lessons about
fear, cowardice, courage, suffering, cruelty, and comradeship. Most of all, we learned about death at an age
when it is common to think of oneself as immortal.
Everyone loses that illusion eventually, but in civilian
life it is lost in installments over the years. We lost it
all at once and, in the span of months, passed from
boyhood through manhood to a premature middle age.
The knowledge of death, of the implacable limits
placed on a man's existence, severed us from our youth
as irrevocably as a surgeon's scissors had once severed
us from the womb. And yet, few of us were past
twenty-five. We left Vietnam peculiar creatures, with
young shoulders that bore rather old heads.

My own departure took place in early July 1966.
Ten months later, following a tour as the CO of an infantry training company in North Carolina, an honor-
able discharge released me from the Marines and the
chance of dying an early death in Asia. I felt as happy
as a condemned man whose sentence has been com-

muted, but within a year I began growing nostalgic for the war.

Other veterans I knew confessed to the same emotion. In spite of everything, we felt a strange attachment to Vietnam and, even stranger, a longing to return. The war was still being fought, but this desire to go back did not spring from any patriotic ideas about duty, honor, and sacrifice, the myths with which old men send young men off to get killed or maimed. It arose, rather, from a recognition of how deeply we had been changed, how different we were from everyone who had not shared with us the miseries of the monsoon, the exhausting patrols, the fear of a combat assault on a hot landing zone. We had very little in common with them. Though we were civilians again, the civilian world seemed alien. We did not belong to it as much as we did to that other world, where we had fought and our friends had died.

I was involved in the antiwar movement at the time and struggled, unsuccessfully, to reconcile my opposition to the war with this nostalgia. Later, I realized a reconciliation was impossible; I would never be able to hate the war with anything like the undiluted passion of my friends in the movement. Because I had fought in it, it was not an abstract issue, but a deeply emotional experience, the most significant thing that had happened to me. It held my thoughts, senses, and feelings in an unbreakable embrace. I would hear in thunder the roar of artillery. I could not listen to rain without recalling those drenched nights on the line, nor walk through woods without instinctively searching for a trip wire or an ambush. I could protest as loudly as the most convinced activist, but I could not deny the grip the war had on me, nor the fact that it had been an experience as fascinating as it was repulsive, as exhilarating as it was sad, as tender as it was cruel.

This book is partly an attempt to capture something of its ambivalent realities. Anyone who fought in Vietnam, if he is honest about himself, will have to admit he enjoyed the compelling attractiveness of combat. It was a peculiar enjoyment because it was mixed with a commensurate pain. Under fire, a man's powers of life heightened in proportion to the proximity of death, so that he felt an elation as extreme as his dread. His senses quickened, he attained an acuity of consciousness at once pleasurable and excruciating. It was something like the elevated state of awareness induced by drugs. And it could be just as addictive, for it made whatever else life offered in the way of delights or torments seem pedestrian.

I have also attempted to describe the intimacy of life in infantry battalions, where the communion between men is as profound as any between lovers. Actually, it is more so. It does not demand for its sustenance the reciprocity, the pledges of affection, the endless reassurances required by the love of men and women. It is, unlike marriage, a bond that cannot be broken by a word, by boredom or divorce, or by anything other than death. Sometimes even that is not strong enough. Two friends of mine died trying to save the corpses of their men from the battlefield. Such devotion, simple and selfless, the sentiment of belonging to each other, was the one decent thing we found in a conflict otherwise notable for its monstrosities.

And yet, it was a tenderness that would have been impossible if the war had been significantly less brutal. The battlefields of Vietnam were a crucible in which a generation of American soldiers were fused together by a common confrontation with death and a sharing of hardships, dangers, and fears. The very ugliness of the war, the sordidness of our daily lives, the degradation of having to take part in body counts made us draw still closer to one another. It was as if in comradeship we found an affirmation of life and the means to preserve at least a vestige of our humanity.

There is also the aspect of the Vietnam War that distinguished it from other American conflicts—its absolute savagery. I mean the savagery that prompted so many American fighting men—the good, solid kids from Iowa farms—to kill civilians and prisoners. The final chapter of this book concentrates on this subject. My purpose has not been to confess complicity in what, for me, amounted to murder, but, using myself and a few other men as examples, to show that war, by its nature, can arouse a psychopathic violence in men of seemingly normal impulses.

There has been a good deal of exaggeration about U.S. atrocities in Vietnam, exaggeration not about their extent but about their causes. The two most popularly held explanations for outrages like My Lai have been the racist theory, which proposes that the American soldier found it easy to slaughter Asians because he did not regard them as human beings, and the frontier-heritage theory, which claims he was inherently violent and needed only the excuse of war to vent his homicidal instincts.

Like all generalizations, each contains an element of truth; yet both ignore the barbarous treatment the Viet Cong and ARVN often inflicted on their own people, and neither confront the crimes committed by the Korean division, probably the most bloody-minded in Vietnam, and by the French during the first Indochina war.

The evil was inherent not in the men—except in the sense that a devil dwells in us all—but in the circumstances under which they had to live and fight. The conflict in Vietnam combined the two most bitter forms of warfare, civil war and revolution, to which was added the ferocity of jungle war. Twenty years of terrorism and fratricide had obliterated most reference points from the country's moral map long before we arrived. Communists and government forces alike considered ruthlessness a necessity if not a virtue. Whether committed in the name of principles or out of vengeance, atrocities were as common to the Vietnamese battlefields as shell craters and barbed wire. The marines in our brigade were not innately cruel, but on landing in Danang they learned rather quickly that Vietnam was not a place where a man could expect much mercy if, say, he was taken prisoner. And men who do not expect to receive mercy eventually lose their inclination to grant it.

At times, the comradeship that was the war's only redeeming quality caused some of its worst crimes—acts of retribution for friends who had been killed. Some men could not withstand the stress of guerrilla-fighting: the hair-trigger alertness constantly demanded of them, the feeling that the enemy was everywhere, the inability to distinguish civilians from combatants created emotional pressures which built to such a point that a trivial provocation could make these men explode with the blind destructiveness of a mortar shell.

Others were made pitiless by an overpowering greed for survival. Self-preservation, that most basic and tyrannical of all instincts, can turn a man into a coward or, as was more often the case in Vietnam, into a creature who destroys without hesitation or remorse whatever poses even a potential threat to his life. A sergeant in my platoon, ordinarily a pleasant young man, told me once, "Lieutenant, I've got a wife and two kids at home and I'm going to see 'em again and don't care who I've got to kill or how many of 'em to do it."

General Westmoreland's strategy of attrition also had an important effect on our behavior. Our mission was not to win terrain or seize positions, but simply to kill: to kill Communists and to kill as many of them as possible. Stack 'em like cordwood. Victory was a high body-count, defeat a low kill-ratio, war a matter of arithmetic. The pressure on unit commanders to produce enemy corpses was intense, and they in turn communicated it to their troops. This led to such practices as counting civilians as Viet Cong. "If it's dead and Vietnamese, it's VC," was a rule of thumb in the bush. It is not surprising, therefore, that some men acquired a contempt for human life and a predilection for taking it.

Finally, there were the conditions imposed by the climate and country. For weeks we had to live like primitive men on remote outposts rimmed by alien seas of rice paddies and rain forests. Malaria, blackwater fever, and dysentery, though not the killers they had been in past wars, took their toll. The sun scorched us in the dry season, and in the monsoon season we were pounded numb by ceaseless rain. Our days were spent hacking through mountainous jungles whose immensity reduced us to an antlike pettiness. At night we squatted in muddy holes, picked off the leeches that sucked on our veins, and waited for an attack to come rushing at us from the blackness beyond the perimeter wire.

The air-conditioned headquarters of Saigon and Danang seemed thousands of miles away. As for the United States, we did not call it "the World" for nothing; it might as well have been on another planet. There was nothing familiar out where we were, no churches, no police, no laws, no newspapers, or any of the restraining influences without which the earth's population of virtuous people would be reduced by ninety-five percent. It was the dawn of creation in the Indochina bush, an ethical as well as a geographical wilderness. Out there, lacking restraints, sanctioned to kill, confronted by a hostile country and a relentless enemy, we sank into a brutish state. The descent could be checked only by the net of a man's inner moral values, the attribute that is called character. There were a few—and I suspect Lieutenant Calley was one—who had no net and plunged all the way down, discovering in their bottommost depths a capacity for malice they probably never suspected was there.

Most American soldiers in Vietnam—at least the ones I knew—could not be divided into good men and bad. Each possessed roughly equal measures of both qualities. I saw men who behaved with great compassion toward the Vietnamese one day and then burned down a village the next. They were, as Kipling wrote of his Tommy Atkins, neither saints "nor blackguards too/But single men in barricks most remarkable like you." That may be why Americans reacted with such horror to the disclosures of U.S. atrocities while ignoring those of the other side: the American soldier was a reflection of themselves.

This book is not a work of the imagination. The events related are true, the characters real, though I have used fictitious names in some places. I have tried to describe accurately what the dominant event in the life of my generation, the Vietnam War, was like for the men who fought in it. Toward that end, I have made a great effort to resist the veteran's inclination to remember things the way he would like them to have been rather than the way they were.

Finally, this book ought not to be regarded as a protest. Protest arises from a belief that one can change things or influence events. I am not egotistical enough to believe I can. Besides, it no longer seems necessary to register an objection to the war, because the war is over. We lost it, and no amount of objecting will resurrect the men who died, without redeeming anything, on calvaries like Hamburger Hill and the Rockpile.

It might, perhaps, prevent the next generation from being crucified in the next war.

But I don't think so.

Part One

THE SPLENDID LITTLE WAR

No great dependence is to be placed on the eagerness of young soldiers for action, for the prospect of fighting is agreeable to those who are strangers to it.
—Vegetius
Roman military writer, 4th century A.D.

Chapter One

Let the boy try along this bayonet-blade
How cold steel is, and keen with hunger of
    blood. . . .

> —Wilfred Owen
> "Arms and the Boy"

At the age of twenty-four, I was more prepared for
death than I was for life. My first experience of the
world outside the classroom had been war. I went
straight from school into the Marine Corps, from
Shakespeare to the *Manual of Small-Unit Tactics,* from
the campus to the drill field and finally Vietnam. I
learned the murderous trade at Quantico, Virginia,
practiced it in the rice paddies and jungles around
Danang, and then taught it to others at Camp Geiger,
a training base in North Carolina.

When my three-year enlistment expired in 1967, I
was almost completely ignorant about the stuff of ordinary life, about marriage, mortgages, and building a
career. I had a degree, but no skills. I had never run
an office, taught a class, built a bridge, welded, pro-
grammed a computer, laid bricks, sold anything, or
operated a lathe.

But I had acquired some expertise in the art of
killing. I knew how to face death and how to cause it
with everything on the evolutionary scale of weapons
from the knife to the 3.5-inch rocket launcher. The
simplest repairs on an automobile engine were beyond
me, but I was able to field-strip and assemble an
M-14 rifle blindfolded. I could call in artillery, set up
an ambush, rig a boobytrap, lead a night raid.

Simply by speaking a few words into a two-way
radio, I had performed magical feats of destruction.
Summoned by my voice, jet fighters appeared in the
sky to loose their lethal droppings on villages and men.

3

High-explosive bombs blasted houses to fragments, napalm sucked air from lungs and turned human flesh to ashes. All this just by saying a few words into a radio transmitter. Like magic.

I came home from the war with the curious feeling that I had grown older than my father, who was then fifty-one. It was as if a lifetime of experience had been compressed into a year and a half. A man saw the heights and depths of human behavior in Vietnam, all manner of violence and horrors so grotesque that they evoked more fascination than disgust. Once I had seen pigs eating napalm-charred corpses—a memorable sight, pigs eating roast people.

I was left with none of the optimism and ambition a young American is supposed to have, only a desire to catch up on sixteen months of missed sleep and an old man's conviction that the future would hold no further surprises, good or bad.

I *hoped* there would be no more surprises. I had survived enough ambushes and doubted my capacity to endure many more physical or emotional shocks. I had all the symptoms of *combat veteranitis:* an inability to concentrate, a childlike fear of darkness, a tendency to tire easily, chronic nightmares, an intolerance of loud noises—especially doors slamming and cars backfiring—and alternating moods of depression and rage that came over me for no apparent reason. Recovery has been less than total.

I joined the Marines in 1960, partly because I got swept up in the patriotic tide of the Kennedy era but mostly because I was sick of the safe, suburban existence I had known most of my life.

I was raised in Westchester, Illinois, one of the towns that rose from the prairies around Chicago as a result of post-war affluence, VA mortgage loans, and the migratory urge and housing shortage that sent millions of people out of the cities in the years following World War II. It had everything a suburb is supposed to have: sleek, new schools smelling of fresh plaster and floor wax; supermarkets full of Wonder Bread and Bird's Eye frozen peas; rows of centrally heated split-levels that lined dirtless streets on which nothing ever happened.

It was pleasant enough at first, but by the time I entered my late teens I could not stand the place, the dullness of it, the summer barbecues eaten to the lulling drone of power mowers. During the years I grew up there, Westchester stood on or near the edge of the built-up area. Beyond stretched the Illinois farm and pasture lands, where I used to hunt on weekends. I remember the fields as they were in the late fall: the corn stubble brown against the snow, dead husks rasping dryly in the wind; abandoned farm houses waiting for the bulldozers that would tear them down to clear space for a new subdivision; and off on the horizon, a few stripped sycamores silhouetted against a bleak November sky. I can still see myself roaming around out there, scaring rabbits from the brambles, the tract houses a few miles behind me, the vast, vacant prairies in front, a restless boy caught between suburban boredom and rural desolation.

The only thing I really liked about my boyhood surroundings were the Cook and DuPage County forest preserves, a belt of virgin woodland through which flowed a muddy stream called Salt Creek. It was not too polluted then, and its sluggish waters yielded bullhead, catfish, carp, and a rare bass. There was small game in the woods, sometimes a deer or two, but most of all a hint of the wild past, when moccasined feet trod the forest paths and fur trappers cruised the rivers in bark canoes. Once in a while, I found flint arrowheads in the muddy creek bank. Looking at them, I would dream of that savage, heroic time and wish I had lived then, before America became a land of salesmen and shopping centers.

That is what I wanted, to find in a commonplace world a chance to live heroically. Having known nothing but security, comfort, and peace, I hungered for danger, challenges, and violence.

I had no clear idea of how to fulfill this peculiar ambition until the day a Marine recruiting team set up a stand in the student union at Loyola University. They were on a talent hunt for officer material and displayed a poster of a trim lieutenant who had one of those athletic, slightly cruel-looking faces considered handsome in the military. He looked like a cross between an All-American halfback and a Nazi tank commander. Clear and resolute, his blue eyes seemed to stare at me in challenge. JOIN THE MARINES, read the slogan above his white cap. BE A LEADER OF MEN.

I rummaged through the propaganda material, picking out one pamphlet whose cover listed every battle the Marines had fought, from Trenton to Inchon. Reading down that list, I had one of those rare flashes of insight: the heroic experience I sought was war; war, the ultimate adventure; war, the ordinary man's most convenient means of escaping from the ordinary. The country was at peace then, but the early sixties were years of almost constant tension and crisis; if a conflict did break out, the Marines would be certain to fight in it and I could be there with them. Actually *there.* Not watching it on a movie or TV screen, not reading about it in a book, but *there,* living out a fantasy. Already I saw myself charging up some distant beachhead, like John Wayne in *Sands of Iwo Jima,* and then coming home a suntanned warrior with medals on my chest. The recruiters started giving me the usual sales pitch, but I hardly needed to be persuaded. I decided to enlist.

I had another motive for volunteering, one that has pushed young men into armies ever since armies were invented: I needed to prove something—my courage, my toughness, my manhood, call it whatever you like. I had spent my freshman year at Purdue, freed from the confinements of suburban home and family. But a slump in the economy prevented me from finding a job that summer. Unable to afford the expense of living on campus (and almost flunking out anyway, having spent half my first year drinking and the other half in fraternity antics), I had to transfer to Loyola, a commuter college in Chicago. As a result, at the age of nineteen I found myself again living with my parents.

It was a depressing situation. In my adolescent

mind, I felt that my parents regarded me as an ir-
responsible boy who still needed their guidance. I
wanted to prove them wrong. I had to get away. It
was not just a question of physical separation, although
that was important; it was more a matter of doing
something that would demonstrate to them, and to myself as well, that I was a man after all, like the
steely-eyed figure in the recruiting poster. THE MA-
RINE CORPS BUILDS MEN was another slogan current at
the time, and on November 28 I became one of its
construction projects.

I joined the Platoon Leaders' Class, the Marines'
version of ROTC. I was to attend six weeks of basic
training the following summer and then an advanced
course during the summer before I graduated from
college. Completion of Officer Candidate School and
a bachelor's degree would entitle me to a commission,
after which I would be required to serve three years
on active duty.

I was not really ambitious to become an officer. I
would have dropped out of school and gone in immediately as an enlisted man had it not been for my
parents' unflinching determination to have a college
graduate for a son. As it was, they were unhappy.
Their vision of my future did not include uniforms
and drums, but consisted of my finding a respectable
job after school, marrying a respectable girl, and then
settling down in a respectable suburb.

For my part, I was elated the moment I signed up
and swore to defend the United States "against all
enemies foreign and domestic." I had done something important on my own; that it was something
which opposed my parents' wishes made it all the
more savory. And I was excited by the idea that I
would be sailing off to dangerous and exotic places
after college instead of riding the 7:45 to some
office. It is odd when I look back on it. Most of my
friends at school thought of joining the army as the
most conformist thing anyone could do, and of the
service itself as a form of slavery. But for me, enlisting was an act of rebellion, and the Marine Corps

symbolized an opportunity for personal freedom and independence.

Officer Candidate School was at Quantico, a vast reservation in the piny Virginia woods near Fredericksburg, where the Army of the Potomac had been futilely slaughtered a century before. There, in the summer of 1961, along with several hundred other aspiring lieutenants, I was introduced to military life and began training for war. We ranged in age from nineteen to twenty-one, and those of us who survived OCS would lead the first American troops sent to Vietnam four years later. Of course, we did not know that at the time: we hardly knew where Vietnam was.

The first six weeks, roughly the equivalent of enlisted boot camp, were spent at Camp Upshur, a cluster of quonset huts and tin-walled buildings set deep in the woods. The monastic isolation was appropriate because the Marine Corps, as we quickly learned, was more than a branch of the armed services. It was a society unto itself, demanding total commitment to its doctrines and values, rather like one of those quasi-religious military orders of ancient times, the Teutonic Knights or the Theban Band. We were novitiates, and the rigorous training, administered by high priests called drill instructors, was to be our ordeal of initiation.

And ordeal it was, physically and psychologically. From four in the morning until nine at night we were marched and drilled, sent sprawling over obstacle courses and put through punishing conditioning hikes in ninety-degree heat. We were shouted at, kicked, humiliated and harassed constantly. We were no longer known by our names, but called "shitbird," "scumbag," or "numbnuts" by the DIs. In my platoon, they were a corporal, a small man who was cruel in the way only small men can be, and a sergeant, a nervously energetic black named McClellan, whose muscles looked as hard and wiry as underground telephone cables.

What I recall most vividly is close-order drill: the hours we spent marching in a sun so hot it turned the asphalt field into a viscous mass that stuck to our boots; the endless hours of being driven and scourged by McClellan's voice—relentless, compelling obedience, a voice that embedded itself in our minds until we could not walk anywhere without hearing it, counting a rhythmic cadence.

> Wan-tup-threep-fo, threep-fo-your-lef, lef-rye-lef, hada-lef-rye-lef, your-lef . . . your-lef . . . your-lef.
> Dress it up dress it up keep your interval.
> Thirty-inches-back-to-breast-forty-inches-shoulder-to-shoulder.
> Lef-rye-lef.
> TothereAH HARCH . . . reAH HARCH . . . by-daleflank HARCH!
> Dress it up keep your dress DRESS IT UP SCUM-BAGS.
> Lef-rye-lef. Dig those heels in dig 'em in.
> Pick-'em-up-and-put-'em-down DIG 'EM IN threep-fo-your-lef.
> DIG 'EM IN LET'S HEAR IT DIG 'EM IN.
> Threep-fo-your-lef, lef-rye-lef.
> Square those pieces away SQUARE 'EM AWAY GIRLS. YOU, SHITHEAD FOURTH MAN IN THE FRONT RANK I SAID SQUARE THAT FUCKIN' PIECE, SQUARE IT AWAY Wan-tup-threep-fo.
> YOU DON'T SQUARE THAT PIECE I GONNA MALTREAT YOU BOY KNOCK UP UP THE SIDE O' THE HEAD threep-fo-your-lef SQUARE THAT PIECE! YOU FUCKIN' DEAF? EYES FRONT! DON'T LOOK AT ME NUMBNUTS! EYES FRONT! SQUARE YOUR PIECE! Now you got the idea, nummie Wan-tup-threep-fo.
> Threep-fo-your-lef, lef-rye-lef, hadalef-rye-lef, lef-rye-lef. Lef-rye-lef, lef-rye-lef, your-lef, your-lef YOUR OTHER LEF SHITHEAD. Lef-rye-lef, lef . . . lef . . .
> Lef-rye-lef.

The purpose of drill was to instill discipline and

teamwork, two of the Corps' cardinal virtues. And by the third week, we had learned to obey orders instantly and in unison, without thinking. Each platoon had been transformed from a group of individuals into one thing: a machine of which we were merely parts.

The mental and physical abuse had several objectives. They were calculated first to eliminate the weak, who were collectively known as "unsats," for unsatisfactory. The reasoning was that anyone who could not take being shouted at and kicked in the ass once in a while could never withstand the rigors of combat. But such abuse was also designed to destroy each man's sense of self-worth, to make him feel worthless until he proved himself equal to the Corps' exacting standards.

And we worked hard to prove that, submitted to all sorts of indignities just to demonstrate that we could take it. We said, "Thank you, sir" when the drill sergeant rapped us in the back of the head for having a dirty rifle. Night after night, without complaint, we did Chinese push-ups for our sins (Chinese push-ups are performed in a bent position in which only the head and toes touch the floor). After ten or fifteen seconds, it felt as if your skull was being crushed in a vise. We had to do them for as long as several minutes, until we were at the point of blacking out.

I don't know about the others, but I endured these tortures because I was driven by an overwhelming desire to succeed, no matter what. That awful word— *unsat*—haunted me. I was more afraid of it than I was of Sergeant McClellan. Nothing he could do could be as bad as having to return home and admit to my family that I had failed. It was not their criticism I dreaded, but the emasculating affection and understanding they would be sure to show me. I could hear my mother saying, "That's all right, son. You didn't belong in the Marines but here with us. It's good to have you back. Your father needs help with the lawn." I was so terrified of being found wanting that I even avoided getting near the candidates who were borderline cases—the "marginals," as they were known in the lexicon of that strange world. They carried the virus of weakness.

Most of the marginals eventually fell into the unsat category and were sent home. Others dropped out. Two or three had nervous breakdowns; a few more nearly died of heatstroke on forced marches and were given medical discharges.

The rest of us, about seventy percent of the original class, came through. At the end of the course, the DIs honored our survival by informing us that we had earned the right to be called Marines. We were proud of ourselves, but were not likely to forget the things we endured to claim that title. To this day, the smell of woods in the early morning reminds me of those long-ago dawns at Camp Upshur, with their shrill reveilles and screaming sergeants and dazed recruits stumbling out of bed.

Those who passed the initial trial went back to Quantico two years later for the advanced course, which was even more grueling. Much of it was familiar stuff: more close-order drill, bayonet practice, and hand-to-hand combat. But there were additional refinements. One of these was a fiendish device of physical torture called the Hill Trail, so named, with typical military unimaginativeness, because it was a trail that ran over a range of hills, seven of them. And what hills—steep as roller coasters and ten times as high. We had to run over them at least twice a week wearing full pack and equipment. Softened by the intervening two years of campus life, dozens of men collapsed on these excursions. The victims were shown no mercy by the DIs. I remember one overweight boy lying unconscious against a tree stump while a sergeant shook him by the collar and shouted into his blanched face: "On your feet, you sackashit. Off your fat ass and on your feet."

Recreation consisted of obstacle-course races or pugil-stick fights. The pugil-stick, a thick, wooden staff, padded at each end, was supposed to instill "the spirit of bayonet"; that is, the savage fury necessary to ram cold steel into another man's guts. Two men would square off and bash each other with these clubs, urged on by some bloodthirsty instructor. "Parry that one, now slash, SLASH! Vertical butt stroke. C'mon, kill the sonuvabitch, kill 'im. Thrust. Jab. That's it, jab. JAB! KILL 'IM."

Throughout, we were subjected to intense indoctrination, which seemed to borrow from Communist brainwashing techniques. We had to chant slogans while running: "Hut-two-three-four, I love the Marine Corps." And before meals: "Sir, the United States Marines; since 1775, the most invincible fighting force in the history of man. Gung ho! Gung ho! Gung ho! Pray for war!" Like the slogans of revolutionaries, these look ludicrous in print, but when recited in unison by a hundred voices, they have a weird, hypnotic effect on a man. The psychology of the mob, of the *Bund* rally, takes command of his will and he finds himself shouting that nonsense even though he knows it is nonsense. In time, he begins to believe that he really does love the Marine Corps, that it is invincible, and that there is nothing improper in praying for war, the event in which the Corps periodically has justified its existence and achieved its apotheosis.

We were lectured on the codes marines are expected to live by: they never leave their casualties on the battlefield, never retreat, and never surrender so long as they have the means to resist. "And the only time a marine doesn't have the means to resist," one instructor told us, "is when he's dead." There were classes on Marine Corps history, or, I should say, mythology. We learned of Lieutenant Presley O'Bannon storming the fort of the Barbary corsairs at Tripoli, of Captain Travis seizing the fortress of Chapultepec—"the halls of Montezuma"—during the Mexican War, of the 5th and 6th Regiments' bayonet charge at Belleau Wood, of Chesty Puller whipping the rebels in Nicaragua and the Japanese on Guadalcanal.

Around seven hundred and fifty men began the advanced course; only five hundred finished. The graduation ceremony took place on a scalding August afternoon in 1963. We stood at attention on the liquefying asphalt of the parade field on which we had spent countless hours drilling.

A squad of field grade officers began taking their places in the reviewing stand, campaign ribbons adding a splash of color to their khaki shirts. The sun glinted off their brass rank insignia and the polished instruments of the band. There was a small crowd of civilians, mostly parents who had come to watch their sons take part in this martial rite of passage. Awards were presented, the usual messages of congratulation read, and someone made a brief duty-honor-country valedictory speech. We stood patiently, sweat trickling from our noses and onto our ties, the heat wilting the creases in our shirts.

Finally, the order to pass in review rippled down the line. We marched past the stand, snapping our heads at the command "Eyes right" while the gold and scarlet guidons fluttered in the breeze and the drums rolled and the band played the Marine Corps Hymn. It was glorious and grand, like an old-fashioned Fourth of July. Bugles, drums, and flags. Marching across the field in battalion mass, with that stirring, soaring hymn blaring in our ears, we felt invincible, boys of twenty-one and twenty-two, all cheerfully unaware that some of us would not grow much older.

I was commissioned on February 2, 1964, and returned to Quantico in May for Officers' Basic School, where new second lieutenants served a six-month apprenticeship before being sent to their first commands. I was assigned to Company H, Basic Class 2-64.

Basic School was fairly pleasant compared to OCS. No more harassment from profane, sadistic drill sergeants. Now they had to call us "sir," although, with the previous summer's experience fresh in our minds, the sight of some old salt with three stripes and a rocker on his sleeves still caused a Pavlovian reaction of terror.

Living conditions were regal. We were housed in two-man rooms in a BOQ that was indistinguishable from a modern dormitory. Large, airy lecture rooms and a gymnasium (named in honor of an alumnus who had been killed in Korea) completed the collegelike atmosphere.

Basic School was a school in fact as well as in name, a halfway house between the campus and the real Marine Corps. Its purpose was to turn us into professional officers. Because of the Corps doctrine that every marine is a rifleman, the course emphasized infantry fundamentals—weapons-training and small-unit tactics. It was dry, technical stuff, taught in the how-to-do-it fashion of a trade school: how to take a hill by frontal assault or envelopment; how to defend it once you have taken it; how to deliver searching and traversing fire with an M-60 machine gun.

For me, the classroom work was mind-numbing. I wanted the romance of war, bayonet charges, and desperate battles against impossible odds. I wanted the sort of thing I had seen in *Guadalcanal Diary* and *Retreat, Hell!* and a score of other movies. Instead of the romance, I got the methodology of war, Clausewitz and his nine principles, lines and arrows on a map, abstract jargon, and a number of bewildering acronyms and abbreviations. To be in battle was to be "in a combat situation"; a helicopter assault was a "vertical envelopment"; an M-14 rifle a "hand-held, gas-operated, magazine-fed, semiautomatic shoulder weapon." I had read somewhere that Stendhal learned his simple, lucid style by studying Napoleon's battle orders. Literature should be grateful that Stendhal didn't live in the present; the battle orders we studied were written in language that made the Rosetta Stone look like a Dick-and-Jane reader.

"*Enemy sit.* Aggressor forces in div strength holding MLR Hill 820 complex gc AT 940713-951716 w/fwd elements est. bn strength junction at gc AT 948715 (See Annex A, COMPHIBPAC intell. summary period ending 25 June) . . . *Mission*: BLT 1/7 seize, hold and defend obj. A gc 948715 . . . *Execution*: BLT 1/7 land LZ X-RAY AT 946710 at H-Hour 310600 . . . A co. GSF estab. LZ security LZ X-RAY H minus 10 . . . B co. advance axis BLUE H plus 5 estab. blocking pos. vic gs AT 948710 . . . A, C, D cos. maneuver element commence advance axis BROWN H plus 10 . . . Bn tacnet freq 52.9 . . . shackle code HAZTRCEGBD . . . div. tacair dir. air spt callsign

PLAYBOY . . . Mark friendly pos w/air panels or green smoke. Mark tgt. w/WP."

I was not the only one to find this eye-glazing. During one particularly dull lecture, a classmate named Butterfield leaned over to me. "You know," he whispered, "the trouble with war is that there isn't any background music."

Our Hollywood fantasies were given some outlet in the field exercises that took up about half the training schedule. These were supposed to simulate battlefield conditions, teach us to apply classroom lessons, and develop "the spirit of aggressiveness." The Corps prized élan in its troops. The offensive was the only tactic worthy of the name. We were taught the rudiments of defensive warfare, while retrograde movements were hardly mentioned, and only then in tones of contempt. The Army retreated, the Marines did not, although they had—at Chosin Reservoir in Korea. The essence of the offensive was the frontal assault: "Hey diddle diddle, straight up the middle." This was the supreme moment of infantry combat; no tricky flanking or encircling movements, just a line of determined men firing short bursts from the hip as they advanced on the enemy at a stately walk.

It was easy to do in the bloodless make-believe of field problems, in which every operation went according to plan and the only danger was the remote one of falling and breaking an ankle. We took these stage-managed exercises seriously, thinking they resembled actual combat. We couldn't know then that they bore about as much similarity to the real thing as shadow-boxing does to street-fighting. Diligently we composed our five-paragraph attack orders. We huddled in pine-scented thickets, soberly playing the roles assigned to us—student platoon leader, student squad leader—and with our maps spread flat, planned the destruction of our fictitious enemy, the aggressor forces. We fought them throughout the spring and summer, enveloped them, went at them with squad rushes, and made frontal assaults against the sun-browned hills they defended, yelling battle cries as we charged through storms of blank cartridge fire.

At the time, counterinsurgency was fashionable in military circles: it had become obvious that the next war, if there was to be one, would be fought in Indochina (that August, when the Tonkin Gulf resolution was passed, we were midway through the Basic course); and combating insurgencies gave the services a special mission in the age of the New Frontier. The Peace Corps could go off to build dams in India or schools in Bolivia, but it was up to the War Corps to do the man's work of battling Communist guerrillas, the new barbarians who menaced the far-flung interests of the new Rome. Finally, counterinsurgency was still surrounded by the Kennedy mystique, even though the young president had been dead for nearly a year. But the glamorous prince of Camelot had given the new doctrine his imprimatur by sending the first Special Forces detachments to Vietnam, glamorous figures themselves in their green berets and paratrooper boots.

The fascination was strongest among the junior officers, who were drawn by the apparent romance of fighting guerrilla bands in far-off places. Beyond that, a feeling of inadequacy came over us whenever we compared the colorful chests of combat veterans to our own, naked except for marksmanship badges. We wanted to dress up that blank khaki with Bronze and Silver Stars, and Vietnam appeared to be the most likely place where we could win them.

The senior first lieutenant who tutored us in counterguerrilla operations had served there for thirty days as a "military observer," which did not exactly qualify him as an expert. He had been wounded, however, and although it had happened under less than heroic circumstances—he was hit in the buttocks while squatting over a latrine—the Purple Heart pinned above his left pocket gave him an air of authority.

Anyway, he sounded authoritative as he revealed to us the mysteries of counterrevolution. His lectures were full of enough jargon to dispel the illusion that guerrilla-fighting was something like Indian-fighting, a rough, seat-of-the-pants form of warfare. On the contrary, it appeared to be a highly specialized art; complex tactics with esoteric names were required to outwit the wily insurgents. We were taught how to batter them into submission with the Hammer and Anvil Movement, to make them dance to their deaths in a Minuet Ambush, to trap them in a Constricting Cordon, and to repulse their attacks with the Triangular Defense.

These strange maneuvers we practiced in the steamy bottomlands that were as close an approximation of Asian jungles as Virginia could offer. Many months later, I would remember, as a grown man remembers the games played in boyhood, how we ran around in those woods, ambushing each other and raiding imaginary guerrilla camps. In our enthusiasm, we tried to make these playact exercises as realistic as possible, even in such minor details as our dress. I have kept a photograph taken of another lieutenant and me just before we set out on a "reconnaissance mission." It shows us wearing what we conceived of as authentic jungle-fighter uniforms: camouflage shirts, camouflage berets fashioned from helmet covers, camouflage paint smeared on our faces. I guess we were little more than overgrown kids playing soldier, but, judging from our grim expressions, we must have thought it serious business.

A few of my classmates became counterinsurgency cultists, immersing themselves in almost all of the literature published on the subject. They made a curious sight, those crew-cut, American-looking officers studying the gospels of Mao Tse-tung as devoutly as the Chairman's disciples in Peking and Hanoi. They were obeying the old injunction "Know your enemy." Most of those studious officers were regulars with career ambitions, and they boned up on that exotic strategy for the same reason medical students read articles on the latest trends in surgery: they thought it would make them better at their profession if and when the time came to practice it in earnest. As for me, I had no desire to be a general. Vietnam mostly interested me as a place where I might find a bit of dangerous adventure, not as a testing ground for new military theories or for my own professional talents, which were modest at best.

Whenever I think back to those days at Basic School, the recollection that first comes to mind is always the same: A double file of green-clad men, bent beneath their packs, are tramping down a dirt road. A remorseless sun is beating down. Raised by our boots, a cloud of red dust powders the trees alongside the road, making them look sickly and ashen. The dust clings to our uniforms, runs in muddy streaks down our sweating faces. There is the rattle of rifle slings and bayonet scabbards, the clattering of mess kits bouncing in our haversacks. Our heads ache from the weight of steel helmets, and the cry "Close it up, keep your interval, close it up" is echoing up and down the long column.

I do not know which was worse, the monotony or the effort—the monotony of putting one foot in front of the other hour after hour or the effort of keeping five paces distance from the man in front "so's one round don't get you all." Even among the most disciplined troops, a route-column has an "accordion effect." It stretches and contracts because of differences in stride. At first, the company moves at an easy pace; then it stops suddenly. We bunch up, bump into each other and wait, leaning far forward to ease the ache in our backs. The column begins to move again, in the jerky fashion of a train pulling out of a siding. Gaps open in the files. We run to close them up, that maddening cry in our ears. "Close it up, damnit, people, keep it closed up." At last, a five-minute break is called. Shedding our packs, we drift off the road and slide down an embankment to lie exhausted on the cool grass. There is just enough time for a few swallows from our canteens, a few drags on a cigarette, before the dread command comes down the line. "H Company, saddle up! Off your ass and on your feet. Saddle up, move out!" We pick ourselves up, and are at it once more. One foot in front of the other. Pick 'em up and put 'em down. Sometimes I could not remember ever having done anything else. My college years receded, and it seemed as if I had spent almost all my life humping a too heavy pack beneath too hot a sun down a road that was too long. The essence of the Marine Corps experience, I decided, was pain.

But there were moments of exhilaration that compensated for the hours of marching on blistered feet. I remember one evening when we were trudging over a hilly firebreak toward a bivouac site. Coming to the top of one rise, I looked ahead at the lead platoon laboring up yet another. They were strung out along the trail like two lengths of chain, one behind the lanky figure of Major Seymour, the company CO, the other behind the bobbing, scarlet pennant carried by the guidon-bearer. When the latter reached the crest of the next hill, the flag caught a breeze, momentarily revealing a gold *H,* then furled again and gradually sank out of sight as he went down the slope. The column followed, shambling through a faint pall of dust that moved with it, uniforms mottled with black patches of sweat, webbed cartridge belts faded to a dull yellow from constant scrubbing, haversacks framed by blanket rolls, the stocks of slung rifles showing as brown daubs on the backs of the marines' olive-drab utilities.

Right of the firebreak, the woods stretched unbroken to the horizon, where the sun hovered over a serrated line of trees: a giant orange balloon floating above a green sea. The air was growing cool and smelled of pine, with the drowsy stillness of a summer evening in the South. I clambered down into the saddle between the two hills, climbed again, went down again, and was gratified to see nothing but level ground ahead. About a quarter of a mile away, the trail joined the hard-surface road that led to the bivouac. It was a welcome sight, that patch of asphalt showing through the trees. Now that it knew it was on the last leg, the company began to march faster, almost jauntily. A few marines near the point started singing the verse to a marching song and the rest of the column answered with the chorus.

I gotta gal that lives on a hill . . .
       Oh, Little Liza, Little Liza Ja-ane.
She won't do it but her sister will . . .
       Little Liza Jane.
       Whoa-oh-oh-oh Little Liza, Little Liza Jane
       Oh, Little Liza, Little Liza Jane.

I gotta gal in Lackawanna . . .
      Oh, Little Liza, Little Liza Jane.
She knows how but she don't wanna . . .
      Little Liza Jane.
      Whoa-oh-oh-oh Little Liza, Little Liza Jane
      Oh, Little Liza, Little Liza Jane.

The song was like a cry of defiance. They had just humped through thirty miles of wilderness in intense heat with forty pounds on their backs, and they were coming in singing. Nothing could subdue them. Hearing that full-throated *Whoa-oh-oh-oh Little Liza, Little Liza Jane* roaring through the woods, I felt proud of that spirited company and happy that I was one of them.

Autumn brought a week in Norfolk for amphibious warfare school: seasick days on the choppy Atlantic, drunken nights on South Granby Street. Then a return to Quantico for training in house-to-house fighting and night attacks, mock battles fought in the wan and fitful glow of illumination flares. Week by week, month by month, we learned our violent craft, each lesson a step in our evolution from civilians to professional soldiers. The change would not be complete until after we had served in Vietnam, for there are facts about war which cannot be taught in training, no matter how realistic and strenuous it is. But Quantico carried the process about as far as possible off the battlefield.

Like all evolutions, ours was accompanied by mutations. The Marine Corps had made highly efficient fighting men of us, and we had begun to look it. Gone were the shaggy, somewhat overweight children who had stumbled off the buses at OCS a long time before. They had been replaced by streamlined marines, whose hardened limbs were adapted for walking great distances or for thrusting a bayonet into a man's ribs with ease.

But the most significant changes were not the physical ones. We had become self-confident and proud, some to the point of arrogance. We had acquired the military virtues of courage, loyalty, and *esprit de corps,* though at the price of a diminished capacity for compassion. There were other alterations. In my own case, it was the way I looked at the world around me. A year earlier, I would have seen the rolling Virginia countryside through the eyes of an English-major who enjoyed reading the Romantic poets. Now I had the clearer, more pragmatic vision of an infantry officer. Landscape was no longer scenery to me, it was *terrain,* and I judged it for tactical rather than aesthetic value. Having been drilled constantly to look for cover and concealment, I could see dips and folds in a stretch of ground that would have appeared utterly flat to a civilian. If I saw a hill—"high ground"—I automatically began planning how to attack or defend it, my eyes searching for avenues of approach and fields of fire. A woodland meadow held no picturesque beauty for me. Instead, it presented a potential menace. If I came upon one, my first instincts were to figure out how to get a platoon safely across the exposed ground and how best to deploy the men: in a wedge, a combat-V, or line of skirmishers, two squads up and one back.

Not all the training dealt in lethal practicalities. In those pre-Vietnam days, the course proceeded leisurely, with plenty of time devoted to the ceremonial side of military life. We learned to put on reviews, the proper way to flourish a sword, how to behave at social functions; in brief, all that spit-and-polish nonsense which is totally divorced from the messy realities of twentieth-century warfare.

In spite of its uselessness, I cannot say that I found it unattractive. The romantic in me responded to the pageantry of a parade, to the tribal ritualism of ceremonies that marked anniversaries or comradeships formed long ago on distant battlefields. In the summer it was Mess Night, which had obscure and ancient origins in the British Army. To the roll of a solitary drum, officers in dress whites filed into the mess. Lit only by candles, it looked as dim and secretive as the dining hall in a monastery. Silver trophies from our ancestors, the Royal Marines, and other English regiments gleamed in a corner case. To THE U.S. MARINE CORPS,

read the inscription on one, FROM THE 1ST BATTAL-
ION, ROYAL WELCH FUSILEERS. PEKING 1900. Toasts
were made, and wineglasses raised, lowered, raised
again, like chalices at some strange Mass.

In the winter it was the Marine Corps birthday ball,
which commemorated the Corps' nativity in a Phila-
delphia tavern on November 10, 1775. The observance
of this rite was the cause of my first offense against
the Uniform Code of Military Justice. I went AWOL
from the Quantico Naval Hospital, where I was
recovering from mononucleosis, to attend the celebra-
tion. I thought it would be a night of beerswilling cama-
raderie, something like the gatherings of Beowulf's
warriors in the mead hall, and I was determined not
to spend it in the aseptic confines of the isolation ward.

Earlier that day, two classmates had smuggled my
dress blues and a bottle of Jack Daniel's into my room.
After eight o'clock bedcheck, I made a dummy out of
my baggy pajamas, stuffed it under the covers, put
on my blues, wrapped the whisky in a paper bag, and
walked freely past the guards. A short taxi ride
through the town of Quantico—a few bars, half a
dozen laundromats, and twice that many uniform shops
fronting the brown Potomac—brought me to Little
Hall, where the party was being held.

I walked inside and into the nineteenth century.
Junior officers wore white gloves and Prussian-blue,
Prussian-collared tunics. Majors and colonels whom
I was accustomed to seeing in functional khakis strutted
around in waist-length dinner jackets with shoulder
boards that advertised their rank in gold and red. A
couple of generals swooped toward the bar, capes billowing behind them. Off to one side, like a row of car-
dinals perched on a branch, scarlet-clad bandsmen sat
stiffly on a row of folding chairs. Through all this military plumage, wives and girl friends glided with a rustle
of expensive gowns. "Good evenin', majuh," one of
these creatures said in her honey-soft, flirtatious-but-
chaste, Tidewater-aristocracy accent. "It's sooo nahce
to see you again, suh. It cuhtainly is a luhvly
pahty. . . ." A full-dress ball. I could not make up my
mind what it looked like—a scene from *The Student*

Prince, a costume party, or the senior prom at a military academy.

I felt disappointment. The atmosphere was more one of a debutante cotillion than of Beowulf's mead hall. And perhaps because there was so much brass around, including the Marine Corps commandant, General Wallace Greene, everyone behaved. The band stuck to a vapid repertoire of Broadway musical scores, and General Greene made a slightly slurred speech which drew some polite applause.

Inconsequential though the ball was, that night in November 1964 holds a special significance for me. I see the hall, crowded with officers in baroque uniforms, filled with fashionably dressed women. Some are dancing; some are filing past a buffet, spearing hors d'oeuvres with toothpicks; some, holding drinks, are engaged in light conversation; all are without forebodings of what awaits them: fear, disfigurement, sudden death, the pain of long separation, widowhood. And I feel that I am looking at a period piece, a tableau of that innocent time before Vietnam.

Chapter Two

For I am a man under authority, having soldiers under me: and I say to this man, Go, and he goeth; and to another, Come, and he cometh; and to my servant, Do this, and he doeth it.
—Matthew 8:9

The old salts used to tell us that the most memorable experience in an officer's life is his first command. It is supposed to be like first love, a milestone on the road to manhood. They claimed, these veteran majors and colonels, to remember almost everything about the first platoons they led on Guadalcanal, or in Tientsin, or in Korea. "Why, it seems like yesterday, lieutenant. . . . I had this rifleman, Lance Corporal . . . poor guy was killed by a Jap machine gun when we were taking

Bloody Nose Ridge. . . . And there was this sergeant in mortars, big redhead, damn if he couldn't put an eighty-one down a smokestack at maximum range."

I do not have such powers of recall. My first command was a rifle platoon in a battalion of the 3d Marine Division, which I joined on Okinawa after graduation from Basic School and a month's leave in San Francisco. There were about forty men in it, but I can remember only a few. What remains in my memory is a partial roster of 2d platoon, C Company, 1st Battalion, 3d Marines:

Corporal Banks, 1st squad leader in place of Sergeant Gordon, who had been temporarily attached to D Company. Banks was a soft-spoken black who had fought in Korea and was therefore regarded as a living relic by his teen-age squad. He was, in fact, not more than thirty or thirty-one.

Corporal Mixon, the 2d squad leader, was thin and almost delicate-looking, with a shy, diffident manner.

Corporal Gonzalez, 3d squad leader—short, stocky, pugnacious but likeable.

Lance Corporal Sampson, an old man of twenty-five whose seven-year career in the Marine Corps was as checkered as a chessboard. He had twice risen to corporal, had been busted down to private both times, and was again on the ascent when I took over the platoon. A sloppy, careless man with a heavy beard that gave him a perpetual five o'clock shadow, Sampson was an archetypal service bum in garrison, but a good field soldier. It was as if he needed the stimulus of hardship or danger to display his better characteristics.

Lance Corporal Bryce, a tall Kansan and one of the most taciturn men in the company. Something seemed to be preying on his mind; whatever it was, he kept it, as he did everything else, to himself. I did not hear him speak more than a few dozen words the whole time I knew him, and in July of 1965, a grenade silenced him completely and forever.

Lance Corporal Marshall, in civilian life a freelance knight of the quarter-mile strip, given to telling tales about back-road jousts won on his chrome-gilt steed, a chopped Chevy with a California rake, four-speed stick, four-eleven rear end, and a fuel-injected mill that idled with a throaty rumble and exploded like Vesuvius when he wound her out, red-lined the tac, and did zee-ro to sixty in five flat, goddamn, leaving the other dudes like they were standing still. Ambition: to save enough money in the Corps to buy an even hairier beast when he got out and spend the rest of his life watching telephone poles whip past in a blur.

PFC Chriswell, the platoon's seventeen-year-old radioman, a reedy, sandy-haired kid who should have been shooting baskets in some small-town gym instead of a rifle ten thousand miles from his home. He had the irritating and unbreakable habit of addressing officers in the archaic third person: "Would the lieutenant like me to clean his pistol?"

PFC Lockhart, quiet, sensitive to the point of tenderheartedness, but a survivor of life on the harsh streets of Chicago's South Side. For some reason, I remember the insignificant fact that he had a hard time doing push-ups.

PFC Devlin, Lockhart's buddy, an all-American-boy, nineteen, with blond hair, blue eyes, and the physique of a middleweight wrestler.

PFCs Bradley and Deane, an inseparable pair of North Carolinians who, like their rebel ancestors, were natural infantrymen. They could walk forever and through anything, shoot straight, and feel nothing but a cheerful contempt for physical adversities.

Corporal Sullivan, whose machine-gun squad was attached to my platoon for a while. He exasperated some of the lifers because he was up for sergeant but refused to behave like one. A sergeant was supposed to be a swaggering tyrant; Sully was a gangly egalitarian, a "goddamned diddy-bopper," as one of his detractors described him, referring to his casual, loose-jointed gait. He had an irreverent sense of humor and gave orders that sounded more like requests. At twenty-two, he was too young for a third stripe, and the fact that he was getting one, the lifers complained, was yet another sign that their Corps was degenerating. "By God, when

I went in we didn't have no pimple-faced buck sergeants. Took you five years just to make E-4."

As for the rest, they are now just names without faces or faces without names.

A few generalizations can be made about all of them. They were to a man thoroughly American, in their virtues as well as flaws: idealistic, insolent, generous, direct, violent, and provincial in the sense that they believed the ground they stood on was now forever a part of the United States simply because they stood on it.

Most of them came from the ragged fringes of the Great American Dream, from city slums and dirt farms and Appalachian mining towns. With depressing frequency, the words 2 *yrs. high school* appeared in the square labeled EDUCATION in their service record books, and, under FATHER'S ADDRESS, a number had written *Unknown.* They were volunteers, but I wondered for how many enlisting had been truly voluntary. The threat of the draft came with their eighteenth birthdays, and they had no hope of getting student deferments, like the upper-middle-class boys who would later revile them as killers. In some cases, a juvenile-court judge had presented a Hobson's choice between the Corps and jail. Others were driven by economic and psychological pressures; the Marines provided them with a guaranteed annual income, free medical care, free clothing, and something else, less tangible but just as valuable—self-respect. A man who wore that uniform was somebody. He had passed a test few others could. He was not some down-on-his-luck loser pumping gas or washing cars for a dollar-fifty an hour, but somebody, a Marine.

The platoon sergeant, William Campbell ("Wild Bill" to his friends), was a veteran of Korea and countless barroom brawls in most of the ports between Naples and Yokohama. He fit the Hollywood image of a Marine sergeant so perfectly that he seemed a case of life imitating art. Six feet three inches and two hundred and twenty pounds of pure mean, he believed in the Marine Corps the way a Jesuit believes in the

Catholic Church, and felt only disdain for the Navy, the Army, the Congress, motherhood, and officers—in that order. It was a sight to watch him walking down a street, straight-backed and swaggering in a uniform bleached white by tropic suns, his eyes glaring scornfully from beneath the bill of a faded cap.

The redhaired giant walked with a slight limp, a souvenir of the frostbite he had suffered in the Chosin Reservoir in 1950. At that time, before names like Khe Sahn, Hue, and Con Thien were added to the Corps' battle-streamers, the fighting withdrawal from "frozen Chosin" was considered to be its greatest contest, a trial by fire and ice. Over the years, the campaign attained the dimensions of an epic—even the most sober military historians compared it to the march of Xenophon's Immortals—and any marine who could say, "I was at Chosin" was likely to be regarded with a great deal of respect. And Campbell was among those few who could.

His relationship to the platoon was that of a chieftain to a warrior clan. Those forty marines constituted his private fiefdom, in the rule of which no one was allowed to interfere. It was his conviction, and he was probably right, that discipline in a regular army is ultimately based on fear. He had inculcated that emotion in the platoon, and it was a fear not of military law, but of him. They had been convinced that risking the possible consequences of obeying an order was preferable to Wild Bill's wrath, the certain consequence of disobeying it. "You are fuckin' up my Marine Corps," he would say to the offender, these words usually preceding an invitation to step behind the barracks.

The platoon did not resent Campbell's violent methods. There is an ineradicable streak of *machismo,* bordering on masochism, in all marines, and I think the platoon was proud that its sergeant was reputed to be one of the toughest in the division. Besides, his man-to-man way of meting out punishment was preferable to the impersonal retribution of the Uniform Code of Military Justice. If nothing else, it kept their records clean and saved them from losing rank or the chance for promotion.

Campbell's abiding passion in life was close-order drill, at which he had gained considerable skill during a tour as a DI at Parris Island, the Marine recruit depot. Drill was an art form to him, and no choreographer could have derived as much satisfaction from staging a ballet as Campbell did from marching his marines around a parade deck. Once, about two weeks after I arrived on Okinawa, I watched him at work. He was standing off to one side of the field, hands on his hips, bawling commands to which the platoon responded with machinelike precision. It was an impressive demonstration of the thing he did best, and when he asked if I would like to give it a try, I said no, I could not do half as well as he, let alone any better. "That's right, lieutenant," he replied with a sneer. "Ain't nobody better'n me."

I had a hard time convincing him that I was the platoon commander. I am not sure if I ever succeeded. He always seemed to tolerate me as an unavoidable nuisance, which is the way he felt about most officers. For all that, I grew to admire and even like him. In the modern army that Robert McNamara had molded into the corporate image of the Ford Motor Company, an army full of "team players" who spoke the glib jargon of public relations and practiced the art of covering their tracks, there was something refreshing about a profane, hard-drinking maverick like Campbell. He played by his own rules, as much as was possible in the service, and he did nothing halfway. He was what he was one hundred percent, with no apologies to anyone, a sergeant of marines.

The battalion was suffering from an epidemic of island fever when I joined it in January 1965. Except for a brief period of cold-weather training in Japan, One-Three had been on Okinawa since September, waiting for something to happen. Their boredom was compounded by isolation. They were stationed at Camp Schwab, "Home of the Third Marines," which, with its stark ranks of one-story concrete barracks and chain link fences, looked more like a minimum security

prison than a home. It was the most remote base on
the Rock, at the edge of the jungled hills that covered
the northern third of the island. The closest thing to
civilization was a short taxi ride away, a squalid collection of honky-tonks with names that read like a lesson in American geography: Bar New York, Club
California, the Blue Hawaii Lounge. The town was
named Heneko, and the marines went there at night
to fight over meager honors, get hustled by the bow-
legged bargirls, and drink in the heavy, reckless way
of young GIs overseas for the first time.

The days followed the time-honored routine of garrison life: reveille, roll call, calisthenics, morning chow,
working parties, noon chow, close-order drill, working
parties, calisthenics, evening chow, liberty call for
those who had liberty, guard mount for those who did
not, evening colors, taps, lights-out.

It was a bleak existence, and did not at all fulfill my
expectations, ever romantic, of what it was like to be
a marine in the Far East. My first lesson in the facts
of life was administered by Fred Wagoner, the company first sergeant, a heavyset man whose thin, gray
hair and steel-rimmed glasses gave him the look of a
stern grandfather. Like most top sergeants, Wagoner
had a reverence for the formalities of military bureaucracy. On the day that I reported into the company,
I had signed some blank fitness report forms and laid
them on his desk before going into an introductory
meeting with the skipper, Captain Lee Peterson. When
I came out, Wagoner stopped me, his eyes baleful and
magnified behind the glasses, which slipped down his
nose; he pushed them back up with a stubby finger,
snorted, and said, "Mister Caputo, you signed these
with blue ink." I replied that I had, my ballpoint was
blue. "Damnit, sir, don't they teach you anything at
Quantico anymore?" he asked rhetorically, shoving
fresh forms at me with one hand and offering his pen
with the other. "Black ink, sir. Everything written in
the Marine Corps is written in black ink."

"Top," I said, "what the hell difference does it make?"

His tone changed to one of indulgent exasperation, as if he were speaking to an idiot child. "Please, sir. Use my pen. Black ink. That's the system, lieutenant, and if I've learned anything, it's that you can't beat the system."

And that is how I spent my first few weeks overseas, learning the system and signing blank forms in black ink, and drinking coffee in the company office with the other platoon commanders. So much for Hollywood and John Wayne. With little to do, I was soon as restless as everyone else. In fact, I was more so. The idleness and tedious housekeeping chores of life in camp got on my nerves because I was eager—some would have said overeager—for a chance to prove myself.

This keenness had been aroused by my status in the One-Three; I was not only its most junior officer, but an outsider as well, an uncomfortable position in what must have been one of the most tightly knit outfits in the service. One-Three was a "transplacement" battalion, part of a unit-rotation system used by the Marine Corps between the Korean and Vietnam wars to maintain both the proficiency and the *esprit* of its Pacific forces. A cadre of veteran officers and NCOs—men like Sergeant Campbell—formed the nucleus of each of these battalions. The ranks were filled with enlisted men who had gone through boot camp together, the junior officer billets with lieutenants who had graduated from Quantico in the same year. Marines assigned to a transplacement unit thus had something in common from the day they joined it; and they generally remained with the unit for the balance of their enlistments, about three years. They spent half that time training with the 1st Division at Camp Pendleton, California, and then sailed to Okinawa for thirteen months' duty in the Far East with the Third. Because they did everything and went everywhere together, shared the same experiences and hardships, a high degree of comradeship developed among them.

Like the marriage of cells in a body, each marine, each squad, platoon, and company was bonded to the other to form an entity with a life and spirit all its own, the battalion.

Such, anyway, was the case with the marines in One-Three. Their individual identities had become inextricably bound up with its identity; they were it, it was them, and in their view, it was the best battalion in the best branch of the service, an elite within an elite. Their clannish, cliquish attitude was almost palpable. I was aware of it from the beginning and was, therefore, painfully conscious of being a stranger. In the mess, I often felt like a guest in some exclusive men's club —not unwelcome, but not a member either.

My "parent unit" was regimental headquarters company, which had assigned me to One-Three for ninety days, the period I was required to serve in a command billet to qualify in my military occupational specialty, or MOS. This meant that I was merely attached to, rather than a part of, the battalion; and when the ninety days expired, I would probably be recalled to HqCo to work in some dull staff job. I was told, however, that this fate might be postponed, even avoided altogether, if the battalion accepted me as one of its own. That, in turn, depended on whether I demonstrated an acceptable degree of competence and won the respect of both my platoon and my fellow officers. Neither would be accomplished easily. The other platoon commanders in Charley Company—Glen Lemmon, Bruce Tester, and Murph McCloy—had anywhere from one to two years' experience, while I had none at all. Compared to them, I seemed inept, an amateur ignorant of the most elementary facts. "Blue ink!" the first sergeant had said, embarrassing me in front of his enlisted clerks. "Don't they teach you anything anymore?" I was alliteratively known as the "boot brown-bar," slang for a raw second lieutenant.

There were rumors floating around camp about a possible deployment to Vietnam. They had begun earlier in the month, when Delta Company was sent to Danang to provide internal security for the American compound there. It was an unexciting mission and, according to the official word, a temporary one. But the unofficial word had it that the rest of One-Three would be on its way to Vietnam soon. Still, as the weeks went by and nothing happened, I began to despair of ever seeing action.

In February, the company was sent up to the Northern Training Area, a jungled, mountainous region, for counter-guerrilla-warfare exercises. This was my first test in the field; anxious to pass, afraid of making the smallest mistake, I bungled it, at least at first. Hesitant and unsure of myself, I gave orders that were often misunderstood by the platoon. Leading patrols in the Okinawan jungles turned out to be far more difficult than it had been in Quantico's forests, which seemed parklike by comparison. I nearly got lost several times, only proving the truth of the old service adage that the most dangerous thing in the world is a second lieutenant with a map and compass. The crowning indignity came during a tactical problem involving an "attack" on a simulated guerrilla base camp. While the platoon was waiting to move to the jump-off point, Campbell lit the smoking lamp, apparently because he felt like having a cigarette. Seeing him do so, I figured it was all right and lit it up. But I had hardly finished the first drag when an enraged instructor emerged from a bamboo thicket.

"What the hell is going on here?" he yelled. "The problem isn't secured. Lamp is out till I say it's lit! You do something like that in Vietnam, you'll draw fire and get your men killed. And take that goddamn thing out of your mouth. You're supposed to set the example."

Chewed out in front of the troops. As if that weren't enough, Joe Feeley, the company executive officer, gave me a lecture later in the day. The instructor had reported the incident to Peterson, who, Feeley said, was willing to make certain allowances because I was green. But another mistake like the one today and the skipper would begin to doubt my competence. "As for your platoon sergeant, *lieutenant,* you had best teach that bullheaded son of a bitch who's the honcho before he gets you in trouble again." Having taken my verbal twenty lashes, I returned to the platoon, remembering the words of a character in a war novel I had read once: "By God, there's nothing like command." By God, there wasn't, and I wondered if I would ever get the hang of it. I did eventually. Resolved to endure no further reprimands, I turned into a regular little martinet, and the platoon's performance for the rest of the exercise, although far from brilliant, was at least respectable.

Looking back, I think that much of my behavior later in Vietnam, good as well as bad, was determined by the rebukes I received that day. They instilled in me a lasting fear of criticism and, conversely, a hunger for praise. The last thing I wanted was to be thought of as inadequate, not quite up to the mark for membership in the tough, masculine world of a Marine rifle battalion. Had I been older or more seasoned, I would have taken Feeley's remark for the unimportant thing it was; but I suffered from a youthful tendency to take things too seriously. That is how I appear in the comments various commanding officers made in their fitness reports on me. I still have copies of these mixed reviews, and they show an ardent, somewhat reckless officer who is trying too hard to live up to what is expected of him. "Lieutenant Caputo is fearless in the face of the enemy"; "an aggressive and eager young officer with a desire to succeed"; "a little too quick on the trigger"; "tends to rush impulsively into things"; "does not plan ahead"; "performed well in combat." Napoleon once said that he could make men die for little pieces of ribbon. By the time the battalion left for Vietnam, I was ready to die for considerably less, for a few favorable remarks in a fitness report. Words.

The exercises lasted two weeks; two weeks of incessant rain during which we gained some familiarity with the miseries peculiar to jungle warfare—leeches, mosquitoes, constant dampness, the claustral effect created by dense forests that dimmed the brightest noon

and turned midnight into the absolute blackness known
by the blind. I cannot say we learned much else that
proved useful. We practiced tactics perfected by the
British during the Malayan uprising in the 1950s, a
conflict that bore only a facile resemblance to the one
in Indochina. Nevertheless, it was the only successful
counterinsurgency waged by a Western power in Asia,
and you could not argue with success. So, as always
seems to be the case in the service, we were trained by
the wrong war; we learned all there was to know about
fighting guerrillas in Malaya.

Some attempts were made to instill in us those anti-
social attributes without which a soldier fighting in the
jungle cannot long survive. He has to be stealthy, aggressive, and ruthless, a combination burglar, bank
robber, and Mafia assassin. One of our instructors in
these lessons was a beefy sergeant whose thick neck
blended smoothly into shoulders that looked as wide as
an M-14 rifle is long. He was always stressing the need
to annihilate every enemy soldier who entered the killing zone of an ambush. The first burst of fire, delivered
at waist level, was to be followed by a second at ankle level, the object being to finish off whoever had
survived the initial volley. To whip us into the vicious
mood required for cold-blooded slaughter, the sergeant
began his first lesson like this:

He came into the classroom, let out a spine-chilling
war cry, and buried a hatchet in one of the wooden
walls. Without saying a word, he wrote something on a
small blackboard, concealing it with his V-shaped back.
He stepped aside, pointing to the writing with one hand
and to a marine with the other. "You, what does that
say?" he asked.

Marine: "It says 'ambushes are murder,' sergeant."

Sergeant: "Right." Shouts "AMBUSHES ARE
MURDER," then returns to the blackboard, writes
something else, and again asks, "What does that say?"

Marine: "And murder is fun."

Sergeant: "Right again." Removes hatchet from wall
and brandishes it at the class. "Now, everybody say it.
AMBUSHES ARE MURDER AND MURDER IS
FUN."

Class, hesitantly, with some nervous laughter: "Ambushes are murder and murder is fun."

Sergeant: "I can't hear you, marines."

Class, this time in unison: "AMBUSHES ARE MURDER AND MURDER IS FUN."

Unshaven and filthy, the company returned to Camp Schwab in time to learn that while it had been murdering fictitious guerrillas, real ones had caused mayhem in Vietnam. The Viet Cong had attacked the American air base at Pleiku, inflicting what was then considered heavy casualties: about seventy airmen had been killed or wounded. A few days later, the first U.S. planes began to empty their explosive bowels over the North. The sustained bombing campaign that came to be known as Operation Rolling Thunder had begun.

The battalion had fallen back into its domestic rut, but the news of these two events—the Pleiku raid and the retaliatory bombing—rekindled the rumors about "going South" and changed the atmosphere in camp from boredom to expectancy. The rumors were denied on February 15, when we got word that One-Three was going afloat in a week, its destination Hong Kong or the Philippines. They were then confirmed on the 17th, when we were alerted to mount out for Danang on the 24th.

Thus began three confusing weeks of alarms and counter-alarms, stand-tos and stand-downs. Charley Company was sent back into the bush for another two days of exercises, presumably as a rehearsal for the live-ammunition drama in which we would be playing by month's end. The weather, bright and warm while we were in garrison, turned sodden, giving us additional practice at being miserable. The platoon was nonetheless enthusiastic, all but Sergeant Campbell.

"Seventeen cotton-pickin' years I been doin' this," he said as we sloshed in the rain across a silty, salmon-colored stream. "Too old for this boy-scout bullshit, lieutenant. I'd like to get back to Parris Island, get my twenty in and get the fuck out. Spend some time with my old lady and my kids for a change."

"Hell, this ain't nothing but red clay, Sergeant

Campbell," said Bradley, who was behind us. "Me and old Deane here usta walk through stuff like this just coming home from school."

"I was talkin' to the lieutenant, turdbird."

"Yes, sir, Sergeant Campbell."

"Like I was sayin', lieutenant, get my twenty in and get out. You know, there's eighty acres I bought in South Carolina and I figure to retire on that."

I laughed, "Wild Bill Campbell, the gentleman farmer."

"Well. sir, go ahead and laugh. But I'm gonna get on the State Troopers when I get out and with that and my retirement, I figure old Wild Bill's gonna have it number fuckin' one while the rest of these turdbirds'll still be walkin' in this shit."

"Shee-hit," someone said. "I ain't gonna be walkin' in this any longer'n I have to. I ain't no friggin' lifer."

"That's because you ain't good enough, you silly little shit."

Finishing the exercises with a ten-mile forced march, we swung through the main gate looking and feeling warlike. But on the 24th, the battalion found itself still on the Rock. For over a week, orders were cut, then countermanded. We heard that the Danang operation had been called off. We were going to Hong Kong after all. Then word came that One-Three was to stage for a landing on the Danang airfield. It was scheduled for March 1. On the 1st, it was postponed to the 3d, and on the 3d to the 5th, when it was canceled altogether. According to the Word, that anonymous source of truths, half-truths, and falsehoods in the service, the battalion would remain on Okinawa until April 8, when it would sail for the Philippines.

I don't know if this series of countermanded orders was a planned deception or simply an example of the confusion that precedes most major military operations. If it was the former, it did not succeed in deceiving anyone but us. The bargirls in Heneko, always founts of accurate intelligence, spoke disconsolately of our impending departure. "You from One-Three Battalion, go Vietnam skoshi-skoshi. I tell you true. Maybe sayonara all Third Marine. Number ten [the worst], no money Heneko no GI here." Another omen appeared in the island's English-language newspaper, which reported that sixty prostitutes had migrated from Saigon to Danang "in anticipation of a rumored landing of U.S. Marines." There were other, more serious indications that the South Vietnamese Army, the ARVN, was nearing collapse. The news in the *Pacific Stars and Stripes* and on the armed forces radio network was a litany of defeats: outposts overrun, relief columns ambushed, airfields raided and shelled.

Despite these signs, we no longer expected our future to be a violent one. Concluding that the past alarms had been drills to test the battalion's "combat readiness," we settled down for a prolonged confinement on the Rock. Boredom reigned again and was combated in the usual ways. On Sunday, March 7, at least half of One-Three's thousand officers and men were enjoying a weekend of I-and-I—intercourse and intoxication—in Kin and Kadena, Ishakawa and Naha, city of the Teahouse of the August Moon.

One who remained on base was Glen Lemmon, the battalion duty officer for that day. Early in the afternoon, a message arrived at HQ, where Lemmon sat, yawning and making entries in the OD's logbook. He read it and, quickly snapping out of his lethargy, picked up the phone to call the CO, Lieutenant Colonel Bain.

Chapter Three

Messenger: Prepare you, generals.
The enemy comes on in gallant show;
Their bloody sign of battle is hung out,
And something to be done immediately.
—Shakespeare
Julius Caesar

About the time Lemmon picked up that phone, Murph McCloy and I were on the terrace of the Officers' Club, drinking beer and admiring the view. The club stood atop a high hill, and the scene below was straight out of *South Pacific*, lacking only a lovesick Ezio Pinza singing to Mary Martin. A turquoise lagoon shimmered in the sun, mahogany-skinned fishermen paddled skiffs across its still surface, and beyond the barrier reef the bright expanse of the East China Sea stretched to the horizon. Content, we lay back in our deck chairs, the sun warm on our faces and the beer icy-cold in our hands.

"P.J., this sure is gracious living," McCloy said. The telephone rang, and Sammy, the club's Okinawan manager, popped out onto the terrace. "Any offasuh from the One-Three Battalion," he paged, "call your OD right now!" McCloy volunteered. I figured it was nothing more serious than another fistfight at the Enlisted Men's Club, but when Murph returned, his face was flushed, as if he had a high fever. In a way, he did.

"P.J., that was Lemmon. He's OD today and he just got the word. We're going South."

"What?"

"We're going to war!" he said, as if it were the most wonderful thing that could happen to a man. Then he left the club at a run.

Nearly a month of hearing the boy cry wolf had

38

made me cautious, so I went inside to call Lemmon myself. He assured me that this was no flap. Had the message right in front of him: One-Three was going South by air. We were to mount out from Kadena Air Force Base sometime tonight and land at Danang the next morning. *Danang tomorrow morning!* The words yanked me out of the sluggishness induced by the hot weather and six beers. I felt an adrenal surge, a tingling in my hands and an empty sensation in my stomach, as if I were in an elevator that was descending too fast.

What was I supposed to do? I had never been to a war before. "Well, neither have I," Lemmon said. "Main thing is to get yourself squared away first." He read me a list of instructions: make up a field transport pack, stow extra gear in a seabag, et cetera. When that was done, hayako down to the company area. Don't worry about the troopers, the NCOs would take care of them. That was all he could tell me. Meanwhile, he had to round up the rest of the officers. "What a day the nummies picked for a mount-out," he said, laughing his strange laugh, which was more a cackle, as dry and harsh as the west Texas plains where he was born. *Heh-heh-heh,* the nummies picked a Sunday; everybody was scattered all over the island, getting drunk or getting laid, and when he reached them in their brothels and bars, they were too stoned to understand what he was telling them.

"I called down at the Kadena O-Club, figuring the boys'd be down there guzzling those French-seventy-fives. Williamson picked up the phone. I told him to hayako his ass back to Schwab because we were going South. He says, 'Oh, bullshit.' I told him, 'No bullshit, Williamson, we're mounting out today, goddamnit.' He tells me, 'Lemmon, I am too shitfaced to go to Vietnam. Send somebody else,' and hangs up. I called him back and got the same crap. Well, little while later, Major Lyons comes in here and I tell him about my problem with Williamson. So Lyons phones Kadena, gets him on the hook and says, 'Mister Williamson, this is the battalion executive officer. If you're not here, sober, in an hour, I'll hang your young ass.'

Heh-heh-heh. Phil, it's really somethin' else, all fucked up. . . ."

Lemmon hung up, leaving me to guess the point of that story, if it had one.

I sprinted back to the BOQ, crashing through the door with a bang loud enough to startle my unflappable roommate, Jim Cooney.

"Christ, what lit the fire under your tail?" He was a few numbers my junior and had just arrived on the Rock, so I composed myself and tried to sound coolly professional.

"Oh, we just got the word to mount out."

"Where to?"

"Vietnam," I said offhandedly, as if I commuted there once a month.

"Yeah?" Cooney replied, unimpressed. He would lose half of his platoon in August, at the Battle of Chu Lai. "Vietnam, huh? No shit."

In spite of the past alarms, I was unprepared for anything more serious than a field exercise. My 782 gear, or field equipment, was strewn about the room and my utility uniforms were being washed by one of the naissons who did laundry at the BOQ, a girl named Miko. Well, there would be no need for starched uniforms in the bush. I dashed into the laundry room, stuffed a few dollars in Miko's hand, gathered up my bundle, and ran out, with Miko crying in pursuit, "Caputosan, must finish, must finish." I called back that I was leaving for Vietnam. "Ah, Vietnam," she said. "Numbah ten. Too bad."

Back in the room, I worked swiftly to make up a field-transport pack. This burden consisted of a haversack, knapsack, blanket, shelter half, poncho, tent pegs, ridge-pole, guy line, an extra pair of boots, changes of socks and underwear, a spare uniform, mess kit, shaving kit, and entrenching tool. Adding a steel helmet, two canteens, side arm, flak jacket, field glasses, compass, knife, and rations, my kit came to sixty-five pounds. The pack felt like a Wells Fargo safe when I tried it on to adjust the shoulder straps. Would we be expected to make long marches through steaming jungles with all that on our backs? I slipped it off and it hit the floor with a thud. Following Lemmon's instructions, I stowed extra combat gear in my seabag and packed my service "A" uniforms, most of my civilian clothes, and, regrettably, my books into a footlocker. I would have liked to bring the books along, but there wasn't enough room in the seabag. I was also sure there would not be enough time to read in Vietnam. I didn't know then that nine-tenths of war is waiting around for the remaining one-tenth to happen. The packing done, I stenciled CAPUTO, P.J. 2LT. 089046 C-1-3 on the footlocker and tagged it for shipment to the division warehouse at Camp Courtney. It would be stored there until I returned to claim it. The possibility that I might not return did not occur to me. I was twenty-three years old, in superb condition, and quite certain that I would live forever.

The scene at the battalion area was chaotic and the atmosphere one of crisis. Enlisted men were running in and out of the squad bays with the frenzied motions of figures in a silent film. Some were in full battle-dress, some still in civilian clothes, and others in only their underwear, odd bits of equipment slung over their naked shoulders. Working parties lugged crates from the supply sheds and piled them in the streets, creating an obstacle course for jeep and truck drivers. A mechanical mule—a heavy-weapons carrier that looked nothing like a mule but rather resembled an oversized toy wagon—dodged one of the stacks, went over a curb, and roared down a sidewalk, a 106-mm recoilless rifle bouncing in its flatbed. Charley Company's area, like the others, resembled an outdoor army surplus store. Scattered everywhere were mortar tubes, baseplates, rows of packs with rifles propped against them, tent canvas, machine-gun belts—the linked cartridges coiled in the metal ammo cans—flak jackets, helmets, and a variety of communications gear. Testing the radios, the operators produced a concert of squawks, bleeps, and static hisses, above which their voices rose in monotonous chants. "Burke Six, Burke Six, this is Charley Six, Charley Six. Read you weak and garbled, say again weak and garbled. Give me a long test-count." ". . . Roger, Charley Six. Long test-count follows . . . ten, niner, eight . . ."

I recall very little of the next few hours. It was all noise and confusion, with officers yelling orders at sergeants, sergeants at corporals, corporals at lance corporals, lance corporals at privates, who, having no one to yell at, did all the work. The chain of command, if nothing else, was functioning smoothly. I remember the theatrical McCloy exclaiming, "The bronzed gods are off to war!" when he saw a marine with bandoliers crossed over his chest, Mexican-bandit style; a supply clerk who said, "These're so's your pecker don't get blown off" as he issued sets of armored shorts; the strange feeling, a mixture of apprehension and anticipation, when I drew my pistol from the armory and saw the .45-caliber rounds, gleaming in the magazines like blunted yellow teeth.

About 2000 hours, more commonly known as eight P.M., Peterson summoned his platoon leaders and staff NCOs to the company office for a briefing. We crowded into the small room, which was soon dense with cigarette smoke and the stench of stale sweat. The tall, boyish-looking Peterson was bent over an acetate-covered map upon which lines and arrows had been drawn in grease pencil. Copies were passed to the platoon commanders. Some of us were so ignorant of Vietnamese geography that the skipper had to begin by pointing out where Danang was. It appeared on the old French Army maps under its colonial name, Tourane.

The briefing turned out to be sketchy. The Communists, Peterson said, had launched a dry-season offensive in I Corps and the Central Highlands and threatened to cut South Vietnam in half. The ARVN had been taking heavy casualties, the equivalent of a battalion a week. South Vietnamese units now guarding vital installations had to be sent into the field, both to make good ARVN losses and to provide enough manpower for a counteroffensive. American ground troops, therefore, had to be deployed immediately to Vietnam as security forces for U.S. bases, which were in imminent danger of being attacked and

Security for the base was to be provided by the 9th Marine Expeditionary Brigade, a task-organized unit consisting of our battalion; 3rd Battalion, 9th Marines; an artillery battalion; and assorted support troops. The brigade was to stage a combined air-sea assault at such-and-such hours the next morning and then establish defensive positions around Danang. Three-Nine would make an amphibious landing north of the city, at a place called Red Beach One, move inland, and occupy Hill 327, which dominated the base from the west. One-Three would take off from Kadena on Air Force C-130s and, after landing, set up a perimeter around the airfield itself. C Company would be in the first wave. There was little else he could tell us. "Any questions?" "Yes, sir, what kind of resistance is expected?" "Light resistance at most, some sniping, some anti-aircraft maybe; nevertheless, you ought to be prepared for heavier opposition. Anything else? Yes, Lieutenant Lemmon?"

"Yes, sir," Lemmon drawled. "How do I get out of this chicken-shit outfit?"

There was laughter from us and a frown from the skipper.

"Knock off the grabass, Glen. Okay, listen up. When you brief your people, make it clear that our mission is defensive only. I don't want anyone going in there thinking he's going to play John Wayne. We're to provide security and that's all. We're not going in to fight, but to free the ARVNs to fight. It's their war."

That said, we went out and passed the word to our platoons. "Defensive perimeter, shee-hit," I heard one rifleman say. "This is a grunt battalion, not a buncha gate guards." Still, it was better than hanging around on the Rock and, on second thought, a traditional Marine Corps operation: American lives and property had to be protected, a beleaguered ally helped, and a foreign enemy taught that the United States meant business. The Marines have landed and all that.

A convoy formed up sometime later. Supplies and equipment were loaded, after which the rifle companies scrambled on board. Then, having hurried all day, we did what soldiers spend three-fourths of their time doing: we waited. Half an hour went by, an hour, two hours. I sat in a jeep near the middle of that long idle column, feeling tired and wondering if it were really me sitting there in a helmet and flak jacket, with a Colt automatic on my hip. Could it have been only a year since I was discussing the relative merits of *Tom Jones* and *Joseph Andrews* in a seminar on the English novel? Since my roommate and I were listening to Bach and Vivaldi as we studied for our graduate record exams? What a waste of time that all seemed now.

A sudden roaring of engines woke me from this reverie. Ahead, about a dozen riflemen were running to board one of the six-bys. Apparently, we had been waiting for stragglers. The convoy began to bump forward, crawling uphill toward the main gate. Colby, Mc-Cloy's platoon sergeant, a straggler who had failed to make it back on time, stood in the street wearing a sport shirt and a silly grin. "So long, Charley Company," he said. "Bye-bye, boys." A marine, knowing that darkness guarantees anonymity, called down from one of the trucks, "Sergeant Colby's missin' movement, hang his ass." Colby just grinned and waved. "Bye-bye, boys." I asked where the hell he had been all day.

"Just gettin' me a little poontang, lieutenant."

"You know we're going South?"

"Yes, sir!" He gave me a wobbly salute. "And I want you to know how much us civilians appreciate what you boys are doing for us."

Down narrow roads the convoy rolled, past cane fields silver-green in the moonlight, past empty beaches stormed long ago by another generation in another war. It was a jolting, rocking ride to the Marine airbase at Futema, our final staging point before going on to Kadena. Bodies and equipment bounced on the steel beds of the trucks or were slammed against the wooden guardrails, but the knocking around did not affect the marines' high spirits. They whooped and hollered, shattering the early morning stillness of the villages along the way. Lights winked on in some of the squat, cement-block huts. Once, an angry woman appeared in a doorway and yelled something. We did not understand the words, but her meaning was clear.

A rifleman responded in pidgin Japanese, "Hey, mamasan, GI okay, joto okay. Number-one skivvy honcho, tachsameo."

The happy warriors. They all sounded as if they were a little drunk. And they were, though it was on the excitement of the event rather than on alcohol. Their battalion had accomplished no mean feat. Without warning or preparation, it had made itself ready for a major combat operation in less than eight hours. Now that that was done, they were free to enjoy the adventure, the sense of release from the petty rules and routines that had governed their lives until now. It was intoxicating to be racing through the darkness toward the unknown, toward a war in a far-off, exotic country. They were done with drills, inspections, and training exercises. Something important and dramatic was about to happen to them.

We had another long delay at Futema. The troops dismounted and stacked arms on a field next to the runway. Sitting back to back or lying with their heads on their packs, they rested on the grass. Cigarettes glowed in the predawn darkness. Battalion HQ had temporarily set up shop in the base operations room. Having nothing else to do, I went in for a Coke. Bedlam reigned. Phones rang, staff officers and clerks bustled around with messages in their hands. Colonel Bain, a big man whose flak jacket made him look bulky as an NFL tackle, said to someone on the telephone, "Well, they'd better let us know if we're going or not." Christ, I thought, don't tell me it's just another flap. A captain whom I had not seen before came up to me and asked if I was doing anything. I made the mistake of telling him I wasn't.

"Good. This is a vehicle manifest, and this," he said —unnecessarily, I thought—"is a piece of chalk. I want you to find these vehicles and mark their centers of gravity with the chalk. Make a cross and put a *CG* under it."

"Yes, sir. But how'm I supposed to know where the center of gravity is?"

"It's marked *CG* in yellow paint. You'll find it."

I considered asking the next logical question: why did I have to mark the centers of gravity when they were already marked? But I had been in long enough to know a peremptory order when I heard one.

I had just started this weighty assignment when the by now familiar command to mount up echoed across the field. The centers of gravity would have to remain unmarked. I ran back to my jeep, only to find it occupied by a staff major. The exalted one handed me my pack, with an expression that seemed to say, "Rank hath its privileges, brown-bar." I found room on a six-by with Gonzalez's squad, who responded cheerfully to the democratic leveling of their platoon commander. "Hey, the lieutenant's comin' along with us enlisted scum," one said. "Make a hole for the lieutenant." They cleared a path through the maze of gear. I moved to the front and flopped down against the rear of the cab. There was the smell of rifle oil, sweat, boot leather, and canvas. The truck engines started again. "Hot damn, movin' out," said Gonzalez, whose left foot would soon be mangled by a land mine.

A big buck sergeant strode past our truck and called out, "Hey, second goddamn platoon, you all ready for them Veet-Cong?"

"Fuckin' A."

"Yeah, watchya gonna do to em?"

"Kick ass and take names!"

"Shee-hit," came the sergeant's reply. He was a vigorous, powerfully built man, and in June a sniper's bullet would smash into his spine, paralyzing him from the waist down.

But that was yet to come. For the moment, riding with Gonzalez's squad, sharing the bone-jarring discomfort, listening to their harsh jokes and laughter, I felt a rush of affection, such as I had never felt for any men. The invisible threads that bound this battalion together pulled at me. For the first time, I thought of it as my battalion, and of myself as one who belonged to it.

We continued for another hour or so, a sinuous column of men and machines rumbling beneath a predawn sky. There is an awesome, elemental quality about an army on the move. It seems to possess its own momentum, a force that cannot be controlled by the men who are its parts, nor even by the men whose orders set it in motion. Inexorably, as if borne upon the current of some powerful river, we were carried closer to the planes that would take us to Vietnam and war.

Rolling into Kadena, the convoy bounced across a broad, dirt field, splitting from single file into several smaller columns abreast. The trucks threw up a gagging dustcloud as they made their sharp turns, charged across the field, then came to a sudden stop at the edge of the runway. Ahead, the C-130s hulked in the gray dawn. A brief period of commotion followed. Heavily laden marines leaped clumsily to the ground. Squad leaders and platoon sergeants stood with upraised arms, shouting commands. *"Fall in on me, second . . ." "Charley Company over here . . . Alpha on the right. . . ."* The jostling mass quickly composed itself into orderly ranks. We marched, by companies, toward the waiting aircraft. Platoons split off and clattered up the rear ramps into the yawning jaws of their assigned planes. The impression was that of dwarfs being swallowed by winged monsters.

My forty-odd men and I had to share space with several large crates and a communications jeep. Moored by a web of chains, the cargo kept us confined to a narrow corridor between it and the fuselage. Some exhausted men collapsed atop the crates, the rest tried to sleep on the deck, using each other as pillows. Thus, we endured yet another wait, one that took us well beyond the scheduled departure time. Rumors of a cancellation circulated. Finally, the crew came on board, passed the usual instructions, and raised the ramp. It locked into place with a metallic clink that reminded me of a cell door closing. Then the plane lumbered noisily down the runway and took off, headed south over the China Sea.

We rested as best we could during the five-hour flight. I retain an image of bodies, weapons, and equipment tangled together; of a young marine smoking and seemingly lost in private thoughts; of another curled up in the fetal position with his flak jacket thrown over him as a blanket against the high-altitude chill; of James Bryce lying utterly still, his mouth half-open, in a prefiguration of the death that would be his six months later.

A warning light flashed. The C-130 lurched into a steep assault-dive to avoid anti-aircraft fire, touched down, and taxied to a stop. "Saddle up, Second," Campbell said. "End of the line." Hoisting their packs, the platoon stood on stiffened legs as the ramp went down. Then, awkward as medieval knights in their armored jackets and shorts, they disembarked and fell in near a drab, metal-sided hangar. The afternoon was hot, damp, and cloudy. At the south end of the field, a few hundred yards away, I could see a group of miniaturized marines erecting a squad tent. Helicopters ferrying supplies from Three-Nine's beachhead flitted around the smooth crest of Hill 327, a geological freak rising abruptly from the rice paddies west of the airbase. The greenish-black wall of the Annamese Cordillera loomed in the distance, its peaks obscured by scudding clouds.

The remaining two companies began to land, the big transports angling out of the lowering sky. Lines of green-clad figures emerged from the planes, then fanned out toward the perimeter. I listened for the sound of gunfire, but heard none. I wasn't sure if I should feel encouraged or disappointed. A young lieutenant in a motley uniform—khaki shirt and green utility trousers—walked up to me and introduced himself. From D Company, he was the landing liaison officer. He asked what outfit I was from.

"That's Charley over there." He pointed to where the squad tent was going up, then shook my hand and said, "Welcome to Danang," as if I were a visiting conventioneer. In a column of twos, we trudged past a warehouse and a squadron of parked H-34 helicopters. The pilots stood watching us with an air of veteran insouciance. They were got up in Terry and the Pirates costumes: camouflage uniforms, rakish bush hats, low-slung revolvers. I gathered that one of the advantages of being in Vietnam was the freedom more or less to dress as you pleased. A little farther on, we received an object lesson in some of Vietnam's disadvantages. One of the planes had been hit by light anti-aircraft fire. There were several jagged holes in one of its wings. The expressions on some faces seemed to ask, "If that's what bullets do to airplanes, what would they do to me?" The answer was provided by a fork-lift off-loading supplies nearby. It carried a stack of aluminum boxes that resembled huge tool chests. They were coffins.

The company was digging in alongside a dirt road, with Lemmon's platoon on the right, Tester's on the left. Mine filled the center. Some of Lemmon's men were talking excitedly; their plane had been the one with the bullet holes in it. They had been *shot at*, their landing had been opposed. A few rounds admittedly was not much opposition, but at least we had been spared the humiliation suffered by Three-Nine. Their entrance into the war zone had been the stuff of which comic operas are made. Like the marines in World War II newsreels, they had charged up the beach and were met, not by machine guns and shells, but by the mayor of Danang and a crowd of schoolgirls. The mayor made a brief welcoming speech and the girls placed flowered wreaths around the marines' necks. Garlanded like ancient heroes, they then marched off to seize Hill 327, which turned out to be occupied only by rock apes—gorillas instead of guerrillas, as the joke went—who did not contest the intrusion of their upright and heavily armed cousins.

Charley Company had been assigned the southern sector of the perimeter, its lines anchored on the left on an asphalt road that led into Danang city, and tied in on the right with A Company. The MLR, or main line of resistance, was opposite the dirt road to our front. It consisted of a chain link fence, a zigzag trench line connecting a series of stone watch-towers—relics from French colonial times—a double-apron barbed wire fence, a minefield, and a triple row of concertina wire. The MLR was manned by an ARVN regional force (militia) battalion, which we would formally relieve in two or three days. Until then, One-Three would serve as a secondary line of defense. Peterson told us that the swath of rice paddies and villages stretching southward had been a Communist stronghold for years and was considered the most likely avenue of approach for a Viet Cong attack. In simple terms, if they hit, they would hit C Company first.

Spurred by that warning, the men worked hard all afternoon, digging foxholes, filling and piling up sandbags, tamping them down with the flat side of entrenching tools. Officers trooped along the line, assigning and changing positions. I was careful to do everything by the book, setting up interlocking fields of fire, emplacing machine guns to cover the platoon frontage—in brief, all that I had learned at Quantico in Rifle Company Defensive Tactics. I was now plying my trade in earnest, but I had a difficult time convincing myself that that was the case. So far, the operation had the playact quality of an exercise. Back on Okinawa, the skipper's briefing about offensives and counteroffensives had created in my mind somber images of shell-cratered fields and devastated towns. But Vietnam, from what I could see of it, did not look like a war-torn country (a scenic defect American firepower would eventually correct). The "Communist stronghold" in front of us reminded me of a tropical park. Groves of bamboo and coconut palm rose out of rice paddies like islands from a jade-colored sea. Carrying poles slung across their shoulders, peasant women in conical hats jogged down a paddy dike past a small boy riding a water buffalo. A group of young girls glided by, provocative creatures in their silk trousers and filmy ao-dais. They smiled politely when a machine-gunner named Bunch waved at them from his foxhole. "Hey, naisson, number one. Joto itchiban." Williams, his squad leader, reminded him that he was no longer on Okinawa. Meanwhile, I scanned the countryside with my binoculars, looking for the red hordes, but the only signs of war were our own

Phantoms, roaring northward with their bomb racks full.

The Beau Geste watchtowers on the MLR contributed to the atmosphere of make-believe. If this was a real war zone, what were those anachronisms doing here? Their only conceivable use would be as registration points for VC mortar batteries. Their occupants were another source of bewilderment. The relaxed behavior of the RFs—Ruff-Puffs they were called—indicated one of three possibilities: no one had warned them that an enemy attack was imminent; they had been told, but were such experienced veterans that mere warnings did not alarm them; or they were the worst soldiers in the world. I was not yet familiar with ARVN fighting abilities, but I inclined to the last possibility. Whatever, they milled around, some without helmets or weapons, and stared curiously at our feverish activity. About half a dozen were asleep under a thatch lean-to; others lounged barefoot near one of the whitewashed towers. A few of the bolder ones slipped through a hole in the chain link and walked along our line, begging cigarettes. "GI, you gimme one cig'rette you." They demanded Salems, but all we could offer were C-ration Luckies so stale that they were said to be of Korean War vintage. These satisfied the RFs, however. Encouraged by their comrades' success, a second mooching expedition set out, but was driven off on Peterson's orders. He passed the word to avoid fraternizing with our allies. According to the intelligence officer, the Ruff-Puffs were politically as well as militarily suspect; their ranks were believed to be riddled with Viet Cong or Viet Cong sympathizers, which amounted to the same thing. Needless to say, we found this intelligence hard to comprehend. That a battalion full of VC in ARVN uniforms could be defending an American airbase against the VC was still beyond our understanding.

At dusk, having neither heard a shot nor fired one in anger, we secured work on our excavations and rigged shelters for the night. This done, the company had its first meal since the previous day's breakfast on

Okinawa. That was already beginning to seem like a long time ago. The marines squatted to open the olive-drab ration cans with the openers attached to their dogtags. Small, blue cooking fires sprang up in front of the hooches, the acrid smell of heat tablets drifting across the bivouac. There was the usual bitching and horse trading that attends a meal of Cees. "Aw, sheehit, I got ham and limas . . . hey, tradeja ham and limas for a canna peaches. . . ." "Yeah, okay I'll take 'em. . . ." "You *like* ham and limas, man, you gotta be a fuckin' idiot. . . ." "All right, then keep 'em, maggot. . . ." "Hey, man, I was only shitinyuh, c'mon, gimme them peaches. . . ." "No way, not just for ham and limas. Price has gone up, my man. Ham and limas *and* your date-nut roll for the peaches."

They were all filthy after a day of muddy digging, and bleary-eyed after nearly two days without sleep. I think they also felt a little let down. The haste with which they had been sent to Vietnam caused them to assume that the situation was desperate. The wagon train was surrounded and the cavalry had to come to the rescue. They had whipped themselves into such a fever of anticipation that reality proved to be an anti-climax. Rather than desperate, the situation appeared to be totally calm. Yes, the wagons were here, in the form of supersonic warplanes, but the Indians were not. Looking at the lackadaisical ARVNs and tranquil rice paddies, we wondered, Well, where is this war we've heard so much about? where are these fabled guerrillas, the Viet Cong? There was one moment of excitement, when something exploded in a paddy field about a hundred yards away. A plume of yellow-brown smoke rose through the trees. A few men reached for their weapons, but relaxed when they learned what had happened: a dog had wandered into a minefield and blown itself to bits.

Night came on quickly. In a matter of minutes, dusk turned into the dark of a moonless midnight. Watches were set: a twenty-five percent alert for the first four hours, fifty percent after that. Helmets and flak jack-

ets on (we had all managed to "lose" the clumsy
armored shorts), the company filed off to the line.
Around nine or ten, when snipers opened up on our
positions, we learned that the Vietnam War was pri-
marily a nocturnal event. The sniping was neither
heavy nor accurate, just a few rounds fired every half
hour or so, but it caused a good deal of nervousness
because no one could tell where it came from. The
bullets seemed to whiz in out of nowhere. The landscape, so bucolic in daylight, gradually assumed a
sinister aspect. To our inexperienced eyes, bushes began to look like men. Still, there was no return fire on
our part: the battalion had been placed under strict
rules of engagement to avoid hitting civilians acciden-
tally. Chambers had to be clear, no firing could be
done except on orders of a staff NCO or an officer.

Our toughest battle that night was waged against
Vietnam's insect life. Mosquito netting and repellents
proved ineffective against the horde of flying, creeping,
crawling, buzzing, biting things that descended on us.
From every hooch came the sound of slaps and cries
of "goddamn little bastards, get outta here." By midnight, my face and hands were masses of welts.

To escape this torture, I made frequent checks of
the platoon lines. It was either on this night or the
next, or perhaps the one after that—those first nights
in Vietnam all blend into one—that I came close to
being shot by one of my own men. As I approached
his foxhole, he stopped me with a bookishly formal
challenge.

"Halt, who goes there?"

"Charley Two Actual" (my code name).

"Two Actual, advance to be recognized."

I took two steps forward.

"Halt. Who is the President of the United States?"

"Lyndon B. Johnson."

"Who is the Secretary of Defense?"

"Robert S. McNamara."

Thinking my responses clearly identified me as an
American, I started to walk forward. Another *halt,*
followed by the sound of a bolt slamming home and

the unpleasant sight of a rifle being leveled at me from ten yards' range brought me up short.

"Two Actual, who is the Undersecretary of Defense?"

"For Chrissake, how the hell do I know."

"Two Actual recognized," said the marine, lowering his weapon. It was Guiliumet. Jumping into his foxhole, I learned the reason for his excessive vigilance. He and the rifleman with him, Paulson, had almost been hit. A shredded sandbag was pointed out to me. "He put it right between us, lieutenant," Paulson said. "Jesus, if I'da been a couple inches the other way, I'da been deep-sixed sure as shit." I flipped off some old-salt comment about a miss being as good as a mile, but made sure to stay away from the wounded sandbag. Looking into the gloom beyond the wire, I saw nothing dangerous, only the empty paddies, gray now instead of green, the inky patches that marked a village or thicket, the scalloped tops of distant tree lines blacker than the black sky. All the same, the sniper had to be out there somewhere—with my head in his sights, for all I knew. Before my imagination got the best of me, I climbed out and continued on my rounds, feeling queasy the whole time. Phantoms, I thought, we're fighting phantoms.

Later, a brisk fire-fight broke out about a thousand yards forward of the perimeter. Grenades and mortars thumped. Small arms crackled like burning timber, and a couple of tracers streaked in silent, scarlet lines above the trees. Artillery boomed in another, more distant battle. All these sounds, the mysterious and fascinating sounds of contact, seemed to answer our earlier questions: the war and the Viet Cong were here all right, waiting for us.

Chapter Four

I'd read of our heroes, and wanted the same,
To play my own part in the patriot game.
                              —Irish ballad

They waited a long time. The battalion did not see
any action until April 22, when B Company was sent
to reinforce a reconnaissance patrol that had fallen
into an ambush a few miles west of Hill 327. In the
meantime, we fought the climate, the snipers, and
monotony, of which the climate was the worst.

The days were all alike. The sun rose about six,
changing color as it climbed, from red to gold to
white. The mists on the rice fields evaporated and the
dawn breeze died away. By noon, nothing moved
beneath the bright sky. Peasants left the fields for the
shade of their villages; water buffalo lay motionless in
the wallows, with only their heads and broad, curving
horns showing above the mud; the trees stood as still
as plants in a greenhouse. A wind fanned out of the
mountains in the midafternoon, a hot wind that lifted
the dust from the roads and the parched paddy fields
lying cracked in the sun, where the rice had been har-
vested. Whenever the wind was up, we could not look
anywhere without seeing dust—dust blowing in clouds,
palls of dust, dust devils that whirled into tents, the
canvas walls billowing like sails, pulling the guy lines
taut, then collapsing suddenly when the funnel passed
through. This was no fine dust, but thick stuff that
clung to everything it touched, to flesh and rifles and
the leaves on the trees. It covered the greasy mess
gear in the galley, so that we had to eat dust as well as
breathe it. And drink it, too, for it sifted into Lister
bags and jerry cans, giving the water the taste of
warm mud. In the late afternoon, the mountains

brought a premature twilight to the coastal plain, but this early dusk was the worst time. The wind dropped and the air was made stifling as the earth released the heat it had absorbed all day. We drank from our canteens until our bellies bulged, and tried to move as little as possible. Sweat ran down our sides and faces. The dust clinging to our skin thickened into a gummy film. Temperatures were irrelevant—the climate in Indochina does not lend itself to conventional standards of measurement. The mercury level might be 98 degrees one day, 110 the next, 105 the day after that; but these numbers can no more express the intensity of that heat than the reading on a barometer can express the destructive power of a typhoon. The only valid measurement was what the heat could do to a man, and what it could do to him was simple enough: it could kill him, bake his brains, or wring the sweat out of him until he dropped from exhaustion. The pilots and mechanics on the base could escape to their cool barracks or air-conditioned clubs, but on the perimeter there was nothing you could do about the heat except endure it. Relief came only at night, and night always brought swarms of malarial mosquitoes and the *crack-crack-crack* of the snipers' rifles.

Boredom was another problem, as it always is in stationary warfare. The battalion relieved the ARVNs, who, less than enthusiastic about being "free to fight" in the counteroffensive, took their time moving out. We would have happily taken their place. Instead of the adventure we had hoped it would be, defending the airfield turned out to be a deadening routine. We stood watch at night, stand-to after sunset, stand-down at first light. By day we repaired the rusted wire, dug fighting holes, filled sandbags. Our positions were shifted frequently, first to the right, then to the left, then right again, according to the ever changing defensive schemes drawn up by the brigade staff. This was not war; it was forced labor. Once, the word was passed to emplace crew-served weapons in bunkers strong enough to withstand direct hits from 120-mm mortars, then the heaviest artillery in the Viet Cong arsenal. The machine-gun squads, displaying a creative flair, erected elaborate works in a style that might be called Sandbag Modern. These architectural projects had no sooner been completed than they were ordered dismantled. The brigade CG, General Karsch, felt that bunkers destroyed a marine's "offensive spirit," which prompted Sullivan to remark that after weeks of working in the hot sun without a bath, his men were about as offensive as they could get.

Karsch and Colonel Bain came out to the perimeter fairly often, and it was interesting to see the contrast in these two officers. The colonel looked, and was, every inch a field marine, a brusque, hulking man with a face that managed to be ugly and attractive at the same time. His nose, banged-up and too big, the seamed flesh and hard, worn eyes told more about where he had been than the words in his service record book and the ribbons on his chest. It was an ugly face, but it had the dignity that is conferred upon those who have suffered the bodily and emotional aches of war. The colonel had paid his dues under fire, and so belonged to that ancient brotherhood to which no amount of money, social pedigrees, or political connections can gain a man admittance.

The tall but paunchy brigadier was another matter. He affected dash by wearing a green ascot with his starched battle jacket. His boots and the stars on his collar gleamed, and a kite-tail of staff officers trailed behind him when he toured the perimeter. The general made some attempts at talking man-to-man to us during his outgoings, but he could never quite bring it off. Once, he came to my platoon command post while I was shaving out of my helmet. As I started to wipe the lather off my face, the elegant figure, all starch and sharp creases, waved his hand deferentially. "No need for that, lieutenant," he said. "Keeping clean in the field. I like to see that. Carry on." I carried on, struck by the insincere friendliness in his voice, like the voice of a campaigning politician.

The overture of the counteroffensive began as March ended. I use the term *counteroffensive* loosely; the racket we heard each night seemed to be a series of disconnected fire-fights rather than an organized battle. Machine guns would fire in short, measured bursts, the bursts growing ever longer until there was only one long continuous rattling that fell suddenly silent; and then the timed bursts would begin again. Once in a while, a mortar round went off with a quick, dull *ca-rump,* a sound which could not be heard without thinking of torn flesh and crushed bones. Heavy artillery drummed all night at irregular intervals, the pale light of the exploding shells flickering above the rims of the distant hills. The fighting sometimes came close to the airfield, but never close enough to touch us, except for the usual sniping; and it was strange to sit safely in our foxholes while other men were killing and dying less than a mile away.

To keep the troops from becoming complacent, the company gunnery sergeant, a broad-chested cheerful man named Marquand, would send them to their positions with prophecies of impending attacks. "They're gonna hit us tonight. I gar-untee you. We're gonna get hit." But nothing happened. Our role in the alleged counteroffensive was limited to making detailed reports of whatever firing we heard forward of our respective platoon sectors. I am not sure who did what with that information, but I think it helped the battalion intelligence officer plot what is known in the jargon as a "sitmap"—a map showing the dispositions of friendly and enemy forces. He showed it to me one day. The MLR was a green line drawn in grease pencil. Beyond it, a swarm of rectangles symbolizing VC battalions and independent companies described a semicircle around the airfield, with the heaviest concentrations to the south and west. A sobering and bewildering sight: the Communists had the equivalent of a division out there, but we had yet to see one enemy soldier. Looking at the map, then out at the paddies, then back at the map, I felt the same queasiness as on that earlier night in Guiliumet's foxhole. It had been a phantom sniper then. Now it was a whole division of phantoms.

Gonzalez was wounded late in the month, our first

casualty. He had been leading a wiring detail and strayed into a minefield which the RFs were supposed to have cleared before we relieved them. Either they had made a bad job of it or the VC said to be in their ranks had deliberately left a few mines in place. They were small antipersonnel mines, designed to cripple rather than kill, and the one Gonzalez stepped on did what it was supposed to do. He was blasted into the air, and his left foot turned into a mass of bruised and bloody meat inside the tatters of his boot. He might have bled to death out there, but Lance Corporal Sampson, crawling on his belly and probing for mines with a bayonet, cleared a path through the field, slung the wounded man over his shoulders and carried him to safety. Sampson was recommended for a Bronze Star. We did not see Gonzalez again. He was evacuated to the States and the last we heard of him, he was recovering in the Oakland Naval Hospital. His foot had been amputated.

He was deeply missed, not because he possessed qualities that made him special, but simply because he had been one of us. Peterson, concerned about the company's low spirits, told the platoon commanders to have a talk with their men. We were to remind them that this was a war zone and that they would have to get used to casualties, because Gonzalez, though the first, would surely not be the last. The thought of giving such a lecture made me feel like a fraud—I didn't know anything about soldiering—but I gave it anyway. The platoon assembled at my command post, as my hooch was grandiosely called, at dusk. Huddled around me like a football team around a quarterback, helmets held under their arms, faces so caked with dust that their eyes seemed to be peering from beneath red masks, they listened patiently to a boot second lieutenant telling them about the hard facts of war. I called for questions when I was finished. There was only one: "José gonna be okay, lieutenant?" I said that he would be, except for the amputation. A few men nodded. They had heard the only thing that was truly important to them and could not have cared less about anything else I had to say. Their friend was going to be all right. I dismissed them then and, watching them file off in twos and threes, I was again impressed by the uncommon affection these common men had for each other.

And there were more casualties. Three-Nine suffered most of them. Only a few were caused by enemy action, the rest by sunstroke and accidents—those mishaps that are an inevitable part of war. Nervous sentries shot other marines by mistake. Accidental discharges accounted for several dead and wounded. Once, a prop-driven Skyraider that had been crippled by anti-aircraft fire made a crash landing on the airstrip. The pilot had jettisoned all of his ordnance except a two-hundred-and-fifty-pounder, which for some reason remained in the bomb rack. A big exception. It exploded, disintegrating him and his plane and injuring several airmen nearby. That other inevitability, disease, also affected us, though not too seriously. Diarrhea and dysentery were the most prevalent. Malaria made its appearance, but the bitter-tasting pills we took kept it under control; they also gave a yellowish cast to everyone's skin. I heard that two marines in the brigade died of blackwater fever. A more common affliction, one which I caught that spring, was called FUO—fever unknown origin. It was characterized by a slight fever, a sore and swollen throat, and a generally worn-out feeling which the heat made all the worse.

These maladies were mainly due to our living conditions. We used to read with amazement the stories about the luxuries lavished on the United States Army. The Ice-Cream Soldiers, we called them, for the marines in I Corps lived hard, the way infantrymen always have. Dust, filth, and mosquitoes filled our hooches at night. Our one cooked meal seemed always to be rice and beans. C rations constituted the other two meals, and there came the moment when I could not look at those tin cans without gagging. Except for the peaches and pears. Peaches and pears were about all we could eat in that climate. We had no field showers at first; there was seldom enough water for drinking, let alone bathing, and much of that was the green-as-pea-soup stuff we drew from village wells. It was purified with halizone tablets, which made it taste like iodine. Even with the tablets, the water loosened everyone's bowels, and if there is any one odor I will always associate with Vietnam, it is the stench of feces and lime in a latrine. Toilet paper was in short supply, except for the small tissues in the ration boxes, and what with waste-matter caking to anal hairs and no baths and constant sweating and uniforms stiff and white with dried sweat, it got so that we could not stand our own smell.

All that aside, it was not an unpleasant time for us, this time of phony war. The miseries of the monsoon were months away, as was the war of attrition, with its murderous game of King of the Hill. We were near enough to danger to maintain the illusion that we really were in danger, and so to style ourselves combat infantrymen. Our self-image was bolstered by the airmen stationed at the base. An unwarlike bunch of mechanics and technicians, they had lived for weeks with nothing between them and the VC but that thin, unreliable line of ARVN militia. Now, with a Marine brigade guarding them, they could crawl into their bunks at night without fear of having their throats slit while they slept. "Man, I can't tell you how glad we are to see you guys here" was a constant refrain. Their clubs were thrown open to us, and we were always assured at least one round of free beers. We were heroes in their eyes, a role we played to the hilt with much talk about ducking bullets out on the perimeter, which they thought of as the edge of the world.

Some risk was involved in the small-unit security patrols we ran through the villages beyond the MLR, but these never amounted to more than healthy outdoor exercise. For diversion, we had occasional liberties in Danang, where we did the usual whoring and drinking. Once we had fulfilled our soldierly duties along those lines, we went to the Grand Hotel Tourane, a whitewashed, charmingly seedy colonial establishment, and ate a decent meal. Then, feeling sated and wonderfully clean in tropical khakis, we moved to the veranda to drink cold beer beneath slowly twirling fans and watch sampans gliding down the Tourane River, rust-red in the sunset.

It was a peculiar period in Vietnam, with something of the romantic flavor of Kipling's colonial wars. Even the name of our outfit was romantic: Expeditionary Brigade. We liked that. And because it was the only American brigade in-country at the time, we had a feeling of being special, a feeling of "we few, we happy few, we band of brothers." Lieutenant Bradley, the battalion motor transport officer, perfectly expressed the atmosphere of those weeks. He called it the "splendid little war."

It was not so splendid for the Vietnamese, of course, and in early April we got a hint of the nature of the contest that was being waged in the bush. Two Australian commandos, advisers to an ARVN Ranger Group, walked into Charley Company's area. They were tough-looking characters, with hatchet-hard faces, and were accompanied by an even tougher-looking Ranger, whose eyes had the burned-out expression of a man no longer troubled by the things he has seen and done. The Aussies looked up Sergeant Loker, Tester's platoon sergeant, who had once served as an adviser with them. There was a noisy reunion. A few of us, curious about these strangers, gathered nearby to listen. The Australians were describing a fire-fight they had been in that morning. The details of this clash have vanished from my memory, but I recall the shorter of the two saying that their patrol had taken a "souvenir" off the body of a dead VC. He pulled something from his pocket and, grinning, held it up in the way a fisherman posing for a photograph holds up a prize trout. It was an educational, if not an edifying, sight. Nothing could have been better calculated to give an idea of the kind of war Vietnam was and the kind of things men are capable of in war if they stay in it long enough. I will not disguise my emotions. I was shocked by what I saw, partly because I had not expected to see such a thing and partly because the man holding it was a mirror image of myself—a member of the English-speaking world. Actually, I should refer to "it" in the plural, because there were two of them, strung on a wire: two brown and bloodstained human ears.

Later in April, we relieved Three-Nine on Hill 327, which was not a single hill but a range of heights that formed a natural wall between Danang and the VC-controlled valley to the west. Happy Valley it was called, for nothing happy ever happened there.

D Company held 327 itself, on the left flank; Hill 268, in the center, was occupied by our company; on the right flank, A Company defended the Dai-La Pass, north of which rose another hill, 368. It was held by 2d Battalion, which, along with regimental HqCo, had landed a few days earlier. Battalion HQ and B Company, in reserve, pitched camp at the base of the high ground, in a field near a squalid village nicknamed Dogpatch. A battery of 105s was emplaced immediately behind them, the howitzers enclosed by circular, sandbagged walls and the barrels elevated so the shells would clear the hills.

The company's new home had much to recommend it. The steep, grassy slopes of Hill 268 were almost unassailable by a large force. Its former tenants had improved its natural defensive features with sandbagged trenches, machine-gun emplacements, and a fortresslike forward observer's bunker. Three-Nine apparently had not thought much about the admonition to preserve offensive spirit. Better still, the heat was less intense up there. And there was no dust, nor any snipers, except for Sixteen-Hundred Charlie, a punctual guerrilla who cranked off a few rounds at four o'clock almost every afternoon. We grew rather fond of him, mainly because he never hit anything. But most impressive was the view, especially when you looked westward. Happy Valley was as beautiful as it was dangerous, a quilt of emerald rice paddies and dusty fields broken by the vagrant lines of paddy dikes and palm groves where the villages were. The Song Tuy Loan flowed through the valley, but we could not see it because of the bamboo clustered thickly along its banks; only an occasional patch of brown water showed through the arched branches of the trees. Far off, duncolored foothills climbed toward the high Cordillera, whose peaks had names like Ba-Na, Dong Den, and Tung Heo. The mountains were always changing but never changing. Their forms shifted in the shimmering heat waves and their colors varied with the light, from pale green, when they caught the rising sun, to an ever darkening green that became blue on the very clear days after a rain had washed the dust from the air. I had never seen such country. so lush and enchanting in the daytime that it reminded me of Shangri-La, that fictional land of eternal youth. But night always brought the sound of artillery, a practical reminder that this was Vietnam, where youth was merely expendable.

Ten days passed, ten days of total idleness. The novelty of our surroundings wore off and the battalion began to suffer from a spiritual disease called *la cafard* by the French soldiers when they were in Indochina. Its symptoms were occasional fits of depression combined with an inconquerable fatigue that made the simplest tasks, like shaving or cleaning a rifle, seem enormous. Its causes were obscure, but they had something to do with the unremitting heat, the lack of action, and the long days of staring at that alien landscape; a lovely landscape, yes, but after a while all that jungle green became as monotonous as the beige of the desert or the white of the Arctic.

We waited and waited for an attack that never came. Finally, in the latter half of the month, someone decided that since the Viet Cong would not come to us, we would go to them. The strategy of static defense was scrapped. The brigade received orders to commence long-range patrols and small-scale search-and-destroy operations beyond the perimeter. "Small-scale" meant up to battalion size. The new strategy went under the rubric of "aggressive defense," but it meant that we were going to share in the fighting. The war would no longer be only "their war," meaning the Vietnamese, but ours as well; a jointly owned enterprise.

This proved to be an effective cure for *la cafard*. The old excitement, dulled by seven weeks of drudgery, pulsed through the battalion again. Since the landing, we had acquired the conviction that we could win this brushfire war, and win it quickly, if we were only turned loose to fight. By "we," I do not mean the United States, but our brigade alone; and by "quickly," I mean very quickly. "I think we'll have this cleaned up in a few months," a staff major told me at the time. Such assurance did not seem outlandish then, nor was it confined to those of us in Vietnam. An old high-school friend, also in the Marine Corps, was aboard ship in the mid-Atlantic when he learned of the Danang landing. As soon as he got back to the United States, he rushed to Washington and requested immediate assignment to "ground forces, Western Pacific."

"I was worried that the war would be over before I got there," he told me years later. (He got his wish; he was sent to Vietnam twice and was twice wounded, first by a mortar, then by a rocket that left him blind in one eye.)

I guess we believed in our own publicity—Asian guerrillas did not stand a chance against U.S. Marines —as we believed in all the myths created by that most articulate and elegant mythmaker, John Kennedy. If he was the King of Camelot, then we were his knights and Vietnam our crusade. There was nothing we could not do because we were Americans, and for the same reason, whatever we did was right.

The new phase opened with B Company's skirmish on April 22. As far as I know, it was the first engagement fought by an American unit in Vietnam. Like so many of the thousands of fire-fights that were to follow, it began with an ambush and ended inconclusively. An eighty-man company from the 3d Reconnaissance Battalion had set out that morning on a patrol through Happy Valley. Third Recon was a band of self-styled swashbucklers whose crest was a skull and crossbones and whose motto proclaimed them to be CELER, SILENS ET MORTALIS—swift, silent and deadly. Slow, noisy and harmless would have been more like it, because about all they ever did was get themselves surrounded or ambushed, or both, and then call for someone to rescue them.

And that is what happened on the 22d. A company of VC, numbering around one hundred and twenty men, opened up on the patrol near the hamlet of Binh Thai. The patrol charged the enemy positions, but the lightly armed reconnaissance troops failed to dislodge the guerrillas, who pinned them down with automatic-weapons fire. A team of ARVN scouts attached to the marines detached themselves and fled in panic. The patrol leader meanwhile radioed an urgent request for reinforcements. After a long delay, while the request went up and down the chain of command, Bravo Company was ordered to saddle up in full combat gear. Led by its delighted captain, the riflemen assembled at the battalion helipad to await the arrival of their helicopters, symbol of the military's New Mobility. The H-34s got there, but not in time to prevent another delay, which, through no fault of the H-34s, rendered the New Mobility meaningless. A regimental staff officer, noticing that the marines were not wearing flak jackets, ordered them back to their tents. At this, Colonel Bain flew into a rage, commenting acidly about "chicken-shit staff officers who care more about uniform regulations than about helping marines in trouble." To show his contempt for these meddlers, he hopped in his jeep and drove to the valley by way of a dirt road. Where the road ended, he continued on foot to the battlefield, through two miles of hostile bush with only a frightened driver and the sergeant major for security. This daring act earned him the admiration of the troops and the enmity of the brigade and regimental staffs.

We in C Company were unaware of the confusion. From our eight-hundred-foot citadel, we could see only the drama of the operation. It was as though we were in an open-air theater, watching a war movie. The marines running at a crouch into the helicopters; the helicopters taking off one by one as they were loaded, each rising in a floating, nose-down climb out of the dust cloud raised by the rotor blades; the deafening roar of the engines diminishing as the aircraft soared to an assembly point directly overhead, hovering, while up ahead Huey gunships strafed the landing zone, skimming low and looking small against the background of the mountains, the bursts from their rapid-fire cannon muted by distance to a whirring noise; then the long, sliding descent of the assault helicopters, which grew larger, then smaller before they vanished beneath the low ridge beyond which lay the landing zone; the white-phosphorus smoke billowing through the trees where Bravo Company made contact, and the taut voice that came crackling over a field radio: "Burke Bravo has four VC KIA, say again four Victor Charlie KIA." There was a fascination in all this. More than anything, I wanted to be out there with them. Contact: that event for which so many of us lusted. And I knew then that something in me was drawn to war. It might have been an unholy attraction, but it was there and it could not be denied.

Off and on, the fire-fight lasted until dusk, but B Company never came up against the main body of VC. The guerrillas had used the delays to break contact with the recon patrol and then fade back into the bush, their withdrawal covered by a few snipers and a small rear guard. Six of these were killed and four captured in a hamlet that was burned down with white-phosphorus grenades. Our casualties were insignificant: a few men were wounded by grenade shrapnel, but only one, from the reconnaissance patrol, seriously enough to be hospitalized. Still, Bravo Company felt that they had undergone their baptism of fire, that soldier's sacrament, and came back in a cocky mood.

Late the following day, Peterson called the officers and platoon sergeants into briefing. B Company's little scrap had inspired the staff to try something more ambitious: a two-company search-and-destroy operation. The enemy unit to be sought and, if found, destroyed, was the 807th Battalion. It was thought to be operating in the foothills around Hoi-Vuc, a village on the far side of the valley. Delta Company was to establish a blocking position near the scene of the previous day's action while Charley Company made a helicopter assault a few miles farther west. The landing zone would be a clearing sandwiched between Hills 107 and 1098, the latter a great, green pyramid known to the Vietnamese by the more poetic name of Nui Ba-Na. From there C would move southeast, following the course of the Song Tuy Loan River, pass through the village of Hoi-Vuc, then link up with D. I recognized the maneuver from my Quantico schooldays: a hammer and anvil movement. C Company was the hammer, and the Viet Cong were expected to flee before its advance like crazed rats, only to be crushed against D Company, the anvil. That is how the plan looked on the captain's map, where the tangled jungle was merely a smear of green ink and all the hills were flat.

Peterson concluded by reading instructions from brigade concerning rules of engagement. The day before, a rifleman in B Company had shot a farmer, apparently mistaking him for a VC. To avoid similar incidents in the future, brigade again ordered that chambers be kept clear except when contact was imminent, and in guerrilla-controlled areas, no fire be directed at unarmed Vietnamese *unless they were running*. A running Vietnamese was a fair target. This left us bewildered and uneasy. No one was eager to shoot civilians. Why should the act of running identify someone as a Communist? What if we shot a Vietnamese who turned out to have a legitimate reason for running? Would that be a justifiable act of war or grounds for court-martial? The skipper finally said, "Look, I don't know what this is supposed to mean, but I talked to battalion and they said that as far as they're concerned, if he's dead and Vietnamese, he's VC." And on that note, we left to brief the squad leaders.

The next few hours were given to the usual preparations, with everyone very cheerful—except the platoon sergeants. When I walked into their tent to pass some last-minute instructions to Campbell, I found them in what struck me as a solemn mood. Campbell seemed especially grim, not at all like himself, and in the weak light of a kerosene lamp, shadows deepening the lines in his face, he looked much older than his thirty-six years. He was writing a letter to his wife and three sons. It was odd how I had never been able to think of him as a husband and father, or as anything other than a sergeant. Now, I made some remark about their morose mood.

"We're not morose," Colby said. "It's just that this company acts like we're going on a boy-scout hike. We were just talking and we think that if somebody

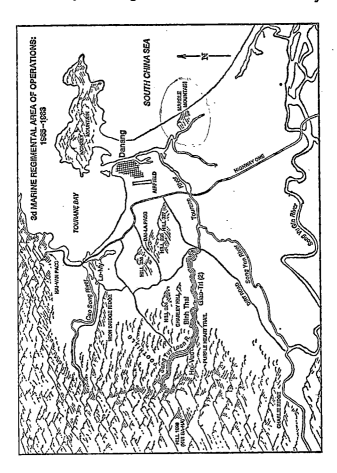

gets killed tomorrow, he oughtta be laid out and the company marched past to look at the body. Then we'll see if anybody's still got something to laugh about."

I said that that sounded pretty morbid.

"These helicopter assaults can get pretty morbid, lieutenant." Colby then launched into a description of some bloody operation he had gone on while serving as an adviser with the ARVN Rangers. "We'd move left and the mortar'd move left. We moved right and the mortars moved right. Stayed with us all the way up that valley. That was down at Tam-Ky, where I got hit, lieutenant. We just got our asses waxed and that's what might happen tomorrow if it's a hot LZ."

I made a graceful retreat, sensing I had touched an exposed nerve in these veterans. But I could no more understand what it was than I could the mood they were in. Full of illusions, I did not realize they had none.

Chapter Five

You wanted combat for what? I don't know really why. Or really know why. Who wants true combat? But here it is . . .
　　　　—Ernest Hemingway
　　　　Across the River and Into the Trees

Widener awoke me in the early morning. Reaching through my mosquito net and shaking me by the shoulders, he said, "It's oh-four-hundred, lieutenant. Time to get outta the rack." Widener, a southern Indianan who had taken Chriswell's place as platoon radio operator, had the shrill, twanging voice of a country-music disc jockey. It was an extremely disagreeable voice at that hour. "Oh-four-hundred, sir. Rack-out time."

"I'm awake, Widener. You can shove off."

"Yes, sir."

I swung off my cot. The hard-packed earthen floor

of the tent felt cool underfoot. My mouth had a metallic taste from having smoked too much and slept too
little the night before. I had, in fact, just managed to
doze off when Widener came in. And yet I was not at
all tired. There had been times in civilian life when I
had slept ten hours and felt less alert than I did on that
early April morning in Vietnam. Miller, the forward
observer attached to C Company, lay snoring on the
cot next to mine. Only the outline of his bulky figure
was visible through the mosquito netting that shrouded
him. The others were awake: Peterson lacing up his
boots, McCloy shaving by flashlight at the makeshift
washstand outside, Lemmon wiping the dampness
from his carbine, Tester doing the same to his rare
and precious SK 50, a submachine gun he had
acquired because his pistol seemed an inadequate
means of self-defense. I fumbled in the darkness for
my boots and jacket, locating both by their smell, the
moldy stink of dried sweat and embedded filth. The
whole tent smelled that way, like a locker room that
has never been aired out. We dressed without talking;
the only sounds were the far-off bumping of artillery
and the clanging of mess kits as the company filed toward the galley for breakfast. Then a battery of eight-
inch howitzers opened up from its position across the
road from battalion HQ. The noise made my heart
contract. The big guns had been brought up a few
days earlier, but I could not get used to their mon-
strous roar, nor to the sound, a demented whooping,
made by the retaining bands that spun off the huge
shells that rushed overhead.

"Big Ivan," said Miller, awakened by the firing.
Ivan was the battery's radio code-name. "That's what
they'll prep the LZ with. They're probably registering
now. Yeah, I'll bet Ivan puts the fear of God into
Charlie."

"I don't know about Charlie," I said, "but it sure
puts the fear of God into me."

"Hey," someone said, "P.J.'s getting nervous in the
service."

McCloy, who was primping himself outside, recited

some Kipling: " 'I'm old and I'm nervous and cast from the service' . . ."

I bristled at the ribbing because it came too close to the truth. I *was* nervous. Afraid that I might make some stupid mistake when the platoon hit the LZ, I had lain awake all night trying to conceive of every contingency and then rehearsing what I would do in each case. Over and over again until, exhausted by the mental effort, I had entertained myself with fantasies of personal heroics. I had even imagined how the accounts of my bravery would sound in the local newspapers: "A Chicago-area marine has been awarded the Silver Star in Vietnam, it was announced today. Philip Caputo, of suburban Westchester, was cited for his courageous actions while serving as a platoon leader with the 3rd Marine Regiment near Danang. The 23-year-old officer single-handedly knocked out a Viet Cong machine-gun nest. . . ." With my brain alternating between feverish dreams of glory and the coldly practical problems involved in securing a landing zone, my feelings had become confused. I hoped we would meet resistance so I could fulfill those dreams, or at least learn how I would behave under fire. At the same time, worried that I might behave badly, I hoped nothing would happen. I wanted action and I did not want it. The result of these conflicting desires was what I felt now, a tense emotional balance which the blasts of the howitzers threatened to upset.

In this state, McCloy's poetry recital irritated me more than it should have. I made some testy comment about the stupidity of shaving before an operation; every nick and scratch would sting like hell in the heat. Murph said something about it being proper and gallant for an officer to go into combat clean-shaven, adding that "The French paratroopers shaved before they jumped into Dien Bien Phu."

"Yeah," Lemmon said, "it sure did them a lot of fucking good."

The eight-inchers started firing another mission as we walked down to the galley, the guns visible, then invisible in the fitful muzzle-flashes. The valley toward the west was a pool of blackness lit only by the red-bursting shells. Toward the east, the China Sea could not be distinguished from the sky, so that the lamps of the fishing junks looked like low-hanging stars and the strip of white coastal sand like the edge of the world. Up ahead, the company was filing past the mess line, the faces of the men dimly seen in the yellow light cast by the lantern burning in the galley. Mess men in greasy dungarees indifferently slopped breakfast onto the trays, and one marine expressed amazement when he saw what it was. "Steak and eggs? I gotta be seeing things. Steak and goddamned eggs?"

"You ain't seeing things," a cook said. "Fattening you up for the slaughter, jarhead. Steak and eggs'll look terrific when your guts are hanging out."

In the fly tent grandly billed as the Officers' and Staff-NCOs' Mess we ate hurriedly amid the pleasant and strangely domestic smell of brewing coffee. The platoon sergeants had recovered from their funk and were cheerful in the resigned way of men who know they have no control over what is going to happen to them. They complained only about the lack of bread and jam. What was the good of luxury like steak and eggs without bread and jam? First Sergeant Wagoner told them not to expect too much, and Campbell said, "Top, you're full of sour owlshit," and everyone laughed a little too hard.

It grew light, not the way it does in temperate climates, with darkness receding slowly before the advancing gray of dawn, but all at once. Breakfast was over, our first decent meal in seven weeks. Walking back to the officers' tent to pick up my gear, I caught the odors of water, wet earth, and woodsmoke on the early-morning breeze. This was the only bearable time of day in Vietnam. I delighted in the coolness while dreading the heat that was promised in the red, rising sun.

We formed into helicopter teams of eight men each and assembled at a wide, level place in the saddle between our hill—we now thought of it as ours—and Hill 327. C Company presented a picture that could have been a symbol of the war: lines of men in rifle-green and camouflage helmets, standing or kneeling on

one knee, waiting for the helicopters that would take
them into combat. Far below and across the road from
the dust-powdered headquarters tents, the eight-inch
battery began pounding the landing zone. It was a
sight that would move me always, even after I became
disillusioned with the war: the sight of heavy guns in
action. They were self-propelled howitzers, awesome-
looking things as big as tanks. Tongues of flame flicked
from the long, black barrels. The shells went hissing
overhead and on over the valley, dim in the shadow of
the mountains. The Cordillera looked especially beautiful at that hour, and, in the clear air, close enough to
touch. It was golden-green high up, where the new sun
touched it, greenish-black lower down, and the line
between light and shadow was as sharp as if it had
been painted on. Looking in the opposite direction, we
could see the helicopters taking off from the airfield.
Climbing into the clean sky, they flew above the
coastal paddy lands and resembled a string of ungainly,
migrating birds. Now the sound of the bombardment
reached us. The explosions of the first shells echoed
and reechoed through the mountains; just as their re-
verberating roar began to fade, there was another burst
and another series of echoes, and still another, until all
we heard was a rumbling, solemn and unbroken. The
guns were firing air-bursts. Gray puffs of smoke blos-
somed above Hill 107, which bulked from the em-
browned elephant grass like the back of a sleeping
dinosaur. Behind it rose Nui Ba-Na, on whose eastern
face the shadow line receded as the sun climbed. Mists
had begun to curl up through the jungle that covered
the mountain's slopes, and they mingled with the
smoke to form a cloud that was shaken and thickened
by each new bursting shell. The scene charmed me:
the dim valley, the hill and the gray puffs blossoming
above it, and, towering above it all, that great mountain with its mysterious name.

The helicopters came in when the bombardment
lifted. They landed three at a time in the small zone,
each chopper creating a miniature hurricane. The crew
chief on the lead aircraft waved my team forward.
Bent double beneath the whirling rotor blades, we ran

through the wind-lashed dust and were hauled aboard. The noise was terrific. The squat, blunt-nosed H-34 shuddered and rattled violently. We had to shout to make ourselves heard. The crew chief, sitting on a folded flak jacket behind his machine gun, motioned to us to strap ourselves into the webbed seats. The engine pitch increased. The helicopter seemed to bear down for a moment, like a high-jumper crouching to spring, then lunged upward. My guts tightened in the abrupt ascent. We went into a banking climb, I saw the rest of the company far below, growing rapidly smaller.

We flew westward, following the course of the Song Tuy Loan. Rice paddies stretched north and south of it, a green and brown mosaic slashed by the mustard-colored ribbon that was the river. Widener and the six riflemen in my team sat stiffly, their weapons propped upright between their knees. Dust clung to their faces like red talcum powder. The crew chief, leaning on the butt of the M-60, was trying to light a cigarette in the wind that blew through the open hatch. It was the first cool, steady wind I had felt since coming to Vietnam and it was wonderful. God, it was going to be hot in the bush. If only it would not be so hot, just this one day. Looking out the hatch, I saw the other helicopters flying alongside in staggered formation. Dark-green against the blue sky, they rose and fell on the wind currents, like ships riding a gentle swell at sea.

After I came home from the war, I was often asked how it felt, going into combat for the first time. I never answered truthfully, afraid that people would think of me as some sort of war-lover. The truth is, I felt happy. The nervousness had left me the moment I got into the helicopter, and I felt happier than I ever had. I don't know why. I had an uncle who had told me what the fighting had been like on Iwo Jima, an older cousin who had fought with Patton in France and who could hardly talk about the things he had seen. I had read all the serious books to come out of the World Wars, and Wilfred Owen's poetry about the Western Front. And yet, I had learned nothing. "All the poet can do today is warn," Owen wrote. Colby and the other platoon sergeants were certainly not poets, but

that is what they had been trying to do the night before
—warn me, warn all of us. They had already been
where we were going, to that frontier between life and
death, but none of us wanted to listen to them. So I
guess every generation is doomed to fight its war, to
endure the same old experiences, suffer the loss of the
same old illusions, and learn the same old lessons on
its own.

The country changed. The Tuy Loan narrowed until it was only a thread bordered by galleries of bamboo
jungle. The paddy lands gave way to creased and yellow foothills that looked like the hills on a terrain
model or a relief map. I checked to make sure the
smoke grenades were securely fastened to my cartridge
belt, and for what must have been the tenth time,
went over the plan for securing the LZ: the nose of the
helicopters will be 12 o'clock; 1st squad will set in
from 12 to 4; 2d squad from 4 to 8; 3d squad
from 8 to 12; red smoke, hot LZ; green smoke, cold
LZ. While I was doing this, the formation changed
course. We were flying parallel to the mountains; the
Cordillera spread out before us, and it was the most
forbidding thing I had ever seen. An unbroken mass
of green stretched westward, one ridgeline and mountain range after another, some more than a mile high
and covered with forests that looked solid enough to
walk on. It had no end. It just went on to the horizon.
I could see neither villages, nor fields, roads, or anything but endless rain forests the color of old moss.
There it was, the Annamese Cordillera, hostile and
utterly alien. The Vietnamese themselves regarded it
with dread. "Out there" they called that humid wilderness where the Bengal tiger stalked and the cobra
coiled beneath its rock and the Viet Cong lurked in
ambush. Looking down, I wondered for a moment if
the operation was somebody's idea of a joke. Our mission was to find an enemy battalion. A battalion—a
few hundred men. The whole North Vietnamese Army
could have concealed itself in that jungle-sea, and we
were going to look for a battalion. Crush it in a hammer and anvil movement. We were going to find a
battalion and destroy it. Search and destroy. I half

expected those great mountains to shake with contemptuous laughter at our pretense.

We crossed the line of departure, a military term for the imaginary line beyond which a unit is committed to an attack. I signaled the squad to lock and load. Rifle bolts were pulled back, rounds chambered, chin straps unbuckled. The helicopters went down in a steep, spiraling descent. The trees below seemed nearly a hundred feet high, and for a long way up their trunks were as gray and bare as bones. The landing zone was just ahead, coming up fast, a circle of brightness in the gloom of the jungle. Flowing through the middle of the clearing, the brown Tuy Loan glinted dully in the sunlight, like a belt of tarnished brass. Now the chopper was skimming over the tops of the trees and the crew chief pumping machine-gun bursts into the undergrowth at the edge of the clearing. The belt of cartridges twitched as it uncoiled from the ammo box. The pilot "flared" the helicopter; that is, he committed it to a landing. The rotors made a *wap-wap-wap* noise, the aircraft settled against the earth, and we were out and running in a skirmish line through the wind-flattened grass.

The other two squads came in, and I was relieved to see them fanning across the clearing without confusion. The lack of enemy fire was another relief. This, I had decided, was the last place I wanted to get into a fire-fight. Happiness is a cold landing zone. Within a few moments, we had cleared the LZ and set up a perimeter in the bordering woods. It was like walking from brilliant sunshine into a darkened room. Through the dense canopy overhead the light fell in splintered shafts, bathing everything below in a greenish twilight. No wind blew. The air was heavy and wet, and the jungle smelled like a damp cellar. We could hear things slithering and rustling in the underbrush. We could hear them, but not see them. It was difficult to see much of anything through the vines and trees, tangled together in a silent, savage struggle for light and air. A war of plant life.

I tossed a grenade. The thick green smoke billowed from the canister and the remainder of the company landed. When the helicopters flew off, a feeling of abandonment came over us. Charley Company was now cut off from the outside world. We had crossed a line of departure all right, a line of departure between the known and the unknown. The helicopters had made it seem familiar. Being Americans, we were comfortable with machines, but with the aircraft gone we were struck by the utter strangeness of this rank and rotted wilderness. Nothing moved in the paralyzed air, and the only sounds were the gurgling of the river and the rustling of those invisible things in the underbrush. It was not at all a tranquil silence. I thought of that old line from the westerns: "It's too quiet." Well, it *was* too quiet. There was a tension in the calm, a feeling of something about to happen. Walking around the perimeter to make sure no one had gotten lost, I crashed through a thicket of elephant grass and heard a taut voice cry out, "Who's there? Who's that?"

"It's the lieutenant."

The voice belonged to Lance Corporal Skates, ordinarily not the jumpy type. I found him a few yards ahead, with his rifle still aimed in my direction. "Okay, it's you, sir. You sure scared the hell out of me, lieutenant."

Lemmon's and Tester's platoons were forming up at the far end of the clearing. Company HQ, marked by a small forest of radio antennae, was in the middle of the column. My own radio crackled just then, and the silence was shattered by Widener's disc-jockey voice.

"Roger, Charley Six, I read back for copy. Charley Two to remain in position until One and Three move out, then follow in trace. Roger, Six. This is Two out." Then, turning to me: "Sir, the Six says . . ."

"I heard what the Six said, Widener. Every VC inside of ten miles must have heard it. Keep your fucking voice down, will you."

"Sorry, sir."

"Don't be sorry, just be quiet."

"Yes, sir."

The company started to file down the river trail. One by one they vanished into the undergrowth; it was as if they were being swallowed whole. Then my

platoon peeled off of the perimeter and formed the
rear guard. We marched for an hour through the gal-
lery jungle that grew alongside the river, and in the
mottled light and dense, damp air, it was like walking
underwater. The trail was narrow and muddy—even
in the dry season nothing ever dried in the bush, it
only became less wet. A maze of bamboo and elephant grass twice the height of a man grew on one
side of the trail, and on the other side there was the
sluggish river, and, west of the river, the mountains.
The saw-edged grass slashed our skin, sweat made the
scratches sting, and the heat pounded against our helmets and wrung the sweat out of us as we might wring
water from a sponge. There were moments when I
could not think of it as heat—that is, as a condition of
weather; rather, it seemed to be a thing malevolent
and alive. We kept walking, slowly, with the high
green wall of the mountains looming above us.

The patrol that morning had the nightmare quality
which characterized most small-unit operations in the
war. The trail looped and twisted and led nowhere.
The company seemed to be marching into a vacuum,
haunted by a presence intangible yet real, a sense of
being surrounded by something we could not see. It
was the inability to see that vexed us most. In that lies
the jungle's power to cause fear: it blinds. It arouses
the same instinct that makes us apprehensive of places
like attics and dark alleys.

Men with active imaginations were most prey to
these fears. A man needs many things in war, but a
strong imagination is not one of them. In Vietnam, the
best soldiers were usually unimaginative men who did
not feel afraid until there was obvious reason. But the
rest of us suffered from a constant expectancy, feeling
that something was about to happen, waiting for it to
happen, wishing it would happen just so the tension
would be relieved.

Something finally did happen that morning, and
when it did I damned near jumped out of my skin. It
wasn't much—a burst of heavy rifle-fire from the head
of the column, the noise magnified by the dense woods.
The men dropped immediately and faced the flanks.
The shooting lasted no more than a few seconds, and

then I heard my heart drumming against my chest. Widener took a call on the radio, a summons from Peterson. I ran forward at a crouch, weaving around prone marines. It felt good to be moving. I found Peterson standing in, of all things, a corn field. The thick bush ended and there was this corn field, a piece of the Midwest in an Asian jungle. A line of riflemen was moving cautiously through the rows of dead stalks. The field ended in a swath of elephant grass, the same color as the corn stalks, and beyond the grass rose a low, wooded ridge. Hill 107 stood about a thousand yards away, to our left rear.

From the ridge, a sniper had opened up on the point. Although the sniper broke contact with the first burst of return fire, Peterson suspected an ambush. An enemy mortar crew atop Hill 107 and a few automatic-riflemen on the ridge could damage the company badly as it moved through the broad corn field. Therefore, we would cross it one platoon at a time, each covering the other, while the skipper called an air strike on the hill.

Lemmon's men moved out first. A machine-gunner sprayed the jungle on the far side of the field. This was called "reconnaissance by fire," a fancy term for what amounted to shooting at bushes to see if they shot back. Two Skyhawks came in low, strafing with rockets. Tester's platoon jogged across the clearing, followed by mine. Earth and smoke erupted through the trees on the hill. The racket was comforting. It broke the unreal stillness and somehow assuaged our fear of the presence that seemed to lurk in every thicket. That may have been the real reason for the air strike and the blind firing into the underbrush: they made noise, and noise made us feel less afraid. It was as though rockets and machine guns were merely technological equivalents of the gourds and rattles natives use to chase away evil spirits.

The excitement over, the column trudged down the ever winding trail. Walk for ten minutes. Stop for five while the point checks out a suspicious-looking area. Drop down and watch the flanks. Get up and walk some more. Stop again. Now what? What the hell is going on up there at the point? Drop down, face outboard, and watch the flanks. Get up, walk again. Stumble down into a gully, up the other side, slipping in the mud. Don't bunch up, the squad and fire-team leaders caution. C'mon people, don't bunch up. Keep your interval. Hold it up. Get down, watch the flanks. Move out. Walk stop walk and the sun is growing hotter by the minute. Take a swig from your canteen. Just a swig. Water discipline. Oh, goddamn that was good. How about one more? Allright, but that's all. Ohhhhh, that was better than the first one. The hell with it. You've got two canteens and you'll drink the poison in that river if you have to. Tilting your head back, you suck at the canteen like a baby at a tit. You don't spit the water out, the way you've been taught to. No, you just gulp it down until you feel your gut distending. Slip the empty canteen back into its cover and five minutes later you are as parched as you were before.

It took us all morning to cover the three miles between the landing zone and the village. Four hours to walk three miles, and the company had not once run into significant enemy resistance. It was the land that resisted us, the land, the jungle, and the sun.

Hoi-Vuc stood on the south bank of the Tuy Loan, near a horseshoe bend in the river. A score of thatch huts and a ruined pagoda that bore the marks of past fire-fights. Peterson ordered a cordon and search: 1st and 3d platoons would encircle the village first, then 2d would poke around in the huts. By this time I was sweating so heavily I could hardly see. I seemed to be looking at the world through a translucent curtain. Half blind, I stumbled off the trail, felt the ground give way and suddenly found myself two feet shorter. I had fallen into a pangee trap. Fortunately, it was an old one. The stakes were loose and rotten and I suffered nothing more than the mocking grin of the marine who helped pull me out.

Pushing its way through a baking stand of elephant grass, the platoon forded the river, shallow now in the dry season. A water buffalo lazing in the wallow downstream raised his broad-horned head as we splashed across. The trail on the opposite bank was wide and wound through a tunnel of arched bamboo. On both sides of the track were fire trenches, spider holes for snipers, pangee traps, and rows of crisscrossed stakes, emplaced at angles, like the *chevaux-de-frise* used in our own Civil War.

The platoon moved cautiously into the village. Shaded by coconut palms, the huts were arranged around an open area where a crone with a face as brown and fissured as a walnut squatted beside a small fire. A pile of long, wooden stakes lay next to her. She was holding one over the fire, apparently to harden its point. There was hardly anyone else around—just a few more old women, their teeth stained reddish-black from chewing betel nut, and a couple of idle old men in white cotton shirts and conical straw hats. An emaciated dog rolled in the dust.

We broke up into teams and started the search, which amounted to a disorganized rummaging through the villagers' belongings. Maybe it was the effect of my grammar-school civics lessons, but I felt uneasy doing this, like a burglar or one of those bullying Redcoats who used to barge into American homes during our Revolution. But I was not completely convinced these thatch and bamboo shacks were homes; a home had brick or frame walls, windows, a lawn, a TV antenna on the roof. Most of the huts were empty, but in one we found a young woman nursing an infant whose head was covered with running sores. She was sitting on a bed of woven straw, and she looked at us with eyes that reflected neither fear nor hatred, nor any emotion at all. It was dim and close inside. The air smelled of wood-smoke. The earthen floor was as hard and smooth as concrete. Widener and I began sifting through bundles of clothes. Two other marines rolled aside a large, rice-filled urn to see if it concealed a tunnel entrance, while a third poked his bayonet through the walls. We had been told that the VC sometimes hid clips of small-arms ammunition in the walls. The girl just sat and stared and nursed the baby. The absolute indifference in her eyes began to irritate me. Was she going

overrun. At Danang, the Viet Cong were believed to be massing for a large-scale raid, like the one that had struck Pleiku. Sniping and infiltration had increased recently.

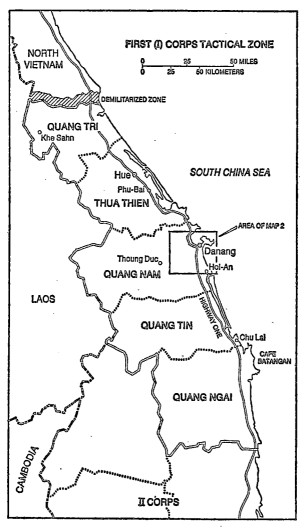

to sit there like a statue while we turned her house upside down? I expected her to show anger or terror. I wanted her to, because her passivity seemed to be a denial of our existence, as if we were nothing more to her than a passing wind that had temporarily knocked a few things out of place. I smiled stupidly and made a great show of tidying up the mess before we left. See, lady, we're not like the French. We're all-American good-guy GI Joes. You should learn to like us. We're Yanks, and Yanks like to be liked. We'll tear this place apart if we have to, but we'll put everything back in its place. See, that's what I'm doing now. But if she appreciated my chivalry, she did not show that, either.

The search turned up nothing significant. Peterson passed the word to break for lunch and be ready to move in half an hour. Gratefully, the marines shed their packs and flopped down in the shade of the trees. A few energetic types collected empty canteens. Campbell, Widener, and I rested inside one of the huts. It must have belonged to a local fat cat because it had a cement floor. I lay with my head against my haversack and drank the juice from a can of peaches. That was about all I could eat. Christ, I had never felt so exhausted, and yet I had walked only three miles, less than one-tenth the distances I had marched at Quantico. It must have been the heat, the incredible Southeast Asian heat. Looking through the door at the white glare outside, I wondered how this sun could be the same one now shining gently in the cool midwestern spring back home.

"Sure takes the starch out of a man, don't it?" Campbell said, as if he had read my thoughts. "Know what I could use right now? A cold bottle of San Miguel. Used to drink that when I was on barracks duty in the Philippines. Had me a little house on Subic Bay, maid and everything. Little Filipino girl. I'd come back from duty, sit back on the couch, and that little Filipino'd crack me a bottle of San Miguel. Ice-cold, lieutenant."

"Jesus Christ, knock it off."

"Ice-cold, lieutenant. Ice-cold bottle of San Miguel'd go down real good about now."

Unable to stand any more of this torture, I walked down to the river, dipped my helmet into the current, and poured the water over my throbbing head. On the way back, I saw an example of the paradoxical kindness-and-cruelty that made Vietnam such a peculiar war. One of our corpsmen was treating the infant with the skin ulcers, daubing salve on the sores while other marines entertained the baby to keep it from crying. At the same time, and only a few yards away, our interpreter, a Vietnamese marine lieutenant, roughly interrogated the woman who had been tending the fire. The lieutenant was yelling at her and waving a pistol in front of her ravaged face. I could not understand a word, but I did not have to be a linguist to guess that he was threatening to blow her head off. This went on for several minutes. Then his voice rose to an hysterical pitch, and holding the forty-five by the barrel, he raised his arms as if to pistol-whip her. I think he would have, but Peterson stepped in and stopped him.

"She is VC, Dai-uy," the lieutenant protested, explaining that the stakes which she had been hardening in the fire were antihelicopter devices; the VC placed them in fields which might be used as landing zones. Peterson said, all right, the stakes would be destroyed; but he was not going to preside over the torture of an old woman, Viet Cong or not. Looking surprised and disappointed, the lieutenant stalked off, warning us that we would learn how things were done around here. The old woman shuffled away, a sack of bones covered by a thin layer of shriveled flesh. The Enemy.

The company moved out half an hour later. We had just begun to cross the dusty, furrowed field outside the village when the snipers opened up. Bullets cracked loudly overhead, or went past our ears with a sucking sound, as when you draw in a breath through clenched teeth. The sniping seemed to be coming from the area we had passed through earlier, but all I could see there were trees. Two or three marines, taking cover behind the crumbled, overgrown walls of a wrecked shrine, fired blindly into the jungle. The VC replied with a few more rounds, the marines answered with another burst, and that ended the quarrel. The company formed into a column and started down the river trail, shambling listlessly in the white, liquid light of a tropic afternoon. Sweat blackened our uniforms, our backs ached from the weight of rifles and packs.

The plan called for us to patrol a short distance along the south bank, then to ford the river and sweep a hilly area on the north side before linking up with D Company. That would complete the operation—if this aimless thrashing around could be called an operation. My platoon had the point. We had gone about two hundred yards when our invisible friends opened up again, this time with a brief but heavy burst of automatic fire. The bullets smacked into the trees, shredding leaves, snapping twigs. The lead squad, Sergeant Gordon's, jumped into a nearby trench and loosed a long, stuttering volley into the underbrush on the far side of the river. One marine quickly emptied his magazine, inserted another and banged away again. A round whipped past me, with a loudness disproportionate to its size. I leaped into the trench beside Lance Corporal Bunch, not altogether sure what I was supposed to do. So, as was my habit, I yelled. When in danger, when in doubt, run in circles, scream and shout. "Slow fire!" I shouted into Bunch's ear. "Slow fire! What the hell are you shooting at?"

"Right there, sir. They're right in there," he said, squeezing off another five-rounds-rapid. I looked over his shoulder, but there was only the placid river and the wall of jungle beyond. It was as if the trees were shooting at us. I wasn't frightened, just confused. Or maybe I was confused because I was frightened. Then I heard Campbell's voice booming above and behind us. "Cease fire, you silly shits! Cease fire!" Several enemy bullets walked up the trail behind him, splattering dust, the last round striking less than an inch from his heel. He kept walking, as casually as a coach at the rifle range. "Cease fire, Second. Can't see what the hell you're shooting at. Let's have a little goddamned fire discipline."

The gunfire spluttered to a stop. I climbed out of the trench, feeling a little embarrassed.

"Didn't know you was in there," Campbell said. I wasn't sure if this was meant as a statement or a reproach. "Those troopers haven't got any fire discipline, lieutenant. Bunch of cotton-pickin' girls."

"Yeah, listen, that was nice going. They almost shot your ass off."

Campbell sneered as only he could. "Now, don't go making me out no goddamned hero. I didn't hit the deck because I wrenched my back getting out of the chopper. Got a bad back. I'm an old man, you know."

Well, I thought, you're some old man.

Peterson came up on the radio. He wanted to know what we were doing, restaging World War II? I felt that old dread of criticism rising up in me, but the skipper let me off with a mild reprimand.

"Just don't go shooting up all your ammo at a couple of snipers," he said. "Okay, let's move it out."

Fifteen minutes later, while crossing an expanse of rice paddies, the platoon was again pinned down by a small group of guerrillas. There could not have been more than three of them, two with carbines and one with an automatic rifle, probably an AK-47. They were on our side of the river this time, in a tree line that was almost out of effective small-arms range. The carbines started it off. There was a double cracking: the sound of the bullet followed by the report of the carbine. The effect was that of a man rapidly and rhythmically clapping his hands. Then the AK put a few rounds across our front and the platoon went down as if they had hit a trip wire. I then saw something rare for that stage of the war: I saw a VC. He was the one with the automatic. Actually, I saw a twitching beige cloud at the edge of the trees; it was the dust kicked up by the recoil of his rifle. I might have seen the guerrilla himself, but I could not be sure. He was too far away to hit any of us, except by accident, but I thought we might get him with an M-60. I ran over and got one of the machine guns into action. As its tracers streamed in long, red arcs toward the woods, a few riflemen from 3d platoon set up a line behind a paddy dike and began firing in the direction of the tracers. My platoon, however, just lay flat, in a state of bewildered paralysis.

I figured this presented an opportunity to redeem my earlier foul-up with Hollywood heroics. Standing up in front of a stunted tree—it was the only tree in the paddy and a stupid place to expose myself—I crooked my arm and pumped it up and down. This was the hand-and-arm signal to move out on the double. Pumping away, I hollered, "C'mon, Second, move your asses. You gonna let a couple of snipers pin a whole platoon down? Move your asses out." Something slapped into the branches not six inches above my head; a fillip from Charlie. A severed twig fell against my helmet and shredded leaves fluttered past my face. Belatedly, I hit the deck. Well, there was nothing random about that. That one had been addressed to me; and so, for the first time in my life, I had the experience of being shot at by someone who was trying to kill me specifically. It was not horrifying or terrifying or any of the things it is supposed to be. Rather, it was perplexing. My first reaction, rooted in the illusion that anyone trying to kill me must have a personal motive, was: "Why does he want to kill *me?* What did *I* ever do to *him?*" A moment later, I realized there was nothing personal about it. All he saw was a man in the wrong uniform. He was trying to kill me and he would try again because that was his job.

Peterson again came up on the radio, and this time he was mad. I knew by the tone of controlled exasperation in his voice. Peterson, who I thought was one of the best company commanders anybody could have served under, hardly ever raised his voice. He calmly asked what the hell I was doing waving my arms around under fire. I explained that I was using a hand-and-arm signal they had taught us at Quantico.

"You're not at Quantico any more. You'll draw fire doing that."

I told him that the VC had just given me the same message in more emphatic terms.

When the skirmish ended, a squad searched the tree line but found only a few spent cartridges. The phantoms had pulled off another vanishing act. Late that afternoon, sunburned, bone-tired, wondering if we had accomplished anything, suspecting that we had not, we linked up with D Company and were flown back to base camp.

Chapter Six

I warrant you, you shall find the ceremonies of the wars, and the cares of it, and the forms of it . . . to be otherwise.

—Shakespeare
Henry V

For the next few weeks, the rifle companies kept to a schedule almost as regular as that of office clerks or factory workers. In effect, we commuted to and from the war. We went into the bush for a day or two or three, returned for a brief rest, and went out again.

There was no pattern to these patrols and operations. Without a front, flanks, or rear, we fought a formless war against a formless enemy who evaporated like the morning jungle mists, only to materialize in some unexpected place. It was a haphazard, episodic sort of combat. Most of the time, nothing happened; but when something did, it happened instantaneously and without warning. Rifle or machine-gun fire would erupt with heart-stopping suddenness, as when quail or pheasant explode from cover with a loud beating of wings. Or mortar shells would come in from nowhere, their only preamble the cough of the tubes.

In those weeks we did not see heavy fighting; the battalion's casualties averaged no more than twenty a month, out of a total combat strength of about a thousand men. But we saw enough to learn those lessons that could not be taught in training camps: what fear feels like and what death looks like, and the smell of death, the experience of killing, of enduring pain and inflicting it, the loss of friends and the sight of wounds. We learned what war was about, "the cares of it, and the forms of it." We began to change, to lose the boyish awkwardness we had brought to Vietnam. We became more professional, leaner and tougher, and a callus began to grow around our hearts, a kind of emotional flak jacket that blunted the blows and stings of pity.

Because of the sporadic, confused nature of the fighting, it is impossible to give an orderly account of what we did. With one or two exceptions, I have only disjointed recollections of this period, the spring of 1965. The incidents I do remember, I remember vividly; but I can come up with no connecting thread to tie events neatly together.

The company is tramping down a dirt road past a Catholic church built long ago by French missionaries. Its gothic style looks out of place in this Asian landscape. Its walls are made of a dark, volcanic-looking rock. The courtyard is enclosed by a stone fence which bougainvillaea covers like bunting and there is a crucifix atop the arched gate. We are marching in a double file through a pall of dust raised by our boots. The dust drifts slowly away from the road and sifts down on the courtyard, dulling the brilliance of the bougainvillaea. It is an extremely hot day, hotter than any we have yet experienced. We have been told that the temperature is over one hundred and ten degrees, but the figure is meaningless. The cruelty of this sun cannot be measured by an instrument. Head bowed, a machine-gunner in front of me is walking with his weapon braced across the back of his shoulders, one hand hanging over the muzzle and the other over the butt, so that his shadow resembles the Christ figure on the cross atop the gate of the church. Farther on, the road runs past a stretch of low, grassy hills and flooded rice paddies. A deserted village lies ahead, a little more than halfway to our objective, an abandoned tea plantation.

Lemmon's platoon is at point, and I can see them through the dust, marching heavy-legged beneath a sky that is as bright as a plate of stainless steel. There is a sudden spattering of small-arms fire, the bullets raising geysers in the flooded paddies. The column stops while Lemmon's men deploy into a skirmish line and charge toward the hills. They splash across the fields, dodge the sudden eruptions of mud and water, then vanish into the elephant grass that covers the high ground. Passing through it, they enter the village. Two squads file back onto the road, a third remains behind to search the huts. We hear calls of "Fire in the hole!" and muffled explosions as grenades are thrown into bunkers and tunnels. But the enemy is not there. The squad returns to the column, and we are marching again, marching in the heat and choking dust.

My platoon is manning an outpost on a hill at the tip of a ridgeline a thousand yards forward of C Company's lines. We have been on the outpost for two days, though it seems more like two weeks. There is nothing to do during the day except sit in the sandbagged foxholes and gaze out at the rice paddies and the mountains beyond. The nights have been hours of nervous wakefulness broken by intervals of fitful sleep. Listening to things—men? snakes? animals?—crawling in the underbrush. Swatting mosquitoes. Trying to see in a blackness that is occasionally lighted by a distant flare.

It is now the afternoon of the third day. I am sitting in the platoon command post with Sergeant Gordon. We have rigged a lean-to over the foxhole to shield ourselves from the sun, but it is still hot. The rubber poncho billows and sags in the spasmodic breezes that blow through the tops of the trees. Gordon, a short, pink-faced career marine, is talking about fear and bravery. He says that bravery is the conquest of fear, which is not an entirely new idea. I am only half

listening to him, anyway. I am trying to read the
paperback Kipling which lies open in my lap, but I
cannot concentrate because Gordon is talking and because an invincible weariness prevents me from reading more than a few lines at a time. Also, I keep
thinking about a girl, a tall, blond girl with whom I
spent my leave in San Francisco five months and a
hundred years ago. I miss her a good deal, but when I
think of her, I find it difficult to remember her face
clearly. She and San Francisco are so far away that
they seem not to exist. Sweat drips off my nose and
onto the Kipling, smudging the print. Gordon chatters
away.

I pick up my field glasses and scan the valley below.
Dampness has smeared the lenses, so all I see is a
blurred, light-dappled green. It is as though I were sitting with goggles on at the bottom of a green river. I
wipe the lenses and my face, but in a few seconds a
fresh flood of sweat cascades into my eyes. I wipe the
lenses again, and sweep the glasses over the empty valley. I have done this dozens of times in the past forty-
eight hours. That is my mission: "To keep the Song
Tuy Loan river valley under observation and report
on all enemy movement and activity sighted." There
isn't any enemy movement or activity, of course. All I
see are the sunstricken paddies, a cone-shaped hill half
a mile away, Hill 324, and the jagged wall of the Annamese range. It is interesting how the color green,
which poets and songwriters always associate with
youth and hope, can be so depressing when there is
no other color to contrast with it. Green. It is embedded in my consciousness. My vision is filled with
green rice paddies, green hills, green mountains, green
uniforms; light green, medium green, dark green, olive
green. It is as monotonous as Gordon's voice.

I interrupt him by reading aloud the stanza to
a poem which has caught my eye:

> And the end of the fight is a tombstone white
>   with the name of the late deceased,
> And the epitaph drear: "A Fool lies here
>   who tried to hustle the East."

Gordon misses the irony, and launches into a discussion of his favorite poem, a ballad called "Rye Whiskey." He begins singing it in a nasal twang.

> *Rye whiskey, rye whiskey, rye whiskey I cry*
> *If I don't get rye whiskey, I surely will die.*

And I think, If you don't shut up, Gordon, you surely will and a lot sooner than you expected. That is what I think, but I don't say it. I recognize that I am in the second stage of the *cafard,* the stage in which you feel a hatred for everything and everyone around you. To get away from Gordon, I go check the perimeter. The marines are all in the same state of mind as I, "fed-up, fucked-up, and far from home." Their arms are tanned a deep brown, but the heat has bled the color from their faces, and their eyes have that blank expression known as the "thousand-yard stare."

It is night on the same outpost, and in at least one marine, PFC Buchanan, boredom has given way to terror. He has fired several shots at something he heard moving in front of his position. I am raging at him: "You goddamned amateur. You're supposed to throw a grenade if there's something there, not fire your weapon. The muzzle-flash could give your position away. You ought to know that." The lecture does not do any good. Buchanan stands in a tense crouch, his rifle resting on the sandbagged parapet, his finger on the trigger. He won't look at me, keeping his eyes fixed on the jungle straight ahead. The vegetation is gray-green in the moonlight. "Buchanan," I whisper, "take your finger off the trigger. Relax. It was probably one of those rock apes they've got up here." He does not move. Fear has overmastered him. Looking down the length of his rifle, he insists that the noise was made by a man. "All right. I'll stay here for a while. I don't want you firing unless you've got a target." I slide down into the foxhole, remove a grenade from my pocket, crimp the pin, and lay it aside.

A while later, Buchanan says in a low voice, "There he is, there he is." I hear a loud, dry rustling, as if someone were crumpling a sheet of crepe paper. Standing up, I look over the parapet and see some bushes moving twenty or twenty-five yards downhill. Whatever is in there is big, as big as a man; but I cannot believe an infiltrator would make so much noise. Unless he is trying to draw our fire. The rustling stops. There is a soft click as Buchanan eases the safety off. Again I tell him that it is probably a rock ape. I no longer completely believe this, and Buchanan does not believe it at all. "That ain't no fuckin' monkey, lieutenant." The rustling begins again. A bush quivers and grows still; the one next to it moves, then the one next to that. Something or someone is crawling along the hillside, parallel to the perimeter line. Before Buchanan can fire, I pull the pin on the grenade. Lobbing it with one hand, I pull Buchanan down with the other. The grenade explodes. A cloud of smoke drifts up through the gray-green underbrush, like dry-ice vapor, and the rustling has stopped. "If there really was a VC out there," I say, "that either killed him or scared the hell out of him." Buchanan at last takes the rifle from his shoulder; the grenade appears to have restored his confidence.

I return to the command post by way of a trail that leads through an avenue of trees with black, greasy trunks. It is dark in there, almost as dark as a vault, and I feel relieved when I am safely back in the CP. Widener is calling the hourly situation report to company HQ. "Charley Six, this is Charley Two. All secure, situation remains the same."

Later, I am startled awake by rifle fire. I seem to have developed an odd ability to sleep and not sleep at the same time. My head is instantly clear, and I know what has happened, just as if I had been awake all the time. There have been a couple of shots from a carbine and a burst from an M-14. The firing has come from my right rear, near Lance Corporal Marshall's position. I climb out of the foxhole and walk in that direction down the trail that leads through the dark avenue of trees. I stop when I see the silhouette of a man thirty or forty feet ahead. I think it is a man. The figure is not moving. He must have seen me at

the same moment. We look at each other for what
seems a long time. I cannot see if he is armed, although I know I heard a carbine. Or did I imagine
it? Am I imagining now? Maybe I am looking at nothing more than a bush shaped like a man. As I have
been trained to do, I look at the outline of the figure
rather than directly at it. If you look straight at an
object at night, your eyes play tricks on you. So I look
at the edges of the form, the figure, the bush, whatever
it is. Yes, it is a man, frozen in mid-stride, apparently
because he is trying to figure out if I have seen him.
I cannot see a weapon, but he could have one; or he
could be carrying grenades. I want to challenge him,
to shout "Dung lai" (halt), but the words catch in my
throat and a weakness creeps into my legs. Transfixed,
I am still watching him as he watches me. Time passes
as in a nightmare that lasts only a few seconds but
seems to go on and on. A marine yells something,
something like "He's over there." The figure moves,
and in one motion I unsnap the flap of my holster,
draw the pistol, pull back the slide to chamber a round,
and take aim. He is gone, crashing through the underbrush downhill. I aim at the sound but hold my fire,
afraid of hitting one of my own men. Then I am aware
that my heart is beating very fast and that the checkered grip of the pistol is slick with sweat.

Marshall comes up to me and tells me what happened. He had been off watch, lying in his hooch,
when he heard movement a short distance away.
There was a challenge from a sentry, followed by a
few shots. Scrambling out of his hooch, Marshall saw
a VC running past, toward the command post; but the
infiltrator vanished into the darkness before anyone
could get a clear shot at him.

After passing the word that there is to be a one-
hundred-percent alert for the next hour, I walk back to
the CP and take over radio watch from Widener. I
am still not sure if the figure I saw and heard was a
Viet Cong, an animal of some kind, or a chimera. The
fear is real enough, though. We pass an uneventful
but nervous night, and I feel like rejoicing when the
sky begins to lighten and I call in the last situation re-

port. "Charley Six, this is Charley Two. All secure, situation remains the same."

Corporal Parker and I are in the division field hospital, visiting PFC Esposito, a grenadier in one of my squads. Esposito is seriously ill and is going to be evacuated to the States. A stocky, dark-skinned boy, he talks about going home after four years in the Marines. He has mixed feelings about it. It will be good to go home, he says, but he regrets having to leave the battalion and Parker, who has been his buddy since boot camp. Esposito appears to be heavily drugged. He lies on his canvas cot, eyes glassy, voice thick. Parker punches him softly in the shoulder and says, "You'll be okay. Hey, we've been together a long time, huh?"

"Yeah, a long time," Esposito says in a voice that sounds like a record playing at too slow a speed.

"Remember that Cuban missile thing back in 'sixty-two? Man, that seems like a long time ago." Turning to me, Parker says, "We're tight, lieutenant. Me and Esposito are real tight."

There are several wounded men in the tent, three marines and half a dozen South Vietnamese. The empty cots are spotted with dried bloodstains. Two of the three marines have been slightly wounded and are relaxing as if on a holiday. The third has a serious head injury. He is heavily bandaged. An intravenous tube is inserted in one of his forearms, a plasma tube in the other, and the tubes hang down from bottles suspended on a metal rack. Another tube is attached to his penis. Various fluids—urine, glucose, blood plasma—course steadily through the plastic tubes. The marine is a big, athletically built man, so tall that his feet hang over the edge of the cot. He lies still, and I can tell he is alive only by the rising and falling of his chest and the low, guttural sounds he makes every few minutes.

A corpsman puts a thermometer in his mouth, checks his blood pressure, then goes to look after the ARVN soldier who lies on the bed next to Esposito. It is a regular hospital bed, elevated so that the soldier is almost sitting straight up. Bandages and plaster casts cover every part of his body except one arm, the lower half of his face, and the top of his head. A shock of thick, black hair droops over the battle dressing wrapped around his forehead and eyes. A number of instruments are attached to the soldier's body: tubes, rubber hoses, clamps, pressure gauges. Wrapped in white, with all those devices on him, he reminds me of one of those hideous experiments in a horror movie.

Parker and Esposito continue reminiscing about their long friendship. Parker's eyes are damp, his voice cracking with emotion, and I feel embarrassed, as if I am listening in on the conversation of two lovers who are about to be separated. I turn to talk to the corpsman, asking him what happened to the South Vietnamese soldier. The corpsman tells me that he has been wounded in the left arm, both legs, the stomach and head and is expected to die in a day or two. The marine is less fortunate.

"He'll probably go through the rest of his life about the way he is now, a vegetable," the corpsman says.

A few moments later, almost as if he were trying to disprove this prognosis, the marine begins to thrash around and make a strange noise, a sort of gurgling snarl. Then I hear a sound like that of a crisp celery stalk being bitten in half. In his spasm, the marine has clamped his jaws on the thermometer. He is trying to swallow it. "Son of a bitch," the corpsman says, running over and pulling the crushed instrument out of the marine's mouth. The big man convulses violently, the bottles sway on the rack while the corpsman removes a Syrette from his kit. He daubs alcohol on the marine's muscular arm and injects the sedative.

"Easy, easy," he says, holding the man down. "Easy, easy. We're going to have to give you a rectal thermometer from now on. Give it to you in the ass before you kill yourself."

The sedative begins to take effect. The marine's spasms subside, the snarling falls off to a succession of moans, and finally he is quiet.

We are lying in a ditch while an AK-47 rivets little

pieces of copper-jacketed death into the road in front
of us. When the firing stops, we run across and return
fire from behind an embankment on the other side.
We shoot without aiming into a field of elephant grass
and up at some low, rounded hills nearby. A few of
us clamber over the embankment, form a skirmish line
and move through the field toward the hills. A rifleman cranks off a couple of rounds at something he has
seen or heard, or something he thinks he has seen or
heard. It is dead-still and broiling in the grass, hot
enough to make it difficult to breathe.

Paulson and I scramble up a knoll and find an
L-shaped bunker dug into its side. Approaching
carefully, I stand next to the entrance and toss a grenade inside. A shudder passes through the ground when
the grenade explodes with compacted force. After the
smoke has cleared, Paulson and I crawl inside and find
a reed mat which has been shredded by the blast. But
the sniper, if he was ever here in the first place, is long
gone. Then we trudge back to the road, feeling blown
out by the wasted effort, like a boxer who has swung
hard and missed.

An hour goes by. Parties of marines are staggering
along, carrying heat casualties who lie in stretchers
we have made by cutting poles with machetes and
then doubling ponchos over the poles. My platoon is
ordered to relieve the 1st at point. Moving up, we
pass Lemmon's men; they are sprawled in a culvert in
the shade of some trees. One marine, slumped at the
shoulders, his arms hanging between his knees, sits on
a log in the classic pose of the worn soldier. Hollow-
eyed, he stares at a point in space. Sweat-smeared dust
coats his face. His helmet lies at his feet. His rifle,
resting on its butt plate, is propped at an angle against
one of his legs. I look at him and know that he is feeling what I am feeling: a tiredness greater than mere
fatigue, deeper than bone-deep, one that reaches down
into a part of myself I cannot name.

Another hour passes, and we can see the convoy that
will take us back to the base camp on Hill 268. The
trucks are lined up near the junction of this road and
the one that leads through the Dai-La Pass. Slim and

straight, an old French watchtower stands in the pass, a ruined monument to a ruined empire. The convoy is about five hundred yards ahead, the olive-drab vehicles miragelike in the heat waves rippling up from the road. Though the sight of it lifts our spirits, our bodies are too jaded to move any faster.

A machine-gunner named Powell begins to stumble and pirouette, like a man mimicking a drunk. Another marine offers to carry the heavy weapon, but Powell shoves him aside and says proudly, "I can hack it. I can hump my own gun." The M-60 clatters to the ground. Powell staggers forward, then falls facedown into the dust. Rolling him over, we see that his skin is hot, dry, and fish-belly white. Heatstroke. We wet his lips and pour what is left of our water over his head. Two marines lift the unconscious Powell and, holding him in a fireman's carry, hurry him to the trucks. He is put in the cab, to keep him out of the sun, but this turns out to be a mistake: The stifling air inside makes his condition worse. He wakes up in a maniacal rage and tries to strangle the driver. It takes three of us to pry his fingers loose from the man's throat. His lips curled back on his teeth, kicking and growling like a captured animal, Powell is dragged into the bed of the truck and strapped to a stretcher with web belts. There are no helicopters available for an evacuation.

The convoy moves slowly. All the while, Powell alternates between unconsciousness and frenzy, and once he manages to snap the belts loose. When we reach the 105-mm battery position, Lieutenant Miller and I put him in Miller's jeep and rush him to the hospital. He is raging again, and the Navy doctor refuses to treat him.

"This isn't a medical problem," he says.

"What the fuck do you think it is, doc," says Miller, "a disciplinary problem?"

"There's nothing I can do for him."

"You goddamned well better do something," I say, putting my hand on the grip of my pistol. It is a silly thing to do, typical of my hot temper and proclivity for melodrama. But it works. The doctor orders Powell to be taken into one of the tents. Half an hour later, the doctor comes out and says, apologetically, that Powell will have to be evacuated to the States.

"I can't figure out why he's even alive. He's got a body temperature of a hundred and nine degrees."

I ask what that means.

The doctor replies that, in effect, the blood in Powell's head is bubbling like water in a boiling kettle. "If he lives, he'll probably suffer permanent brain damage."

Riding back to the company area in Miller's jeep, I think, We've lost a man, not to the enemy, but to the sun. It is as if the sun and the land itself were in league with the Viet Cong, wearing us down, driving us mad, killing us.

The company is going out again to the area around Hoi-Vuc, a village that is becoming synonymous in our minds with the war. It is under VC control, day as well as night, and we are almost certain to run into something there. This is the scheme: A Company will make a helicopter assault near the village, in a field that has been given the unwarlike code name of LZ Duck. C Company will move by truck to a jump-off point near the Song Tuy Loan River. From there we will proceed on foot for three or four miles, guiding on the river, and set up a blocking position. It's the same old hammer and anvil plan, but we have learned that, in the bush, nothing ever happens according to plan. Things just happen, randomly, like automobile accidents.

We ride past battalion and regimental HQ. Clerks and typists stand at the roadside, turning their heads to shield their eyes from the dust thrown up by the trucks. They cheer and watch us with the envy rear-echelon troops often feel for infantrymen. As is frequently the case before an operation, we are filled with a "happy warrior" spirit and tend to dramatize ourselves. With our helmets cocked to one side and cigarettes hanging out of our mouths, we pose as hard-bitten veterans for the headquarters marines. We are starring in our very own war movie, and the howitzer battery nearby provides some noisy background music.

The convoy slows to a crawl as it passes through Dogpatch. The filth and poverty of this village are medieval. Green pools of sewage lie in the culverts, the smell mingling with the stench of animal dung and nuoc-maum, a sauce made from rotten fish. Lean dogs snarl and snap at each other in the dirt streets. Water buffalo bellow from muddy pens shaded by banana trees whose leaves are white with dust. Most of the huts are made of thatch, but the American presence has added a new construction material: several houses are built entirely of flattened beer cans; red and white Budweiser, gold Miller, cream and brown Schlitz, blue and gold Hamm's from the land of sky-blue waters.

Crowds of children and teen-age boys run alongside the convoy. Many of the children have distended bellies and ulcerous skin, decades of wisdom in their eyes and four-letter words on their lips. They run alongside, begging, selling. "GI gimme one cig'rette you." A cigarette is flipped into the crowd and the boy who catches it is immediately tackled by his friends. He disappears beneath a pile of tiny arms and legs, clutching, kicking, clawing for the cigarette. "Hey gimme candy you." A C-ration tin is thrown down. "Hey booshit. Fuck you GI this no candy. Numbah ten." The kid's friends laugh as he throws the can against the side of a truck. "Gimme cig'rette gimme candy you buy one Coka. One Coka twenny P you buy." Some marines drop piaster notes and coins into the sea of hands holding up bottles of Coca-Cola; but they do not accept the sodas. In this Alice in Wonderland war, Coke is a weapon. The VC sometimes poison it or put ground glass in it and give it to the children to sell to Americans. Or so we've been told. "Twenny P GI I say you twenny P. This no twenny P Fuck you cheap Charlie." The teen-agers are less mercenary. Like adolescent boys everywhere, they are fascinated by soldiers and armies. One of them shouts, "Mahreene numbah one. Kill buku VC." A marine who is not much older than the boy makes a pistol with his thumb and forefinger. "You VC," he says. "Bang. Bang." The boy grins and mimics a soldier

firing a rifle from the hip. "Hokay, hokay. Kill buku
VC."

The older people of the village remain aloof. The
men smoke gnarled cheroots and stare at us without
seeming to notice us. The women stand in the door-
ways, nursing infants, spitting red streams of betel-nut
juice into the dust. We are not a novelty to them.
They have seen foreign soldiers before. The whores are
the only adults who pay any attention to us. Dogpatch
has acquired several whorehouses since the brigade
landed. Boom-boom houses, they are called in the
local slang. The girls are pathetic to look at, dressed
in Western-style pants and so heavily made up that
they look like caricatures of what they are. They make
obscene gestures and signal prices with their hands,
like traders on the floor of a commodities market.

It is midafternoon. The company is strung out along
the trail on the north bank of the river. There is no
front in this war, but we are aware that we have
crossed an undefined line between the secure zone and
what the troops call "Indian country." The hamlets
here are empty except for the very old and the very
young. Pangee traps yawn at the side of the trail, and
there is that tense, oppressive stillness. We are about
halfway to the blocking position when the point platoon, Tester's, is ambushed. The VC open from a
trench line across the river. The automatic fire sounds
like paper ripping; bullets scythe the leaves above our
heads, and someone up front yells "Ambush left!"
There is another ripping sound as 3d platoon returns
fire. The exchange quickly falls off to a few desultory
shots, then just as quickly swells again. Things pop and
crack in the air. The call "Second platoon up! Second
up!" comes down the column. Bent double, I run up
the trail and almost bowl over a marine who is aiming
his rifle from behind a tree. He is aiming at a patch
of clothing that flashes briefly in the green tangle on
the opposite bank. He pulls the trigger, cries "Goddamnit!" when nothing happens. His rifle has jammed
or in his excitement he has failed to chamber a round.
"Goddamnit," he says to no one in particular. "I had
him in my sights."

At the same time, part of 3d platoon is stumbling down the steep bank; the rest are splashing across the river, yelling and shooting, charging wildly toward a hamlet on the other side. Sniper fire crackles, and a marine who is struggling to cut through the web of brush on the riverbank spins and goes down. Another rifleman calls for a corpsman. The action lasts two or three minutes at most, yet I have seen and heard everything with an unusual clarity, which seems to have something to do with the fact that I might have been shot at any moment.

Peterson orders my platoon and Lemmon's to form a perimeter around the paddies on this side of the Tuy Loan. Meanwhile, 3d platoon pursues the VC, but they have again evaporated. Someone says there are blood trails leading off into the jungle. I want to believe this. I want to believe these wraiths are really men who bleed.

Our single casualty, Lance Corporal Stone, has been hit superficially in the hand. The force of the AK round impresses him, however. "It just grazed me," he says to the corpsman bandaging his wound, "but that thing turned me right around." Tester's men make a sudden rush on the hamlet. A phosphorus grenade bursts in a cloud of thick, white smoke, and a hut begins to burn. Another goes up. In minutes, the entire hamlet is in flames, the thatch and bamboo crackling like small-arms fire. The marines are letting out high-pitched yells, like the old rebel yell, and throwing grenades and firing rifles into bomb shelters and dugouts. Women are screaming, children crying. Panic-stricken, the villagers run out of the flame and smoke as if from a natural disaster. The livestock goes mad, and the squawking of chickens, the squeal of pigs, and the bawling of water buffalo are added to the screams and yells and the loud popping of the flaming huts.

"They've gone nuts, skipper," Tester says. "They're shooting the whole place up. Christ, they're killing the animals."

He and Peterson try to stop the destruction, but it is no use: 3d platoon seems to have gone crazy. They

nel, who had come in by helicopter to pass some word or other, the only real damage it did was to our peace of mind. On the morning of the second day, intelligence having received a report of enemy movement south of us, C Company was lifted out to make a helicopter assault near a hill marked on the map as Hill 270.

The flight was a short one and took us over a part of the Annamese range. The manuals we had used in guerrilla-warfare courses cheerfully stated that the modern, civilized soldier should not be afraid of the jungle: "The jungle can be your friend as well as your enemy." Looking at the green immensity below, I could only conclude that those manuals had been written by men whose idea of a jungle was the Everglades National Park. There was nothing friendly about the Vietnamese bush; it was one of the last of the dark regions on earth, and only the very brave or the very dull—the two often went together—could look at it without feeling fear.

We had been airborne less than ten minutes when the H-34s started down toward the landing zone, a field bounded on the north by tangled woods and a stream whose still, brown waters, flecked with white, reminded me of dirty milk. To the south, a low ridge separated the LZ from a swamp, beyond which rose the dusky slopes of Hill 270. Circling down, the helicopters began to draw ground fire; the rounds made a noise like corn popping as they whipped past the aircraft. The fire was not heavy, but it produced in us the sensation of helplessly waiting for a bullet to pierce the fuselage and plow through a foot or groin. Trapped, we were little more than pieces of human cargo, with no means of defending ourselves and nowhere to take cover. The door gunner, sitting on a folded flak jacket, was tensed behind his machine gun; but he could not return fire without the risk of hitting another aircraft. Hearing that *pop-pop-pop* outside, I could only think of what a pilot had once told me: "If a chopper gets hit in the right place, it has the flying characteristics of a falling safe." Nevertheless, the experience—our first of a hot LZ—was not entirely unpleasant. There was a strange exhilaration in our helplessness. Carried willy-nilly down toward the landing zone, with the wind slapping against our faces and the trees rushing in a green blur beneath us, we felt a visceral thrill. It was like the feeling of being on a roller coaster or in a canoe careening down a wild rapids; the feeling, half fear and half excitement, that comes when you are in the grip of uncontrollable forces.

Suddenly we were on the ground. I leaped out of the door and was grateful when my boots touched the soft, damp earth. I was back where an infantryman belonged, on his feet and in the mud. Bent at the waist, we dashed toward the woods at the northern edge of the clearing. Opposite, Lemmon's men were assembling in a swale of elephant grass at the base of the low ridge. The grass rippled in the wind churned up by the helicopters' rotor blades. The VC were still taking potshots at the landing zone; we heard the rounds smacking overhead and the distinctive crack of Russian SKS carbines. The two sounds occurred almost simultaneously, so it was impossible to tell where the snipers were. But now that we were back in the foot soldier's natural element, the firing did not seem half so frightening. It was just the usual, sporadic harassing fire, and we had learned by this time that it was not serious sniping, rather a VC tactic intended to fray our nerves. We ignored it.

The last wave came in, dropped Tester's platoon, and flew off. There was a brief crackling as the VC turned their rifles on the aircraft, but none of the H-34s was hit. Watching them climb until they were just specks in the sky, some of us felt a momentary but deep longing to go with them back to the small comforts and relative safety of what was called, for lack of a better term, the rear. It was the same feeling we had experienced on the first operation, a sense of being marooned on a hostile shore from which there was no certainty of return. Drawn up in mass formation back at base camp, C Company had looked formidable—two hundred heavily armed marines. But there in the LZ, surrounded by those high, jungled hills, it seemed such a small force.

Forming a column, my platoon started toward its first objective, a knoll on the far side of the milky-brown stream. It was an objective only in the geographical sense of the word; it had no military significance. In the vacuum of that jungle, we could have gone in as many directions as there are points on a compass, and any one direction was as likely to lead us to the VC, or away from them, as any other. The guerrillas were everywhere, which is another way of saying they were nowhere. The knoll merely gave us a point of reference. It was a place to go, and getting there provided us with the illusion we were accomplishing something.

The platoon stumbled through patches of ankle-high creepers, then filed down a trail into the yellow-green scrub that bordered the clearing. The sniper fire continued to pop behind us. Two shots, half a minute of silence, another shot, fifteen seconds of silence, two more shots. The woods became dense, muffling sound until we could no longer hear the small arms. A solid wall of vegetation hemmed both sides of the trail, the trees so still they did not look real. A marine slipped in the mud, his rifle and equipment clattering as he fell. The column started to bunch up and the NCOs passed the word to "keep it spread out, people, five paces between each man." It was a phenomenon I had seen before: in the jungle, men tended to draw together, seeking the reassurance that comes from being physically close to one another, even though that increased the risk of the proverbial one round killing several men at once. I think this bunching happened because even the illusion of being alone in that haunted, dangerous wilderness was unbearable. We were supposed to know better, but officers were as prey to this fear as the men. On a previous patrol, I had lost sight of the marine in front of me; he had slipped around a sharp bend in the trail. Although I knew he was only a short distance ahead, I felt lost, almost terrified, and ran around the bend until I again saw the comforting sight of his back.

And so, stretching and contracting, the column trudged at an exasperatingly slow pace. Finally we came to the stream. Holding his rifle above his head, the point man began to wade in the chest-deep water, which was stagnant and dark in the shade of the over-hanging trees. I recoiled from the idea of stepping into it, though I was teased by memories of the Michigan trout stream I had fished on summer vacations. I remembered the narrow stretches where it flowed so fast that it had worn the rocks on the bottom to the smoothness of polished marble and how my teeth ached when I drank its cold water. Lost in this reverie, I only half heard the call coming up from the rear of the column. "Hold it up, Second. Tell the lieutenant to hold it up."

"What the hell for?" I called back.

"Hold it up, lieutenant."

Sweat spilled into my eyes, and I felt irritation ris-ing. "Goddamnit, I said what the hell for?"

A drenched red-faced marine came jogging up the trail. It was one of the company clerks who doubled as runners on operations.

"Mister Caputo, the captain says for you to get your platoon back to the LZ on the double," he said, breath-ing hard. "There's some VC up on the ridge and we're going to assault."

Instantly, irritation turned into elation. An assault! "How many?"

"Sir, that's all the skipper told me, that you should double-time back to the LZ. But I think there's maybe a platoon of them up there. One of the pilots spotted them."

Facing about so that the rear squad was now the point, the platoon headed back at a run. Helmets bouncing against our heads, canteens against our hips, rifle slings and bandoliers jiggling, we sounded like a platoon of junkmen. We had covered half the distance, a hundred yards perhaps, when I heard an erratic volleying and the sounds that signaled solid contact: the stuttering of machine guns and the bursts of M-79 grenades, a 40-mm grenade fired from a riflelike launcher. Breaking out of the jungle, we ran into the clearing and a brisk fire-fight. Bullets plucked at the air and, though they were flying at a safe distance overhead, we instinctively fanned out and went forward with our shoulders hunched, as if we were walking against a strong wind. Dogtrotting across the field, stumbling on the low creepers, we found it difficult to tell what was going on. Sixty or seventy yards ahead, Lemmon's men were moving up the ridge; small groups advanced in rushes while others fired up at the crest. Dust spots appeared where bullets pecked the earth, and then a whorl of gray smoke rose from behind the ridgeline, followed immediately by the flat explosion of an M-79. The runner led me to Peterson, who was standing with studied calm next to his radio operator. The skipper told me to put my platoon in defilade beside a hill that stood at a right angle to the ridge.

This we did. Tester's platoon was in front of mine, strung out in a long file against the hillside. Hot and winded, we squatted to wait while 1st platoon made a frontal assault, that quintessential Marine maneuver. It was nothing like those choreographed attacks we had practiced at Quantico or on Okinawa. The marines were more or less on line, bunched into knots in some places, spread apart in others. Some men were falling behind, some pushing out ahead and firing from the hip. A few seemed to be scrambling hand over hand where the slope was very steep. My imagination persuaded me that I saw the Viet Cong on the ridgeline. If I did, I did not see them for long. Several greenclad figures suddenly appeared on the crest. Then I heard a rhythmic popping that recalled the sound of a rifle range. The company radioman said that the VC had been driven off and were now fleeing across the swamp. Lemmon wanted to hit them with mortars before they gained the cover of the jungle on Hill 270.

Sergeant Johnson's 60-mm mortar crew ran out into the middle of the LZ, and, quickly setting up the tube, put three rounds in the air. "Right five-zero!" someone called out. Johnson, a Korean War veteran with a face as seamed as a well-worked mine shaft, relayed the correction to the crew and three more shells hissed over the ridge to burst with a succession of dull *crumps* in the swamp beyond.

Peterson ordered Tester's platoon and mine to start moving up; we were to sweep around the guerrillas'

flank, then move into the marsh and mop up. We
would be covered by an artillery barrage, which he
would call in on Hill 270 in case another VC force
was dug in there. While Johnson's mortars continued
to fire, we started up the hill, Tester's platoon in the
lead. It was slow, hot going through waist-high stands
of elephant grass. An occasional ricochet sang past us,
but the action had slackened to desultory exchanges
between Lemmon's machine-gunners and some snipers
up on 270. Then our ears caught a faint, vibrating
hiss, which in seconds became a sound like canvas
tearing, followed by the most godawful noise I had
ever heard, a screech such as a millsaw makes when it
strikes a knot. It was the artillery, 155-millimeters, and
because the target was close, we felt as well as heard
the shell-bursts. The ground quivered, the shock wave
slapped like a gust of wind, smoke and clods of earth
boiled up from the swamp and 270's forward slope.
At that range, there was a good chance of a round
falling short—that is, falling on us—and we crouched
as low as dignity would allow. Listening to the 155s
rending the air with howls and roars, I could only
wonder what it was like to be under the bombardment,
to be one of those Viet Cong, naked against the blast
and splintering steel of one-hundred-pound shells. And
for a moment, I pitied them. I doubt that I have any
more compassion than the next man, but in those days,
I tended to look upon war as an outdoor sport, and
the shelling seemed, well, unfair. The runner had said
there was perhaps a platoon of guerrillas on the ridge,
meaning twenty or twenty-five men at most. We were
two hundred and, to add to our numerical superiority,
we were dumping a ton of high-explosive on them.
But this was early in the war; later, I would be able
to see enemy soldiers incinerated by napalm and feel
quite happy about it.

The bombardment lifted and C Company was ordered to move down into the swamp. We were to clean
out any remaining pockets of resistance and look for
enemy corpses, the number of which would be the
measure of our victory. According to the tactics manuals, this phase of the action was the "pursuit." The

word suggests an exhilarating chase, but in this case it meant a vicious, mudbound manhunt. The swamp, a great pool of rust-red mire about twice the size of a football field, was broken by islands of thorn bushes and razor-sharp grass that slashed the skin and tore our uniforms. The mud was waist-deep in places. It tugged at our boots, almost pulling them off when we lifted our feet to walk; and with each step the rotten-egg stench of escaping marsh gas rose into our nostrils. All of us were soon covered with leeches, black things as big as a man's thumb.

In the maze of thickets, it was impossible to keep any kind of formation. Units got mixed up; platoons disintegrated into squads, squads into fire-teams, until the company had no more organization than a crowd at a train station. It was also difficult to find the bodies. Some had probably been entombed in the mud. A few wounded VC, judging from the blood trails they left, appeared to have crawled into those nearly impenetrable thickets; we left them there, to die slowly or to rot if they were already dead. One or two may have been blown apart by the artillery: here and there, bits of flesh and tattered clothing hung from the underbrush. After fifteen or twenty minutes of searching, the first body was discovered. Two marines, each holding onto an ankle, dragged the corpse away, its brains spilling out of the huge hole in its head like gray pudding from a cracked bowl.

With the mud, heat, leeches, and clawing thorns, and the risk of a wounded VC lobbing a grenade from his hiding place, the mood of the company turned savage. This was especially true of 1st platoon; they had done the actual killing, and once men begin killing it is not easy to stop them. So we were not surprised or outraged when we learned how that first Viet Cong—the one with his brains blown out—had died. Though badly wounded in the fire-fight, he was still alive when a search party found him. Without warning, one of the marines, PFC Marsden, a grenadier in Lemmon's platoon, shot the man in the face with a pistol. The summary execution apparently surprised Marsden himself: the moment after he fired the shot, he looked at the pistol as if it had gone off by itself and said, "Now what did I do that for?" There were two other versions of the incident: that the enemy soldier was already dead when Marsden shot him; that the marine had fired in self-defense when the VC tried to throw a grenade. Whatever the truth of the matter, in that dangerous swamp it seemed a perfectly natural thing to do. And given the order General Greene, the Marine Corps commandant, had issued on an inspection tour of Vietnam the previous month, it seemed the approved action. Addressing a group of marines, Greene had told them they had a single, simple mission to accomplish in the war: "You men are here to kill VC." Well, that is what Marsden had done; he killed a Viet Cong, wiped out one small part of the Communist forces. He had accomplished his mission.

The mop-up continued. A second corpse was found. With PFC White, a 1st platoon machine-gunner known as Pappy because he was a venerable twenty-nine, I was on the trail of a third. A sliver of blood, flecked with bits of flesh and intestine, led into a patch of brown marsh grass.

"He's got to be in there, sir," White said, cradling his M-60. "We flushed at least a dozen of them off that ridge, and I know we hit one of them right around here."

I drew my pistol and we pushed into the stuff. The grass was nearly head-high, making it difficult to see more than a few yards ahead. The blood trail grew thicker, splashed like fresh red paint on the brown grass, which was flattened where the wounded man had crawled through it. We followed the trail for several yards, then stopped to listen. Hearing nothing but the muffled rattle of a rifle some distance away—probably a marine clearing a thicket before searching it—White and I went on. Stumbling forward, I almost tripped over the VC. He was lying on his back, with one arm thrown over his chest, the other out at an angle, his eyes wide and staring at a sky he did not see.

"Knew we got one of them around here," White said.

The enemy soldier appeared to be about eighteen or nineteen. He had been hit in the worst, most painful place a man can be hit, in the place that is the center of so many aches, the ache of fear, of hunger, sometimes even of love. We feel so many things in our guts and that is where two 7.62-mm bullets had caught him. Judging from the distance he had crawled, a good thirty yards, he had had ample time to feel pain and perhaps to realize that death was not decades, but only moments, away. It was surprising he had lasted that long. A modern, high-velocity bullet strikes with tremendous impact. No tidy holes as in the movies. The two in his belly were small—each about the size of a dime—but I could have put my fist into the exit wounds in his back. An enormous amount of blood had poured out of him and he was lying in it, a crimson puddle in which floated bits of skin and white cartilage.

There was nothing on him, no photographs, no letters or identification. That would disappoint the boys at intelligence, but it was fine with me. I wanted this boy to remain anonymous; I wanted to think of him, not as a dead human being, with a name, age, and family, but as a dead enemy. That made everything easier. Two marines came up, collected the VC's gear —a carbine and a web cartridge belt with a canteen attached—then dragged the corpse away. "He's heavy," one of the riflemen said. "You wouldn't think a little dude could be so heavy."

By this time the company had reached the base of Hill 270, and patrols were moving up its slope in an attempt to make contact with the remnants of the enemy platoon. Rifle fire chattered a short distance away. Some of my marines were running toward a column of smoke rising from the underbrush at the fringes of the swamp. "Hey, lieutenant," one of them called, "over here."

The smoke came from a burning case full of papers. Apparently one of the VC had remained behind long enough to destroy documents. We stamped out the fire but failed to salvage anything. The guerrilla had been hit, however; there were bloodstains on the bushes nearby, and we followed them to a dry stream bed that led up the hill. When I saw the dim, evil-looking jungle farther on, I decided that this was not a job for a small patrol. For all I knew, a hundred-man ambush lay waiting up there in the luxuriant growth. So I assembled the platoon, and the forty of us started up the stream bed.

The bottom was strewn with boulders, moss-covered and slippery, and ribbons of dark water trickled between them. Fresh bloodstains, red against the green moss, speckled the rocks. The platoon moved slowly, stopping every few yards to listen for the sound of breathing or the rustle of underbrush. But we heard only the rattling of our rifle slings and the grating of our boots against the rocks.

The stream bed grew deeper, its banks rising several feet above our heads. A gray-green twilight filtered through the jungle canopy. Plant life grew in snarled profusion along both banks; tree branches, vines, and tendrils were locked together, trying to strangle each other in a struggle to climb out of the shadows and reach the sunlight. Water oozed from the sides of the ravine, and the dead air was thick with the smell of rotting wood and leaves. It seemed as though we were walking through a sewer.

We still heard nothing, and then we lost the trail. Perhaps the VC's wound had clotted. Or perhaps he had crawled into the bush and was waiting up ahead, waiting to take a few of us with him. He could do it, too, and without much trouble. Confined to the narrow corridor of the stream bed, the platoon was in frontal enfilade: this meant that the enemy's line of fire, if he was in front of us, would come down the length of the column; a single burst from an automatic rifle would topple the first four or five men like bowling pins. Where are you? I said to myself. Where are you, you little son a bitch? It was odd; I had begun the patrol with the idea of capturing the guerrilla, but now all I wanted to do was kill him. Waste the little bastard and then get out of that dank, heat-rotted ravine.

Rivera, the point man, held up his hand and dropped to one knee. He signaled me to come up.

"Look over there, lieutenant," he said, pointing at a sampan that rested atop a platform built into one of the sheer walls of the ravine. Several square, rusty cans, filled with rice, were stacked beneath the platform. There was other stuff—clips of small-arms ammunition, cotton bandoliers, canteens, and cartridge belts. A few yards farther up, the stream bed made a sharp bend.

"He ain't far if he's around," Rivera whispered.

I wiped my hands on my trousers and fought the urge to light a cigarette. At that moment, I wanted a cigarette more than anything in the world. My imagination—that cursed imagination of mine—conjured a vision of the VC lying in wait just around the bend. If only that damned bend had not been there. Rivera looked at me with an expression every infantry officer, at one time or another, has seen on the faces of his men; it was an expression that asked; Well, what are you going to do now, mister officer? In the end, I had two choices: to turn back or go on, at the risk of running into an ambush. I chose the latter, partly out of the "spirit of aggressiveness" the Marine Corps had inculcated in me, partly from curiosity, and partly out of pure personal ambition. I have to admit that; I *wanted* to get into a fight, I wanted to prove myself the equal of the other officers in C Company. Lemmon had seen the lion's share of action that day, and I envied the tough little Texan. He would probably win a letter of commendation or maybe a medal. I wanted to win one myself.

"Listen," I said to Rivera, "I'll get a fire-team and we'll check what's around that bend. You take point. If you see that VC, blow his shit away."

"Yes, sir."

Six of us crept up while the rest of the platoon waited. The bottom of the ravine, covered with moss and worn flat by the floods of countless monsoon seasons, was as green, smooth, and clammy as a lizard's skin. Rivera slipped around the bend, raised his hand in the signal to halt, and pointed his rifle at something ahead. My eyes caught a patch of yellow in the surrounding foliage, then the outline of a hut. It was a

small base camp, the hut elevated on poles over the
stream bed.

We moved in, nervously checking for trip wires
and booby traps. The camp could have accommodated
a few men at most, with beds made of tautly woven
reeds, built on top of each other like bunk beds. The
mosquito netting was ratted and torn. I felt an admiration for the VC: it took a lot of dedication to live in a
place like that where you could hardly see the sun,
where the air was dense enough to cut, and mosquitoes rose in clouds from the stagnant pools.

Odd bits of equipment and many documents were
scattered around the camp. It appeared as though the
guerrilla—assuming he had come through there—
had been hurriedly searching for something. On the
other hand, he might have strewn the stuff around to
turn our attention from pursuing him. If that was his
purpose, he had succeeded. The jungle looked even
thicker ahead, and the ravine as dark as a cave. My
aggressive spirit faded. I was not going any farther.
Charlie would live to fight another day, or, if he had
been badly wounded, would crawl into some thicket to
die.

We started to sift through the documents, among
which were a large number of notebooks with neat,
numbered paragraphs written in them. They looked
like operations orders, which led me to wonder if we
had stumbled upon the headquarters of a small unit. I
was about to congratulate myself for making a valuable intelligence find when one of my marines said,
"Hey, lieutenant, look at this."

It was a small packet of letters and photographs.
One photo showed the VC wearing their motley uniforms and striking heroic poses; another showed one
of the guerrillas among his family. There were also
several wallet-sized pictures of girl friends or wives.
The notes written in the corners of these were probably
expressions of love and fidelity, and I wondered if the
other side had a system, as we did, for notifying the
families of casualties. I hoped so. I did not like to
think of those women, dreaming of returns that could
never be, waiting for letters that would never come,

wondering at the lack of news, imagining a dozen reasons for it, all but the one they feared the most, and their growing dread as each long day without word darkened into longer night.

A small group of marines gathered and stared at the letters and photographs. I don't know what they felt, but I was filled with conflicting emotions. What we had found gave to the enemy the humanity I wished to deny him. It was comforting to realize that the Viet Cong were flesh and blood instead of the mysterious wraiths I had thought them to be; but this same realization aroused an abiding sense of remorse. These were men we had helped to kill, men whose deaths would afflict other people with irrevocable loss. None of the others said anything, but later, back at base camp, PFC Lockhart expressed what may have been a collective emotion. "They're young men," he told me. "They're just like us, lieutenant. It's always the young men who die."

We lingered for several minutes, trying to make some sense out of it. The company had only done what it was expected to do and what it had been trained to do: it had killed the enemy. Everything we had learned in the Marine Corps told us to feel pride in that. Most of us did, but we could not understand why feelings of pity and guilt alloyed our pride. The answer was simple, though not apparent to us at the time: for all its intensity, our Marine training had not completely erased the years we had spent at home, at school, in church, learning that human life was precious and the taking of it wrong. The drill fields and our first two months in Vietnam had dulled, but not deadened, our sensibilities. We retained a capacity for remorse and had not yet reached the stage of moral and emotional numbness.

Or so it was for the majority of the men. There were exceptions. At least one marine in the company had already passed beyond callousness into savagery. We had just started back down the ravine, after setting fire to the camp, when we bumped into a patrol led by Sergeant Loker. They were dead beat and looked as if they had been caught in a cloudburst. Stopping to rest, Loker squatted and lit a cigarette.

"Did you burn that place back there, sir?"

I said that I had.

"We passed by it earlier, but I left it alone. You remember how pissed the skipper was when we burned that ville. He said he didn't want any more villes burned down."

"That's a base camp, Sergeant Loker, not a village."

Shrugging, he said, "Okay, lieutenant. You're the boss." He took a long drag on his cigarette, looked away from me for a moment, then turned to face me again. Sweat was dripping off his trim, black moustache.

"You hear about Hanson, sir?"

"No. What about him?" Hanson was a rifleman in 1st platoon.

"I caught the little sonuvabitch cutting the ears off one of those dead VC. He had a K-bar and was trying to slice the guy's ears off. The little jerk. Lordy, I took him up by the stackin' swivel and told him I'd run his ass up if I ever caught him doing that again."

An image of Hanson flashed in my mind: a quiet boy of about nineteen, tall and thin, with dark blond hair, he was so American-looking he could have posed for a Norman Rockwell in the old *Saturday Evening Post*. I tried to imagine him performing the act Loker had just described, but couldn't.

"Does Mister Lemmon know about it?"

"Yes, sir. I don't figure anything'll happen to the kid this time. I didn't give him a chance to finish the job. But how do you figure a little jerk like that?"

I did not say anything, although I wanted to remind Loker about his two Australian friends. Perhaps Hanson had been among those who saw the Aussies proudly displaying their trophy, and perhaps his young, half-educated mind had formed the idea that that sort of thing was all right. Still, there had to be something fundamentally wrong with a man who could muster the cold-blooded nerve to mutilate a corpse with a knife. Marsden's act was at least comprehensible, but Hanson's was beyond understanding. I did not want to hear anything more about it. My quota of emotional shocks had been filled for that day.

Slogging back into the swamp, we saw the enemy dead lying in a neat rank, as if for an inspection. A photographer—I think he was with the *Stars and Stripes*—was taking pictures of them from various angles. Amazingly, there were only four of them. *Four.* We had fought for an hour and a half, expended hundreds of rounds of small-arms ammunition, twenty mortar shells, and a full concentration of 155s to kill four men. I remarked on this to someone in company headquarters, who said, "There were a lot of pieces and blood trails around, so we estimate eight VC KIA." When I asked how that figure had been arrived at, the marine replied, "Oh, I guess somebody just counted up the arms and legs and divided by four."

I handed the documents to Peterson and gave him a report of our excursion to the Viet Cong base camp. He seemed pleased, which, of course, pleased me. The platoon was then ordered to outpost a hill at the western edge of the marsh. We were to keep a lookout for A Company, which was supposed to link up with us later in the day. They had captured five prisoners in a skirmish near Hoi-Vuc.

The platoon was exhausted by the time it had hacked its way to the top of the three-hundred-foot hill. A perimeter was formed, after which the marines collapsed, resting their heads against their helmets and packs. I then performed that time-honored platoon commander's duty, a foot inspection. The men removed their mud-caked boots and peeled off their drenched socks. From the knees down, their legs were covered with leeches and their skin was shriveled and white, like the skin of old men.

As I moved from one man to the next, I became aware of a subtle difference among them, and I might not have noticed it if I had not known them so intimately. They had taken part in their first action, though a minor one that had lasted only ninety minutes. But their company had killed during those ninety minutes; they had seen violent death for the first time and something of the cruelty combat arouses in men. Before the fire-fight, those marines fit both definitions of the word *infantry,* which means either a "body of soldiers equipped for service on foot" or "infants, boys, youths collectively." The difference was that the second definition could no longer be applied to them. Having received that primary sacrament of war, baptism of fire, their boyhoods were behind them. Neither they nor I thought of it in those terms at the time. We didn't say to ourselves, We've been under fire, we've shed blood, now we're men. We were simply aware, in a way we could not express, that something significant had happened to us. Moving around the perimeter, I caught snatches of conversation as the men talked about the experience; some were trying to master their emotions by talking them out; others masked their feelings under a surface toughness. "D' ja see that Charlie Marsden greased?" "Yeah, blew his friggin' brains out. Dude in first platoon told me you could see the back of his teeth through the hole in his head." "Yeah, forty-five at close range'll fuck up your health record every time." "They found an I.D. on one of the Charlies says he was only fifteen. Fifteen, man. A goddam kid." "Fifteen, shee-hit. Listen, all these gooks look younger'n they are. It was probably a phony I.D." "Well, they wasn't much older than any of us. I don't know, but I felt kinda sorry for 'em. No shit." "No shit? You think they would've cried their eyes out if it was the other way around? No way. Fuck it. They woulda zapped us, so we zapped them. Sorry about that."

Most of the men were too worn out to talk for long. Eventually a sullen silence fell over them. The reaction was setting in, a general feeling of disappointment and depression. The fire-fight, our first experience of combat, had not turned out the way we had imagined it would. Used to the orderly sham battles of field exercises, the real thing proved to be more chaotic and much less heroic than we had anticipated. Perhaps it had been heroic for Lemmon's platoon, but for the rest of us, it amounted to a degrading manhunt; pulling bodies out of the mud had left us feeling ashamed of ourselves, more like ghouls than soldiers.

And the mutilation caused by modern weapons came as a shock. We were accustomed to seeing the human body intact; to us, a corpse was an elderly uncle lying in a coffin, his face powdered and his tie in place. Death admits to no degrees: the elderly uncle who dies decently in bed is no less dead than the enemy soldier whose head has been blown apart by a forty-five-caliber bullet. Nevertheless, we were sickened by the torn flesh, the viscera and splattered brains. The horror lay in the recognition that the body, which is supposed to be the earthly home of an immortal soul, which people spend so much time feeding, conditioning, and beautifying, is in fact only a fragile case stuffed full of disgusting matter. Even the brain, the wondrous, complex organ that generates the power of thought and speech, is nothing more than a lump of slick, gray tissue. The sight of mutilation did more than cause me physical revulsion; it burst the religious myths of my Catholic childhood. I could not look at those men and still believe their souls had "passed on" to another existence, or that they had had souls in the first place. I could not believe those bloody messes would be capable of a resurrection on the Last Day. They did, in fact, seem "more" dead. *Massacred* or *annihilated* might better describe what had happened to them. Whatever, they were gone for good, body, mind, and spirit. They had seen their last day, and not much of it, either. They died well before noon.

Finding no signs of immersion foot (a skin disease similar to trench foot) among the men, I returned to the platoon CP to have a look at myself. Campbell and Widener were there, resting under a poncho they had stretched between two trees. It was noon, without a breath of wind, and the sky seemed like a blazing aluminum lid clamped over the world. But the sun felt good against my bare feet.

Campbell talked to himself as he burned a leech off one of his legs. "There you go," he said, touching the black, swollen thing with the tip of a lighted cigarette.

"A little hot-foot for you." The leech curled up and dropped off. "There, got the little fucker. Got any on you, lieutenant?"

"Haven't checked yet," I said.

"Well, you just let your old platoon sergeant look for you. Got to drop your drawers, sir."

I took my trousers down, and, feeling a little ridiculous, stood while Campbell examined. Only one leech was on me, and I watched with pleasure as it recoiled under the heat of the cigarette.

"That's it, lieutenant. Guess leeches don't like your blood type. There was more'n one on old watashiwa."

The Japanese word, which means "yours truly," reminded me of the battalion's peacetime days on Okinawa. That seemed a very long time ago.

Standing on the brow of the hill, I was able to see the battalion's positions on Hill 268 and 327. They were a good eight or nine miles off, but the clear air and some accident in the contours of the land made them appear only a short walk away. The tops of both hills, scoured of underbrush to clear fields-of-fire, rose red and bare from the surrounding green. The tents showed as black dots and the trenchworks as a dark, irregular line running across the red earth. That distant, dusty camp represented civilization to me. Showers. A cot to sleep on. Hot chow.

Instead, I sat down to the usual C rations. It was difficult to eat because of the heat, because I was sick of Cees, and because I kept remembering that boy that White and I had found: the still-staring eyes, like those of a dead fish, the grinning, half-opened mouth.

We were idle for the rest of the day. Occasionally I swept my field glasses over the valley to the west, looking for a sign of A Company. It was hopeless. Nothing could be seen through the green opacity of the jungle except a cluster of huge, oblong boulders standing on a hillside like enormous tombstones. In the end, A Company never made the linkup, having been forced to turn back by impenetrable forests. The jungle had won another round.

Toward evening, a helicopter landed on the island

of solid ground where the four bodies lay. They had stiffened into odd positions and were beginning to smell. Together with the captured documents and equipment, the corpses were loaded onto the aircraft. It took off, its slow, vertical ascent reminding me of a balloon rising on an updraft. I assumed it was taking the bodies to the Danang cemetery, where the enemy dead were said to be buried in mass graves.

Peterson called me on the radio and ordered the platoon to move back to the landing zone; the company would set up its night defensive position there. Hitching their packs and slinging rifles, the marines stumbled down the hill, plodded across the marsh once again, and filed up the ridge where the VC had broken before 1st platoon's assault. Except for some spent cartridge casings, there was nothing to show that a fight had taken place. The swamp where men had died was empty. Its red mud had seeped into the shell craters, filling them, and the smoke from the burning camp had cleared away. Tired, sweating, mud-spattered, the platoon climbed over the ridge at a processional pace. Frogs, crickets, and birds started singing their evening chorus. Artillery began its nightly refrain, guns thudding in the distance, shells whispering through the air, then exploding with an echoing boom that sounded like the beat of muffled drums.

While 1st platoon set up an ambush nearby, 2d and 3d formed a perimeter around the landing zone. Watches were set, listening posts sent out, radios calibrated to the night frequency, foxholes dug: the usual routine. When those things were done, the marines settled back to smoke a last cigarette before darkness fell. A few took advantage of the remaining daylight to clean their rifles. There was a burst of laughter at some joke or other. Finally, the sun dropped below the notched rim of the mountains, the Asian mountains that had stood since the beginning of time and probably would still be standing at the end of it.

Chapter Eight

I have made fellowships—
Untold of happy lovers in old song.
For love is not the binding of fair lips . . .
But wound with war's hard wire whose stakes
  are strong . . .
                    —Wilfred Owen
                    "Apologia Pro Poemate Meo"

The company passed an uneasy night. A thick fog rolled in around two in the morning, the hour when the VC usually attacked. Sentries saw all sorts of imaginary terrors in the swirling whiteness; one marine, mistaking a bush for a man, fired several shots that kept everyone's nerves on edge for an hour afterward. Blinded by the mists, we had to rely on our hearing, though that sense was often deceived by small animals thrashing loudly in the dry grass surrounding the landing zone.

Once, we heard drums beating in the distance. It might have been the VC, but it was probably Montagnard tribesmen signaling each other. Regardless, it was a chilling sound that seemed the essence of all that was frightening and mysterious about the jungle. Sometime later, a marksman in Lemmon's ambush fired at a guerrilla he had spotted through a starlight scope, a device used for night sniping. He thought the VC had been hit, but wasn't sure. In the fog and blackness, listening to the strange night noises, none of us was very sure about anything. It seemed dawn would never come.

When it did, we felt enormously relieved. "I'm sure glad that's over," Sergeant Gordon said as he came down from a brush-covered knoll where he had been on listening post. "It was like being inside a safe in there. Couldn't see a thing, and every time I tried to get a little sleep, something'd start crashing around and we'd think it was a goddamned infiltrator. We were scared shitless half the time."

For A and C Companies, the last two days of the operation were the same as the first: hours of monotonous walking punctuated by brief duels with unseen snipers. Two marines were wounded, neither seriously. Several men fell victim to our other enemy, the sun.

On the afternoon of the fourth day, we passed through Giao-Tri, the hamlet 3d platoon had destroyed earlier. A few villagers were still there, searching for their belongings among the mounds of ashes and charred skeletons of their homes. One old man shuffled along, carrying a partially burned pot. He and the others—there were about six altogether —stopped to look at us as we marched by. I can still see them, dressed in ragged cotton clothes, standing against a background of rubble and blackened trees, watching us with a passivity that was not submission. A sense of guilt and compassion came over me at first. Burning their hamlet had been a demonstration of the worst in us, and I would have been grateful for a chance to show the best that was in us. Instinctively, I wanted to do something for them because of what we had done to them. We could not have done much except, perhaps, give them our food and cigarettes. I would have gladly done that, emptied my pockets and pack, and ordered my platoon to empty theirs, but the villagers' stony coolness inhibited me. They did not seem to want us to do anything. They just stood there, silent and still, showing neither grief nor anger nor fear. Their flat, steady gazes had the same indifference I had seen in the eyes of the woman whose house I had searched in Hoi-Vuc. It was as if they regarded the obliteration of their village as a natural disaster and, accepting it as part of their lot, felt no more toward us than they might feel toward a flood. Such passivity struck me as inhuman. It might have been a stoical mask, concealing deep feelings of sorrow or rage; but if that was the case, their ability to control their emotions was just as inhuman. In this way, my pity for them rapidly turned into contempt. They did not behave the way I expected them to behave; that is, the way Americans would under similar circumstances. Americans would have done something: glared angrily, shaken their fists, wept, run away, demanded compensation. These villagers did nothing, and I despised them for it. Their apparent indifference toward what had happened made me indifferent. Why feel compassion for people who seem to feel nothing for themselves? For I had no conception of the ordeal that constituted their daily existence. Confronted by disease, bad harvests, and above all by the random violence of endless war, they had acquired a capacity to accept what we would have found unacceptable, to suffer what we would have considered insufferable. Their survival demanded this of them. Like the great Annamese Mountains, they endured.

In the early evening, the company reached the dirt road that ran past the "French fort," a stone and concrete ruin overlooking the rice paddies west of Hill 327. According to legend, its French-Moroccan garrison had been wiped out by the Viet Minh in the early fifties. None of us reflected on their fate or saw a warning in the fort's bullet-chipped walls.

Slumped by the roadside in the waning light, we waited for the convoy that would bring us back to base camp. A file of peasant girls came down the road, carrying-poles balanced on their shoulders. Swinging their arms vigorously, the baskets at the ends of the poles swinging in rhythm with their arms, they hurried to reach their village before curfew. The "rules of engagement" specified that Vietnamese caught outside after dark were to be considered VC and either shot or captured. The trucks rolled up shortly afterward. The marines mounted up, happy to be riding instead of walking, and yet conscious that the trucks made them more vulnerable to an ambush or being blown up by a mine. Their sense of relief was almost palpable when the convoy cleared the Dai-La Pass. They were out of Indian country, out of immediate danger, released from the tensions that had cramped them for four days.

I was riding with Corporal Mixon's squad and a machine-gun team, about fifteen men altogether. The U.S. Army calls the infantry the Queen of Battles, but these worn rifle-men looked anything but regal. From the knees down, their legs were caked with dried mud; their old-style leather boots—the new canvas jungle boots had not yet been issued—were rotting on their feet; their web gear, like their uniforms, was faded and frayed.

Packed as tightly as commuters on a bus, bumping against each other as the trucks bounced down the rutted road, we passed battalion headquarters. To men grown used to the bush, it looked incredibly domestic. Laundry hung on lines strung between tents, and smoke curled cheerfully from the stovepipe in the roof of the mess shack. Some tankmen in the armor company attached to the battalion were sitting idly atop one of their thirty-ton monsters. A group of marines with towels wrapped around their waists padded on rubber sandals toward the field showers. And in the foxholes behind the barbed wire along the perimeter, other marines lounged at ease, waiting for night.

The convoy turned onto the new road the engineers had built to connect headquarters with the rifle company camps on Hills 327 and 268. The road, climbing a succession of sharp curves, was thick red dust in the rainless heat of the dry season. We went up slowly, with a gradual, shallow drop on one side and a steep rise on the other. Choked by the dust and eager to get back to camp, we marked our progress by watching the trucks at the head of the column. They vanished around a hairpin turn, reappeared higher up, running straight across the face of the hill, vanished around the next curve, then reappeared again, higher still. The drop-off grew deeper, its slope sheering to a brush-matted draw a long way down. The steep rise on the opposite side of the road began to level off and we caught sight of the grassy spurs and rock outcroppings near the crest. Looking below,

I could see the tail of the column and the dust trail behind it, describing a series of S's down the hillside. The headquarters tents, the tanks, guns, and men in the field at the bottom of the hill looked like pieces in a boy's scale-model army.

The convoy came to an abrupt halt in the bull-dozed field that served as the company assembly area.

"Off the trucks and fall in!" Gunnery Sergeant Marquand's voice boomed across the field. "You'll turn in your pyrotechnics"—signal flares and illumi-nation grenades—"to your platoon guides. Fall in, people. Quicker we get this done, quicker you'll get to crap out."

Tailgates clanged loudly as the marines dismounted and formed up, without any fuss and without their usual boisterousness. They were not dispirited; sober, rather.

The platoon sergeants barked the ritualistic com-mands—"Dress right dress, ready front, at ease!" Looking at the company, at their old-young faces and cracked and muddy boots, I sensed that another change had come over them since March. A close outfit from the start, C Company had become even more tightly knit in Vietnam, and in a different way. Their old fellowship had an adolescent quality to it; it was like the cliquishness of a football team or a fraternity. The emotion in them that evening was of a sterner kind; for Vietnam had fused new and harder strands to the bonds that had united them before the Danang landing, strands woven by the experience of being under fire together and the guilt of shedding first blood together, by dangers and hardships shared. At the same time, I knew I had become less naïve in the way I looked at the men in the battalion. I now knew my early impressions had been based not on reality but on a boyhood diet of war movies and blood-and-guts novels. I had seen them as contempo-rary versions of Willie and Joe, tough guys who at heart were decent and good. I now realized that some of them were not so decent or good. Many had petty jealousies, hatreds and prejudices. And an arrogance tempered their ingrained American idealism ("one marine's worth ten of these VC").

It wasn't that I had become critical of them; not the most exemplary character, I was in no position to criticize. Rather, I had come to recognize them as fairly ordinary men who sometimes performed extraordinary acts in the stress of combat, acts of bravery as well as cruelty.

Sergeant Colby had a somewhat different view. One night I told him I could not understand what had been going on in Hanson's mind. "When I was in Korea," Colby said, "I saw men sight their rifles in by shooting at Korean farmers. Before you leave here, sir, you're going to learn that one of the most brutal things in the world is your average nineteen-year-old American boy." But I refused to believe him. I only knew I had acquired a great deal of affection for those young marines, simply because we had been through a few things together. They were the men with whom I had shared the heat and dust, the tense, watchful nights, the risks of patrolling some desolate jungle trail. There were more admirable men in the world, more principled men, and men with finer sensibilities, but they slept in peaceful beds.

Liberty!

The officers and platoon sergeants were in the headquarters tent for the captain's daily briefing, and First Sergeant Wagoner had just uttered the magic word.

Did you say liberty, Top?

Snorting and adjusting his glasses, Wagoner said yes, ten percent of the battalion would be allowed Cinderella liberty (ending at midnight) in Danang.

"But nobody can go ashore except on the regularly scheduled liberty-bus run," he added.

"Okay," someone asked, "when is the regularly scheduled bus run?"

With a straight face, Wagoner replied, "As far as I know, there isn't any."

Tester, short, tow-headed, ever cheerful, the company's litterateur—he had brought a small library to

Vietnam—leaned back laughing on his campstool. "And I thought *Catch-22* was fiction."

"What's Catch Twenty-two?" the Top asked.

"It's a satire about army bureaucracy," I explained.

Wagoner looked puzzled. "Army? What's that got to do with us? We're in the Marine Corps, not the Army."

Despite the lack of a regularly scheduled bus run, liberty call was sounded that afternoon. And about twenty-five enlisted men from C Company were trucked into Danang. McCloy, Peterson, Sergeant Loker, and I drove in the captain's jeep, charged with the task of making sure the troops stayed out of serious trouble.

We left camp looking crisp in our tropical khakis, but were sweating and dust-powdered by the time we entered the city. Although it looked good to eyes that had been staring at nothing but rice paddies and jungle, Danang was no Hong Kong. It might have possessed an exotic charm before the war; vestiges of those days remained in the quiet districts where whitewashed houses stood in the shade of palm and tamarind trees. But for the most part, Danang had become a garrison town, teeming with refugees from the countryside, armed soldiers in battle dress, whores, pimps, camp followers, and black marketeers.

Thatch huts clustered in dense squalor on the outskirts and merged into warrens of shacks with rusting, sheet-metal roofs. Big-bellied children squalled in the mud alleys between the shanties, the alleys reeking like cesspools. Doc Lap Street, one of the main avenues, was the preserve of the more fortunate. Middle-level army officers, civil servants, and merchants lived there in stucco cottages surrounded by stucco walls covered with bougainvillaea. Flame trees with bright-red blossoms shaded the street. Doc Lap led us into the city's center, a chaotic place full of flyblown restaurants, brothels, and shops whose metal shutters were rolled down while the owners rested in the flattening, afternoon heat. In a vegetable market nearby, peasant women jostled each other at the stalls, bargaining in rapid, singsong voices.

Lance Corporal Reed, Peterson's driver, piloted the jeep through the squadrons of pedicabs that jammed the street. He stopped in front of a row of bars with names like the Velvet Swing and the Blue Dahlia. The trucks behind us bumped to a halt. Released from almost six weeks of constant combat operations, the marines leaped to the ground and whooped into the bars. Their exotic names notwithstanding, the bars were ordinary inside: a Formica-topped bar, a stereo set pilfered from an American PX playing songs about Georgia and Tennessee, a row of booths where dark-haired girls cooed to boys a long way from Georgia and Tennessee, "GI, buy me one drink."

"Yea, sure. One drink. What's your name?"

"My name Co-Phoung. Come from Say-gone. You buy me one drink now."

"I said all right. If I buy you one drink, then we go to your place."

"For sure. You me we go to my house. Number-one short-time. But first you must to buy me one drink."

Outside, cyclo-drivers pimped on the street corners, eyes darting lizardlike from beneath their cork sun helmets as they surveyed the khaki crowds passing by. "Hey, you GI," they hissed, straddling their three-wheeled cycles, "you ride my cyclo to good place. Very cheap. Good place. No VD. No VC." Old women with faces like dried dates squatted on the sidewalks, peddling black-market cigarettes or currency or trinkets or cheaply made jackets with the words *Danang —I've Served My Time in Hell* sewn on the backs.

Once in a while, a man missing an arm or a leg or an eye, some forgotten victim of some forgotten battle, would hobble up holding out a faded fatigue cap. There wasn't any Veterans Administration in Vietnam, and its legions of maimed soldiers, like Falstaff's peppered survivors, were left "for the town's end, to beg during life."

Walking down a street with McCloy and Loker, I gave a few piasters to one of the beggers. He no sooner said "Cam Ong" (thank you) than a mob of small boys with very old eyes accosted us.

"You gimme money you."

"No money. Go on, di-di."

"Gimme cig'rette. One cig'rette one Salem you gimme." They mimicked the motions of a man smoking a cigarette.

"Di-di, you little bastards," Loker snarled. "Di-di mau." (Get out of here and quickly.)

But they stayed with us, chorusing "Cheap Charlie, numbah-ten cheap Charlie." All the time it was steaming hot and the air smelled of the fish piled up and rotting on the quay by the Tourane River.

We sought refuge in Simone's, a bar named after its owner, a French-Cambodian-Thai adventuress who had been born in Bangkok and whose ambition was to marry an American and get to the States. Five or six marines from my platoon were in the place, well on their way to becoming drunk and broke. Loker immediately started talking to Simone. He was much taken by her, although he had no intention of taking her to the States. She knew it and so talked to him noncommittally. McCloy introduced me to two girls from Simone's stable. They had the incredible names of Yum-Yum and Yip-Yap and were plump, pleasant, and reasonable. But I was shy about whoring in front of my men.

Two of the marines, Marshall and Morrisson, wanted to know if I would have a drink with them and the others. I agreed; for some time, I wanted to break down the barriers between officer and enlisted, to drink with the troops and get to know them as they were among themselves.

The experiment in military democracy did not work out. We all had too much to drink and talked a lot of nonsense. Morrisson kept throwing one of his beefy, hairy arms around my neck and slurring, "Lieutenant, me and you could win this war together. Just the two of us." Then he asked if I would talk to Peterson about a brilliant battle plan he and his buddies had worked out.

"We were talking and figured we could whip Charlie's ass if we made a night parachute jump over the Laotian border and then worked our way back to Danang on foot. See, sir, the Cong would never catch us if it was only four or five of us. We'd just move through the boonies creepin' and crawlin' and ambushin' Cong along the way. We'd waste the shit out of 'em. You just gotta talk to the skipper about it."

"Old Moe could do it," said one of the other marines. "He's a shitbird in garrison, but a real evil dude in the boondocks."

"Morrisson," I said, "that's just about the craziest idea I've ever heard."

"That's because I'm a crazy motherfucker, lieutenant. I'm a badass. You know that and I know that. Man, I been busted so many times I couldn't make lance corporal if I stayed in the Crotch for thirty years."

Another marine, reeling on his feet, raised his beer glass. "Tell him, Moe. Tell him. Eat the apple and fuck the Corps."

"Stow it, scumbag," Morrisson said. "Like I was saying, sir. I am a crazy badass, but it's crazy badasses that win wars."

But I had heard all I wanted to hear about Private Morrisson's military theories, and I turned to Marshall, who had been quietly standing by. The talk that followed was hardly better. Marshall's favorite subject was cars. It may have been his only subject. I was almost totally ignorant about cars and listened stupefied as the others nodded knowingly while Marshall rambled on about torques, revs, gear ratios, mills, bores and strokes, overhead cams and rockers and tachs, and how it was really cool to rap your lakers in the parking lot of an A&W root beer stand.

When he had finished his automotive soliloquy, he asked what kind of car I drove, his eyes bright with anticipation: an officer would own at least a Jaguar XKE. Sadly I confessed I did not own a car. I had never owned one.

Marshall appeared to feel genuinely sorry for me. "No shit, lieutenant?"

"No shit. But I always wanted a 'fifty-seven Chevy."

"Yeah—I mean, yes, sir. Well, let me tell you about 'fifty-seven Chevies . . ."

And on he went. Baffled and ultimately bored by

his jargon, pestered at intervals by Morrisson, who still wanted me to consider his mad scheme, I decided there was a good reason for barriers between officers and enlisted men. I managed to extricate myself from the group and left the bar with McCloy.

Murph, who had also done a tour in Vietnam as an observer, was bent on introducing me to the mysteries of Danang. We started by having dinner at a restaurant with the CO of the ARVN battalion McCloy had served with, the 11th Rangers. The meal was unmemorable except for the chayo—rice paper stuffed with vegetables—and the sharp nuoc-maum sauce. Happily, the nuoc-maum tasted better than it smelled. After washing the meal down with iced tea, we left to satisfy other physical needs.

Striding confidently through a maze of narrow, sinister-looking streets, McCloy led me to a two-story house with flaking yellow walls and green shutters. "This is it," he said, climbing the stairs. The inside of the brothel was a scene from a Fellini film: a large, stifling room with a dirt-encrusted floor; half-naked whores lounging on straw beds and languidly waving wicker fans at the clouds of flies that buzzed around their heads. In one corner, a bony creature of indeterminable age lay on her back, staring at the ceiling with opium-glazed eyes. McCloy's confidence began to crumble.

"It wasn't like this last year," he said in his soft Kentucky drawl. "Maybe I've got the wrong place."

One of the women got up and shuffled toward us. Her mouth was a smear of lipstick, and red circles were painted on her sallow cheeks. "Boom-boom, GI?" purred the clownlike thing, pointing at a staircase. "Fuck-suck?"

"Khoung, khoung," I said, backing away from her. "No, no." I turned to McCloy. "Murph, I don't care if this is the *right* place. Let's get the hell out. We'll get a dose just breathing in here."

Just then, three marines from Charley Company came down the stairs laughing and tucking their shirts into their trousers. They stopped cold when they saw us. McCloy's fair complexion turned red, and I felt a flush of embarrassment creeping up my own face. Officers are not supposed to be saints, but they are expected to be discreet. That is to say, they are not supposed to be seen whoring or getting drunk. We had just been seen. I had no idea of what to say, but Murph solved the problem with his usual aplomb. Looking at the marines sternly, he said, "Lieutenant Caputo and I are checking to make sure you men are taking care of yourselves. We hope you've taken precautions."

"If you mean did we use rubbers, yes, sir, we did," said one of the men, a black lance corporal.

"Very good. We don't want you men coming down with VD. Well, carry on."

"Oh, we'll carry on, sir."

Without a further word, McCloy made a crisp turn and walked out the door.

"Neatly done," I said.

"P.J., I didn't go to the Naval Academy for nothing."

We then went to the Blue Dahlia, a dimly lit place with a lush garden outside and a bevy of lush, Chinese bargirls inside. It was a hangout for the Australian advisers stationed at Danang. Three of them were with the 11th Rangers, and I had to endure listening to them and McCloy reminisce about jungle skirmishes in the "old days."

Like most Australians, they were champion drinkers. Two bottles of Johnnie Walker were eventually brought out from their private stock. In the spirit of Australian-American friendship, they poured us each a tumblerful of the clear, golden-white whiskey. Neat, of course. No water, no ice. Then they filled their glasses, emptying one bottle and part of the other. Then one of the Aussies, a lean, leathery warrant officer, did something I had never seen before and have never seen since: he took his glass, which held at least eight ounces, and drained it in one gulp.

"Baawuagh! Bloody good stuff that," he said, pouring himself another. Compared to his heroic swallow, I had taken a delicate sip. The Aussie whacked me on the back. "Look, mate, I thought you was a U.S. Ma-

rine. Thought you blokes was supposed to be tough.
C'mon now, drink it down. We got lots more."

With a twenty-three-year-old's ideas about manhood, and challenged to defend the reputation of the
U.S. Marines, I chugged it all down. Within seconds,
the room began spinning slowly, like a helicopter's
rotor blades when the engine has just started. "That's
the way," the warrant officer said. He poured me a
couple of ounces more. Someone said "Cheers" and I
said "Cheers" and had another drink. The faces in the
spinning room multiplied by two and my mouth felt
the way it does after a dentist's Novocain injection; the
clipped, Australian voices seemed to be coming
through a mile-long tube. "C'mon, mate, 'ave another.
Drink it down now. 'Ey, that's the stuff. Cheers.
You're bloody all right."

Feeling considerably less than bloody all right, I
woke up in the chamber of one of the Chinese bargirls.
I could not remember how I had gotten there. My uniform was strewn on the floor. Her ao-dais was folded
neatly on a chair. Lying naked next to me, she said
with a giggle that I was "buku drunk" and had fallen
asleep. But was I okay now and did I want a number-
one short-time?

"Sure. How much?"

"Four thousand P."

Except for the hard, commercial look in her eye,
she was a beautiful girl, more full-figured than a
Vietnamese, but with the same long, straight black
hair. Without reflecting on the fact that four thousand
piasters was worth more than thirty dollars, I said,
"Sure. Why not? Four thou it is." Fumbling in my
wallet, I produced a stack of orange bills with tigers
and dragons on them. She counted it out carefully,
then rolled over on top of me and gave me a short-
time that was number one but still not worth four
thousand.

When we were finished and dressed, she walked me
back across the street to the Blue Dahlia. McCloy was
still there, sitting with a girl on his lap. Incredibly, the
Australians were working on another bottle of Scotch.

"And how was Lang?" the warrant officer asked. It was the first time I had heard the girl's name.

"Lang was fine, but expensive."

"Yeah, they're spoiled in this place."

There was a pounding on the door. "Shit," the Aussie said, "it's the fucking MPs. You two Yanks under the couch over there." He shoved McCloy and me toward a sofa backed against one wall. Apparently, the bar was in a district off limits to Americans after a certain hour. We squeezed ourselves under the couch, and I recall seeing two pair of gleaming black boots with white laces not six inches from my face. The whiskey and the ludicrousness of the situation made me giddy. McCloy had to clamp a hand over my mouth to keep me from laughing. The MPs stomped around the room for a few minutes until they were satisfied that no Americans were there. The door slammed behind them.

Their departure was a signal for ours. Thanking the Aussies for the whiskey and the hiding place, we shoved off and walked in the humid night to the Grand Hotel. Peterson and Loker were there, drinking rum on the veranda with a Norwegian merchant sailor. A glassy-eyed Peterson introduced us to the Norwegian, a big, blond man with red and blue veins in his face.

"Phil and Murph, this sailor is one helluva good man," the skipper said, thick-tongued. "He's one helluva good man because he's a Scandinavian and *I'm* a Scandinavian and proud of it. Scandinavians are the greatest people in the world."

Acknowledging the superlative qualities of Scandinavians, Murph and I sat down. The sailor offered to buy a round of rum. I accepted, having sweated out the whiskey on the walk to the hotel. Then I bought a round. Then the Norwegian bought another round. In a stupor, I was watching the lights of the fishing junks bobbing on the silky black ribbon of the Tourane River when four giant MPs swept onto the veranda and arrested all of us but the sailor. We had violated a curfew law, they said. Unmoved by our protest that we were field marines who did not know anything about curfew laws, the MPs hauled us off to the Danang brig.

All I remember about our brief stay in that place is standing unsteadily in front of a full-length mirror above which a sign commanded: LOOK SHARP! CHECK YOUR CREASES, BOOTS, AND BRASS. I checked my creases—they had dissolved in the heat; my boots—they were filthy; my brass—it was tarnished.

After some argument, the MPs were talked out of putting us behind bars. Lance Corporal Reed was somehow summoned to fetch us, and we were released. We climbed into the skipper's jeep, picked up two truckloads of roaring, drunken marines, and rattled back to camp. Everyone was laughing and singing. Well, not everyone. Peterson had passed out.

The Cinderella liberty exacted a retribution that was not the stuff of fairy tales. All the celebrants suffered from crippling hangovers the next day. Three days later, half of them discovered they had VD and filed down to the battalion aid station to bare their buttocks while a corpsman pumped them full of penicillin.

My memories of my last two weeks with the battalion are all of a piece. C Company went out on two or three more operations during that period. The always hot, sometimes dangerous days in the bush alternated with monotonous days of waiting in camp. A couple of brief, sordid liberties, much like the first, relieved the boredom.

Once, I led a difficult platoon-sized patrol near Charlie Ridge. I like to think of it whenever I hear some general who spent his tour looking at maps and flitting around in helicopters claim that we could have won the war. First we had to hack our way through a patch of bamboo and elephant grass ten feet high, the worst, thickest patch of jungle we had encountered. Working in shifts, the point man and I chopped at the growth with a machete. When we had cut as much as we could, three or four marines would come up and flatten the wall of brush by hurling their bodies against it. That done, the rest of the platoon would move forward a few yards. Then the point man and I would start out again. All this in bake-oven heat. Coming out of the jungle, we entered a swamp, which we had to cross by hopping from one small island of solid ground to the next. Corporal Mixon lost his footing once, fell into a quicksand pool, and had sunk up to his chest before he was hauled out, covered with muck and leeches. The patrol route took us over the swamp, then up an eight-hundred-foot ridge. The only trail up the ridge was an overgrown game-track. It was easy at first, but then the slope became so steep we had to climb hand over hand, clutching at the bone-gray roots of mahogany trees, hand over hand a foot at a time, gasping and sweating in the moist air. Sometimes a man fell, toppling several of those behind him as he rolled downhill. Thorn bushes clawed us, cordlike "wait-a-minute" vines coiled around our arms, rifles, and canteen tops with a tenacity that seemed almost human. When we finally reached the crest, I checked my map and watch: in five hours, and without making a single enemy contact, we had covered a little over half a mile.

Lemmon was wounded on an operation a few days later. The company was camped in a landing zone named LZ Oriole and Lemmon's platoon had been sent out ahead to scout a hill that overlooked the LZ. Halfway up, the platoon got into a short, sharp firefight with a group of VC guarding a large base camp. One of the guerrillas, concealed behind a rock outcropping, tossed a grenade as Lemmon led a charge against the camp. The grenade struck him in the chest, bounced off, landed between his feet, then rolled into a hollow and exploded. Fragments struck Lemmon in the face, and the force of the blast almost bowled over Sullivan, who was behind him, carrying a machine gun.

The platoon rushed the camp. They found it empty of Viet Cong—the djinns had vanished again—but filled with enough uniforms, equipment, and new AK-47s to equip a full-strength company. The marines cheerfully destroyed the weapons and gear, fired the camp, then pulled back while our artillery pounded the hills behind them.

Lemmon had escaped with minor scratches, Sullivan with only a peppered uniform. But the experience had made an impression on both men. Experiences like that usually do. Sullivan, who was now a sergeant and the father of a two-month-old boy, did not want any more close calls. "Man," I heard him say as the platoon filed back into the LZ, "I felt that blast hit me like a hot wind. It plastered my uniform against my skin. No more of that shit for me. I'm a daddy now."

Lemmon did not say anything at first, just kept shaking his head. I can still see his angular face, as white as porcelain except for the bloody patches where the shrapnel had struck him. He was silent for several minutes, then it all came out of him in a rush.

"Phil, I'm never going to forget that one. I saw that thing coming down at me. I could see the son of a bitch who threw it. I was going up after him with my carbine and then that thing came sailing over." Dragging on his cigarette, he shook his head several times. All the while, his face did not lose that strange, sick whiteness. Smoke from the burning camp billowed through the trees on the hill up ahead. We could not see the camp, only the smoke and the occasional orange flashes of the flames. Rising from the hills beyond were the gray-black plumes of the shells that had covered Lemmon's withdrawal. "I thought I was finished," he continued. "It bounced right off my goddamned chest, and when I saw it down between my legs, all I could think of were my credentials. 'It's going to blow my balls off'—that's all I could think of. Then the thing just rolled away and went off."

D Company, which was on our left flank during the operation, ran into some trouble later in the day. They were shelled with 60-millimeters in a place appropriately nick-named Mortar Valley and about six men were seriously wounded. But they evened the score when they attacked another base camp and killed five VC, including a North Vietnamese political officer. Meanwhile, my platoon was sent off on an all-night ambush, an experience I recall for its sheer misery. No enemy soldiers entered the ambush but thousands of insects did. We lay awake for eight hours, enduring the bites of mosquitoes and stinging fire ants.

Worn-out and red-eyed, we returned to the battalion's lines the next day and were greeted by a strange rumor: our role in the war was to end in September when the regiment would be rotated back to Okinawa. Some of us accepted the rumor as fact, under the illusion that we were hurting the VC badly. It was an illusion partly created by the ever-optimistic reports issued by higher headquarters or printed in the *Stars and Stripes* and partly by our own persistent belief that we would win quickly. Not as quickly as we had first hoped, but within, say, six months or a year.

"I have the feeling the VC are getting demoralized," I wrote in a confident letter to my parents. "They have taken to their camps in the hills because they're afraid of us. Now, we're chasing them into their mountain hideouts."

At the end of May, I was ordered to report back to my parent unit, Regimental Headquarters Company. After attending a week-long course in Yokosuka, Japan, I would be assigned to the staff as assistant adjutant. An adjutant is an administrative officer. I hated the idea of leaving One-Three. It was a first-rate infantry battalion, with a unique spirit and personality. The staff, on the other hand, seemed to be nothing more than a military organization, a soulless, bloodless thing. Papers. Reports. Pins on a map. I made a few attempts to get the assignment changed; all were unsuccessful. So I packed my gear and complained bitterly. Lemmon, whose ideas about war had changed radically since his narrow scrape, could not understand my disappointment.

"I don't know what you're bitchin' about, P.J. I'd give anything for a week out of this hole. Yeah, a week in Yokosuka in a clean bed with one of them Japanese honey-wa's."

Feeling desolate, I padlocked my seabag and then said good-bye to the platoon, to Morrisson the dare-

devil; to Sampson, who had been awarded a Bronze
Star for rescuing Gonzalez and was then reduced to
PFC for going AWOL in Danang; to Butler, who had
livened the dull days in camp with his singing; to
Mixon, Marshall, Skates, and Parker, and, of course,
Sergeant Campbell. "Sorta hate to see you go, lieutenant." he said. "Now old Wild Bill's gonna be the platoon commander and the platoon sergeant and have to
do all the work by himself."

Part Two

THE OFFICER IN CHARGE OF THE DEAD

How many dead? As many as ever
    you wish.
Don't count 'em; they're too many.
Who'll buy my nice fresh corpses,
    two a penny?
                    —Siegfried Sassoon
                    "The Effect"

destroy with uncontrolled fury. At last it is over. The
hamlet which is marked on our maps as Giao-Tri (3)
no longer exists. All that remains are piles of smoldering ash and a few charred poles still standing.
By some miracle, none of the people have been hurt.
I hear women wailing, and I see one through the
smoke that is drifting across the river. She is on her
knees, bowing up and down and keening in the ashes
of what was once her home. I harden my heart against
her cries. You let the VC use your village for an ambush site, I think, and now you're paying the price. It
is then I realize that the destruction of Giao-Tri was
more than an act of madness committed in the heat
of battle. It was an act of retribution as well. These
villagers aided the VC, and we taught them a lesson.
We are learning to hate.

And you've lost your youth and come to manhood, all in a few hours. . . . Oh, that's painful.
That is indeed.

—Howard Fast
April Morning

Our next operation took place in a desolate area southwest of Danang. It was true Indian country, a region of
fallow fields, sun-seared hills, and abandoned villages
lying near a pale-green height called Charlie Ridge.
The operation, which lasted four days, was yet
another attempt to trap the Viet Cong between two
rifle companies, ours and Captain Miller's A Company.
This time we partially succeeded, though it was more
by accident than design.
    We spent the first day blundering around in the bush
and skirmishing with the usual snipers. Once, while
taking a break, we were hit with automatic-weapons
fire. Although it almost killed Peterson and the colo-

Chapter Nine

Your dextrous wit will haunt us long
Wounding our grief with yesterday.
Your laughter is a broken song;
And death has found you, kind and gay.
                    —Siegfried Sassoon
                    "Elegy"

I came back from Japan on June 15, and was picked up at the airfield by Lance Corporal Kazmarack, the adjutant's driver. It was a damp, overcast day. An early-morning rain had turned the dust on the roads to mud. The tents at regimental and battalion head-quarters—the two HQs occupied the same camp—looked strangely clean. Pools of water had collected on the tent tops, and marines were draining them off by pushing poles against the bulges they made in the canvas ceilings. The water made a pleasant sound as it slid off in silvery sheets and splashed on the ground. Kazmarack turned off the road, the jeep skidding in the mud, and drove through an opening in the barbed wire. Two marines sat in a sandbagged emplacement, their ponchos still slick and shining from the rain. I flinched when an eight-inch howitzer from the battery across the road fired a round. You have to hear an eight-incher to appreciate it. Smiling, Kazmarack said, "No sweat, sir, that's outgoing."

"I know it's outgoing," I said, put out with myself for flinching and with the driver for noticing it. "It's sure goddamned loud, though."

"Wait till tonight, lieutenant. Those mothers and the one-five-fives'll be banging away all night. You'd think the Red Chinese Army was out there instead of a bunch of guerrillas."

He pulled up near the adjutant's tent and climbed out to get my valpack from the back seat. "Well, here valpack on the wooden pallet that lay alongside the cot. The tent was filthy. It was pitched next to the road, and the dust raised by passing convoys and tanks rolled right into it. Dead bugs were strewn across the hard-packed, dirt floor. Outside, a trench offered shelter in case of a shelling, or a fighting position in the unlikely event of a ground attack. A foot of water lay in the trench.

In the afternoon, I rode up to Hill 268 to pick up some of the personal gear I had left behind.

When you have lived in the intimate world of an infantry company, you come to know those who have shared that world with you as well as you know your own family. Walking into C Company's bivouac, I sensed immediately that something had happened. No one said anything to me or looked at me in a strange way. Still, I could sense it, just as a man can walk into his house after being gone for a while, hear familiar words from familiar people, see the usual objects in their usual places, yet know instinctively that things are not the same as when he left.

The camp did not look any different. The galley, the headquarters, officers' and platoon sergeants' tents were still pitched end to end on the narrow shelf on the reverse slope of the hill. Farther down was the broad red scar of the landing zone, and the enlisted tents below that. The defensive positions on the forward slope had not been changed. I saw the old, traversed trench line cutting across the hillside in a series of sharp angles; the foxholes with their weathered, sandbag parapets; sentries in flak jackets sitting in some of the foxholes; the dugout where I had slept many nights, and the heavy-timbered FO's bunker, its radio antennae waving in the breeze like steel reeds.

I walked past the galley. Some marines were cleaning their rifles under the tarp that extended from the galley like an awning. There were the familiar smells of oil and solvent, and the metallic sound made by the cleaning rods and bore brushes as they were drawn through the barrels of the rifles. A transistor radio was playing the country-music program broadcast every af-

ternoon by the Armed Forces station in Saigon. Some
men from my old platoon saw me. They waved and
asked what it was like "in the rear." I said I didn't
know, I had just reported in.

I went up to get my gear, increasingly haunted by
the feeling that things were not the same. There was
something peculiar about the men; they seemed a little cool and distant, and I wondered if it was because
they now regarded me as an outsider. In the NCOs'
tent, Campbell and Green, Lemmon's platoon sergeant, were playing cribbage, as they did whenever
the company was in camp. Lemmon, Tester, and
McCloy were in the officers' tent next door. Tester
was saying something about his gear, by which he
meant the Teac tape recorder he had bought in Hong
Kong before the battalion was sent to Vietnam. He
had had to leave it in storage on Okinawa, and he
was worried about it. "I just hope those clowns don't
wreck my gear," he said to Lemmon as I walked in.
Glen, his hawklike face still showing the marks of the
grenade shrapnel, did not say anything. McCloy was
reading a World War II saga titled *Panzer Leader*.
"That gear would cost me twelve hundred bucks in
the States. I picked it up for six . . . hey, P.J.'s back,"
Tester said, interrupting himself. "Caputo, shove off.
This is a line company. It's off limits to rear-echelon
pogues."

"Bruce, I feel lousy enough about being there. Don't
make it worse."

"Uh-oh, Caputo's pissed. Caputo's going to beat the
shit out of me."

"Well, I don't know what you feel lousy about,"
Lemmon said. "You ought to be happy you're at
regiment." He did not look at me. Sitting on an empty
crate, a bush hat pulled low over his forehead, he
was dealing cards to himself and an imaginary op-
ponent. "Fact is, I don't know why you were in a
hurry to get back to the Nam. Hell, Walsh over in
Alpha Company and Mike Repp in Delta went to
Okinawa last month for flight physicals and I don't
think they're back yet. You should have stretched it
out."

"I saw Walsh and Repp," I said. "Anyway, I stretched it out as long as I could."

"Ah, Phil, you're still a boot brown-bar. Suppose you stayed a few extra days. What could they do to you? Make you a grunt and send you to Vietnam?"

Lemmon's Texas accent was naturally harsh, but there was a new edge in his voice, a bitterness that had not been there before. And like the enlisted men I had seen earlier, he had a vaguely distant air.

"Well, I want to know about Japan," said Tester, who seemed more or less his old self. "What I want to know is, did you get your socks blown off? Did one of those honey-wa's blow your socks off? That's what I want to know."

So I told him about the weekend in Tokyo and the half-Russian, half-Japanese girl who stayed with me in the Palace Hotel. Her name was Ayako, she was a bargirl in Yokosuka, and just before we got on the train for Tokyo, she turned to me and said, "Philsan, I will spend two days with you and you will not have to pay me. I will love you for two days and then I will not love you."

"Jesus, you got it for nothing?" Tester asked. "Why *did* you come back?"

Lemmon shook his head as he dealt the cards. "Gollee, if I had that going, I'd still be there. Like I said, what could they do to me? Make me a grunt and send me to Vietnam?"

"For openers, Glen, they could throw you in the brig," I said.

"Shit, the brig's better'n this. You can't get killed in the brig."

"Well, I don't plan on getting killed. There's not much chance of getting killed at regiment anyway."

"You don't know about Sullivan?"

"No."

"He's dead."

Sullivan flashed in my mind. Tall, skinny, looking even younger than his twenty-two years, he was handing me a cigar. I was up in one of the old French blockhouses, looking out at the rice paddies through my binoculars. Sullivan, reaching up as far as he could, was handing a cigar to me. He was smiling, the smile cracking the dust that caked his face. "Hey, lieutenant," he was saying, "just got a letter from my old lady in Pennsylvania. It's a boy." That had been in March or early April, when the battalion was still on the airfield perimeter; and picturing Sullivan as he was then, I felt something draw tight inside myself, tighter and tighter until I thought it would snap.

"How?" I asked.

"A sniper got him. This guy wasn't just some Cong popping off with a carbine. He could shoot. We were set in south of the Song Tuy Loan, near the Song Yen River. It was hotter'n a bitch, and Sullivan volunteered to fill canteens. He'd just got down to the river when the sniper cranked off a round. We figure he was using one of those Russian rifles with a scope, because he got Sullivan with one shot. Went in one side and came out the other. Plowed one helluva hole right through him. He was probably dead before he hit the deck."

I asked when it had happened and felt like a deserter when Lemmon said, "A few days after you left." Not that my presence would have made any difference; I just felt I should have been with them.

"Three companies were out on a battalion-sized operation," Glen went on. "And you're lucky you missed that one because it really got screwed up. Ingram got it, too, you know."

"KIA?"

"No, but he got hit pretty bad. A round caught him in the back and chipped his spine, I think. Last we heard, a meningitis infection set in and he's in a wheelchair. I think he's in a hospital in Tennessee somewhere, near his hometown. He might not ever walk again."

And then I saw an image of Ingram, big, barrel-chested, striding out of the galley on the morning of the company's first operation, striding powerfully and singing in his rich baritone, and that emotional wire inside me tightened again and broke. I felt it break just as surely as you can feel a bone or a tendon break; and afterward, there was only a cold, empty, sick feeling in the pit of my stomach. Ingram crippled and Sullivan dead. Dead. Death. *Death.* I had heard that word so many times, but I had never known its meaning.

"The thing was," Lemmon was saying, "Ingram asked for it. That goddamned Ingram . . . you know how he was. Thought he was too big or tough to get hurt. Right after Sullivan got hit, somebody spotted the sniper in a tree line near a ville, Duyen Son. It was a ways off, so we fired a three-point five at him. A willy-peter round, and that's when it got all fucked up.

"A couple of gunships saw the WP and I guess they figured we were marking the target for an air strike. They started strafing the ville and putting rockets into it. One of my squads heard women and kids yelling and crying in there, and we moved out to get those people out of there. We ran right into an ambush. Got hit from three sides. Ingram was walking around like he's on the drill field. I told him to get his ass down. He says, 'I'm a Marine NCO, sir, and I ain't gonna go low-crawlin' on my belly.' How do you like that bullshit, Phil? So he got it in the back, and then my radioman gets his arm shot to shit. Anyhow, we got into the ville to rescue those civilians, but we couldn't get the Hueys to cease firing. They started strafing and rocketing us. That was something else, getting hit with your own planes. . . ."

Evacuating the casualties had been another nightmare, Lemmon said. The landing zone was under enemy machine-gun fire, and the medevac helicopters were unable to land. Then Gallardo, a corporal in 1st platoon, ran into the LZ and guided the choppers in with hand signals. His canteens were shot off his hip, bullets were whacking at his feet, but he stayed out there until the birds were down and the casualties loaded on board.

"Sullivan's body was laying out there all the time. The skipper couldn't look at him and the others. Like I said, that was a bad hole in Sully, in the side of his chest. That round made pulp out of his insides, and Peterson was really shook about it. He just turned around and walked away so he didn't have to look at him."

"Well, that's the way he is," I said. "He really loves this company."

"Yeah," Lemmon said, "a little too much I think."

We talked about other things. Then I picked up my gear and left. Outside, I ran into Colby.

"Hey, Lieutenant Caputo," he said. "Seeing how the other half lives?"

"You guys won't lay off that, will you? I didn't ask for the staff."

"I know, sir. Guess you've heard about Sergeant Sullivan by now."

"Just now. Mister Lemmon just told me."

"Well, sir, it was bound to happen. I'm just sorry it had to happen to Sully."

"Yeah, sorry about that and everything. You told me once that you were going to make everybody look at the first man who got KIA. Did you do that, Sergeant Colby?"

"Of course not, sir."

Kazmarack drove me back to regimental HQ, down the winding dirt road. The troops were lining up for the evening meal. I was not at all hungry, but went to the officers' mess anyway. There was nothing else to do. The mess was luxurious compared to what I was used to. Two squad tents were joined together and stretched over a frame of two-by-fours. There were screens to keep dust and insects out of the staff officers' food, and a plywood floor, and three tables arranged in a U. Tacked to one of the two-by-fours was the regimental crest, a black shield with a red and gold *3* superimposed on a bayonet, and a banner that proclaimed THIRD MARINES. FORTES FORTUNA ADJUVAT. In contrast to the fairly democratic atmosphere in a rifle company mess, the one at regiment was rigidly hierarchical. Seating at the U-shaped table went according to rank. The regimental CO, Colonel Wheeler, and the executive officer sat at the head. Next came the majors, then the captains, then the lieutenants, with the ends reserved for second lieutenants. There were only two of us on the staff, and, as the other one was off somewhere, I ate alone.

That suited my mood. I did not feel like talking to anyone. Sullivan was much on my mind, Hugh John Sullivan, dead at the age of twenty-two and before he had had the chance to see his son. Colby had been right; it was bound to happen. But I wondered why it had to happen to a decent young man who always had a joke to tell, and not to some cynical old veteran. I wondered why it had to happen to a husband and father, and why it had to happen in the way it did. Like many inexperienced soldiers, I suffered from the illusion that there were good ways to die in war. I thought grandly in terms of noble sacrifices, of soldiers offering up their bodies for a cause or to save a comrade's life. But there had been nothing sacrificial or ceremonial about Sullivan's death. He had been sniped while filling canteens in a muddy jungle river.

I saw him as Lemmon had described him, lying on his back with the big, bloody hole in his side. I imagined that his face must have looked like the faces of the dead Viet Cong I had seen the month before: mouth opened, lips pursed in a skull-like grin, eyes staring blankly. It was painful to picture Sullivan like that; I had grown so used to seeing his living face. That is when I felt for the first time, sitting in the mess over a greasy tray of greasy food, the slimy, hollow-cold fear that is the fear of death; the image of Sullivan's dead face had suddenly changed into an image of my own. That could be me someday, I thought. I might look like that. If it happened to him, there's no reason it can't happen to me. I did not think it necessarily would happen, but I realized it could. Except in an abstract sense, the chance of being killed had never occurred to me before. As a young, healthy American raised and educated in peacetime, or what passes for peacetime in this century, I had been incapable of imagining myself sick or old, let alone dead. Oh, I had thought about death, but only as an event that would happen far in the future, so far that I had been unable to consider it as a real possibility. Well, it had suddenly become a possibility, and a proximate one for all I knew. That was the thing: I could not possibly know or suspect when it would come. There was only a slight chance of being killed in a headquarters unit, but Sullivan probably had not felt any intimations of mortality when he walked down to that river, a string of canteens jangling in his hand. Then the sniper centered the cross hairs on his telescopic sight, and all that Sullivan had ever been or would ever be, all of his thoughts, memories, and dreams were annihilated in an instant.

I came to understand why Lemmon and the others had seemed so distant. It had nothing to do with my no longer belonging to the battalion. It was, rather, the detachment of men who find themselves living in the presence of death. They had lost their first man in battle, and, with him, the youthful confidence in their own immortality. Reality had caught up with them, with all of us. As Bradley put it later that evening: "I guess the splendid little war is over."

Some combat veterans may think I am making too much of a single casualty. Later, I was to see fairly active fighting, and I know that experiencing heavy or constant losses tends to diminish the significance of one individual's death. But at the time we lost Sullivan, casualties were still light; it was the "expeditionary" period of the war, a period that lasted roughly from March to September 1965. The loss of even one man was an extraordinary event. Perhaps, too, we were less emotionally prepared for death and wounds than those who came later; the men who fought in Vietnam at this time had joined the service in peacetime, before the toll built up to a daily announcement. A small statistic illustrates what I mean: One-Three's total losses between March and August of 1965 amounted to about one hundred and ten killed and wounded, or ten percent. During one battle in April 1966, a single company from that same battalion lost one hundred and eight men in only one hour. But most important, in this early period the men in One-Three were very close to one another. They had been together for years and assumed they would remain together until the end of their enlistments. Sergeant Sullivan's death shattered that assumption. It upset the sense of unity and stability that had pervaded life in the battalion. One-Three was a corps in the old sense of the word, a body, and Sullivan's death represented the amputation of a small part of it. The corps would go on living and functioning without him, but it was aware of having lost something irreplaceable. Later in the war, that sort of feeling became rarer in infantry battalions. Men were killed, evacuated with wounds, or rotated home at a constant rate, then replaced by other men who were killed, evacuated, or rotated in their turn. By that time, a loss only meant a gap in the line that needed filling.

Chapter Ten

"He'd never seen so many dead before."
The lilting words danced up and down his brain,
While corpses jumped and capered in the rain.
No, no; he wouldn't count them anymore.
—Siegfried Sassoon
"The Effect"

True to Kazmarack's prediction, my first night at headquarters was noisy. The big guns across the road fired H-and-I missions until dawn. H-and-I stood for "harassment and interdiction," a type of artillery fire directed at road junctions, hilltops, anywhere the enemy was likely to be. It was supposed to fray the Viet Congs' nerves and keep them off balance. I don't know if the artillery achieved its purpose, but by morning my nerves were plenty frayed. I had been jolted awake a dozen times by the roaring howitzers. Well, the artillery was on our side, when the shells didn't fall short.

Frazzled, I spent the next day breaking in as assistant adjutant. Schwartz and I plowed through what seemed a truckload of paperwork. Documents had to be inventoried and audited, messages, directives, and regimental orders filed. Looking at all the red tape, I decided that the life of a staff officer was going to be even worse than I had feared. Later, Schwartz briefed me on my extra assignments—additional duties, as they were called. Junior staff officers were given a number of them because nobody else would do them. We were therefore known as SLJOs: shitty little jobs officers. Schwartz listed mine. In addition to assistant adjutant, I was to be: Regimental Casualty Reporting Officer, Regimental Secret and Confidential Documents Officer, Regimental Legal Officer, Regimental Mess Officer.

On paper, it looked like a heavy work load. In fact, Schwartz said, it would not amount to more than three or four hours a day. Then why was I there? Couldn't one of the clerks handle it all? No, because regulations called for an officer to handle these duties. All right, why couldn't Captain Anderson handle them? He was an officer. Yes, he was, but that's what the assistant adjutant was there for—so the captain didn't have to handle it.

Schwartz left for 2d Battalion a few days later, and I took over. He had been right about not having more than three or four hours' work a day. Sometimes there was less than that. I spent my ample leisure time looking for things to do or reading the cheap paperbacks donated by the Red Cross—*Fighting Red Devils,* "the true-life story of Britain's guts and glory paratroopers in World War Two," or just sitting at my desk, sweaty and thoroughly bored.

At night, the junior officers took turns standing watch in the operations tent. The more junior you were, the later the watch. Generally I drew 2400 to 0200 (midnight to two A.M.) or 0200 to 0400. That did not amount to much work, either. All we did was monitor the radios, call the operations officer, Major Conlin, when something unusual happened, and log the situation reports in the unit diary. The sitreps came in about once an hour: disembodied voices crackled over the radio or the EE-8 field phones, and spoke in the Captain Midnight code-word gibberish that passes for language in the military. "Crowd Three this is Burke Three. Burke Alpha Six reports Alpha Two Scorpion in position at grid coordinates Alpha Tango Hotel Hotel Echo Yankee Yankee Lima. All units report Alpha Sierra Sierra Romeo Sierra." All secure, situation remains the same.

As fighting increased, the additional duty of casualty reporting officer kept me busiest. It was also a job that gave me a lot of bad dreams, though it had the beneficial effect of cauterizing whatever silly, abstract, romantic ideas I still had about war.

My job was simply to report on casualties, enemy as well as our own; casualties due to hostile action and those due to nonhostile causes—the accidents that inevitably occur where there are large numbers of young men armed with lethal weapons or at the controls of complicated machinery. Artillery shells sometimes fell on friendly troops, tanks ran over people, helicopters crashed, marines shot other marines by mistake.

It was not the simple task it seemed. The military has elaborate procedures for everything, and keeping records of the dead and wounded is no exception. The reports were written on mimeographed forms, one for KIAs, one for WIAs, and a third for nonhostile casualties. Each form had spaces for the victim's name, age, rank, serial number, and organization (his unit), and for the date, the description of his injuries, and the circumstances under which they occurred. If he had been killed, the circumstances were almost always described in the same way, and the words could have served as an epitaph for thousands of men: "killed in action while on patrol vicinity of Danang, RVN."

The KIA reports were long and complicated. Much information was required about the dead: their religion, the name and address of their next of kin, beneficiaries of their servicemen's life insurance policies, and whether the money was to be paid in a lump sum or in installments. All reports had to be written in that clinical, euphemistic language the military prefers to simple English. If, say, a marine had been shot through the guts, I could not write "shot through the guts" or "shot through the stomach"; no, I had to say "GSW" (gunshot wound) "through and through, abdomen." Shrapnel wounds were called "multiple fragment lacerations," and the phrase for dismemberment, one of my very favorite phrases, was "traumatic amputation." I had to use it a lot when the Viet Cong began to employ high-explosive weapons and booby traps. A device they used frequently was the command-detonated mine, which was set off electrically from ambush. The mines were similar to our Claymore, packed with hundreds of steel pellets and a few pounds of an explosive called C-4. If I recall correctly, the gas-expansion rate of C-4 is 26,000 feet per second. That terrific force, and the hundreds of steel pellets propelled by it, made the explosion of a command-detonated mine equivalent to the simultaneous firing of seventy twelve-gauge shotguns loaded with double-0 buckshot. Naturally, anyone hit by such a weapon was likely to suffer the "traumatic amputation" of something—an arm, a leg, his head—and many did. After I saw some of the victims, I began to question the accuracy of the phrase. *Traumatic* was precise, for losing a limb is definitely traumatic, but *amputation,* it seemed to me, suggested a surgical operation. I observed, however, that the human body does not break apart cleanly in an explosion. It tends to shatter into irregular and often unrecognizable pieces, so "traumatic fragmentation" would have been a more accurate term and would have preserved the euphemistic tone the military favored.

The shattering or fragmenting effect of high explosive occasionally caused semantic difficulties in reporting injuries of men who had undergone extreme mutilation. It was a rare phenomenon, but some marines had been so badly mangled there seemed to be no words to describe what had happened to them. Sometime that year, Lieutenant Colonel Meyers, one of the regiment's battalion commanders, stepped on a booby-trapped 155-mm shell. They did not find enough of him to fill a willy-peter bag, a waterproof sack a little larger than a shopping bag. In effect, Colonel Meyers had been disintegrated, but the official report read something like "traumatic amputation, both feet; traumatic amputation, both legs and arms; multiple lacerations to abdomen; through and through fragment wounds, head and chest." Then came the notation "killed in action."

The battalion adjutants phoned in reports of their units' casualties, and I relayed them to the division combat casualty reporting center. That done, I filed copies of the reports in their respective folders, one labeled CASUALTIES: HOSTILE ACTION and the other CASUALTIES: NON HOSTILE. I believe the two were kept separate because men killed or wounded by enemy fire were automatically awarded Purple Hearts, while those hit by friendly fire were not. That was the only real difference. A man killed by friendly fire (another misleading term, because fire is never friendly if it hits you) was just as dead as one killed by the enemy. And there was often an accidental quality even about battle casualties. Stepping on a mine or stumbling over the trip wire of a booby trap is a mishap, really, not unlike walking in front of a car while crossing a busy street.

Once the reports were filed, I brought Colonel Wheeler's scoreboard up to date. Covered with acetate and divided into vertical and horizontal columns, the board hung behind the executive officer's desk, in the wood-framed tent where he and the colonel made their headquarters. The vertical columns were headed, from left to right, KIA, WIA, DOW (died of wounds), NON-HOST, VC-KIA, VC-WIA, and VC-POW. The horizontal columns were labeled with the numerical designations of the units belonging to, or attached to, the regiment: 1/3 for 1st Battalion, 3d Marines, 2/3 for 2d Battalion, and so forth. In the first four vertical columns were written the number of casualties a particular unit had suffered, in the last three the number it had inflicted on the enemy. After an action, I went into the colonel's quarters, erased the old figures and wrote in the new with a grease pencil. The colonel, an easygoing man in most instances, was adamant about maintaining an accurate scoreboard: high-ranking visitors from Danang and Saigon often dropped in unannounced to see how the regiment was performing. And the measures of a unit's performance in Vietnam were not the distances it had advanced or the number of victories it had won, but the number of enemy soldiers it had killed (the body count) and the proportion between that number and the number of its own dead (the kill ratio). The scoreboard thus allowed the colonel to keep track of the battalions and companies under his command and, quickly and crisply, to rattle off impressive figures to visiting dignitaries. My unsung task in that statistical war was to do the arithmetic. If I had been an agent of death as a platoon leader, as a staff officer I was death's bookkeeper.

Sometimes I had to verify the body counts. Field commanders occasionally gave in to the temptation to exaggerate the number of Viet Cong their units had killed. So the bodies were brought to headquarters whenever possible, and I counted them to make sure there were as many as had been reported. That was always pleasant because the corpses had begun to decompose by the time they reached headquarters. Decomposition sets in quickly in that climate. Most pleasant of all was the job of identifying our own dead. The battalion adjutants usually did that, but whenever there was confusion about the names of the dead or when the descriptions of their wounds were incorrectly reported to regiment, I had to do it. The dead were kept in a fly tent adjacent to the division hospital. They were laid out on canvas stretchers, covered with ponchos or with rubber body-bags, yellow casualty tags tied to their boots—or to their shirts, if their legs had been blown off. One of the simplest ways to identify a dead man was to match his face against his photograph in a service record book. Some of them did not have faces, in which case we used dental records, since teeth are almost as reliable a means of identification as fingerprints. The latter were used only when the casualty had been decapitated or his jaw shattered to bits.

The interesting thing was how the dead looked so

much alike. Black men, white men, yellow men, they all looked remarkably the same. Their skin had a tallowlike texture, making them appear like wax dummies of themselves; the mouths were opened wide, as if death had caught them in the middle of a scream.

They smelled the same, too. The stench of death is unique, probably the most offensive on earth, and once you have smelled it, you can never again believe with conviction that man is the highest being in earthly creation. The corpses I have had to smell as a soldier and war correspondent smelled much worse than all the fish, birds, and deer I have scaled, skinned, or gutted as a sportsman. Because the odor of death is so strong, you can never get used to it, as you can get used to the sight of death. And the odor is always the same. It might vary in intensity, depending on the state of decomposition, but if two people have been dead for the same length of time and under the same conditions, there will be no difference in the way they smell. I first made that observation in Vietnam in 1965, when I noticed that the stench of a dead American made me just as sick as that of a dead Vietnamese. Since then, I have made it again and again in other wars in other places, on the Golan Heights and in the Sinai Desert, in Cyprus and Lebanon, and, coming full circle back to Vietnam, in the streets of Xuan Loc, a city much fought over during the North Vietnamese offensive in 1975. All those dead people, Americans, North and South Vietnamese, Arabs and Israelis, Turks and Greeks, Moslems and Christians, men, women, and children, officer and enlisted, smelled equally bad.

My first day on the job as a casualty reporting officer was June 21, 1965. Early that morning, a patrol from 2d Battalion fought a small action with the VC near Iron Bridge Ridge. Around noon, my field phone buzzed; it was the 2d Battalion's adjutant reporting four friendly casualties, one dead, three wounded. I put some hostile-action forms on my desk and said, "Okay, go ahead." One by one, beginning with the KIA, he gave me their names and service numbers and the descriptions of their wounds. There was a lot of static on the line, and he had to spell the names phonetically: "Atherton. Alpha Tango Hotel Echo Romeo Tango Oscar November. First name John. Middle initial double-u, as in Whiskey . . . gunshot wound upper body . . . killed in action while on patrol vicinity of Danang . . ." His voice had the rote, practiced sound of a radio announcer reading the stock market results.

I wrote quickly. It was extremely hot in the tent. Sweat dribbled off the tip of my nose and onto the forms, smudging the print. The forms stuck like flypaper to the forearm of my writing hand. One of the reports became badly smeared, and I asked the adjutant to read the information back to me. He was halfway through when the switchboard operator broke in. "Crowd One Alpha"—that was my new code-name—"this is Crowd Operator breaking . . . breaking . . . breaking." That meant he was going to cut me off to clear the line. "Crowd Operator, this is One Alpha working working," I said, meaning I had not yet completed my call. "One Alpha this is Crowd Operator. Cannot hear you. Breaking." There was a click. "You dumb son of a bitch," I yelled into the dead phone. Sweating heavily, I cranked the handle of the EE-8. After ten or fifteen minutes, the operator answered and reconnected me to 2d Battalion. Their adjutant came back on the line and picked up where he had left off. ". . . Multiple fragment wounds, lower half of both legs. WIA, evacuated . . ."

When the reports were called into division and filed, I went over to operations to find out how many enemy casualties there had been. Webb Harrisson, one of the assistant operations officers, leafed through a small pile of messages. "Here it is," he said. "Four Charlies, all KIA." I walked into the colonel's tent and made the proper changes on the scoreboard with my grease pencil. The Ex-O, Lieutenant Colonel Brooks, looked at the figures. He was a bald, stocky man whom the troops had nicknamed Elmer Fudd because he resembled the comic-book character.

"Keeping the old board up to date, are you, lieutenant?" he asked.

"Yes, sir," I said, thinking, What the hell does it look like I'm doing?

"How recent are those figures?"

"As of this morning, sir."

"Very good. Colonel Wheeler is giving a briefing for General Thompson this afternoon and he'll want the latest casualty statistics."

"Yes, sir. Who is General Thompson?"

"He's from MACV." Military Assistance Command Vietnam, Westmoreland's headquarters.

Sometime later, a jeep drove into headquarters carrying the dead Viet Cong and two civilians who had been injured in the fire-fight. The civilians, both women, rode in the back of the jeep. One was old and frail-looking, and had minor scratches on her arms. The other, in her early or mid-thirties, lay on her stomach in the back seat. Pieces of shrapnel had lodged in her buttocks. The bodies were on a trailer hitched to the jeep.

The driver parked behind the adjutant's tent and unhitched the trailer. It tipped forward, the hitch clanging against the ground and the bodies tumbling over on top of each other. A half-severed arm, with a piece of bone protruding whitely through the flesh, flopped over the side of the trailer, then flopped back in again. Stretcher-bearers came up and carried the young woman to the regimental aid station. The old woman shuffled along behind, spitting blackish-red betel-nut juice into the dust.

I checked to make sure there were four bodies. There appeared to be. It was difficult to tell. Tossed around in the trailer, they had become entangled, one barely distinguishable from another. Three of them were entangled, anyway. The fourth did not have arms below the elbow, and his legs had been shot or blown off completely. The others had been mangled in other places. One had been hit in the head, his brains and the white cartilage that had moored them to his skull spilling onto the bottom of the trailer. Another, hit in the midsection, had been turned inside out, the slick, blue and greenish brown mass of his intestines bulging out of him. There was a deep, dark red pool of blood at the low end of the trailer. I turned away from the sight and told the driver to get the bodies out of there.

"Sorry, sir," he said, starting up his jeep. "I was told to leave the bodies here. I've got to get back to the motor pool."

"Who the hell told you to leave the bodies here?"

The driver shrugged. "Some officer told me, lieutenant. I've got to get back to the motor pool."

"All right, shove off."

The marine drove away. I went into the tent and told Kazmarack to take the corpses to the cemetery where the enemy dead were buried. Kazmarack called it the body dump, and it was more that than a proper cemetery.

Captain Anderson said, "Leave the bodies here, Mister Caputo."

"Sir, they're going to smell pretty bad in another few hours."

"The colonel wants the bodies here."

"What the hell for?"

"He wants the clerks around here to look at them. There isn't much action around here, so I guess he wants them to get used to the sight of blood."

"You're kidding, captain."

"No, I'm not."

"Well, I don't think much of that idea. Christ, let's just bury the poor bastards."

"Lieutenant, I think what you think doesn't make much difference. The Old Man wants these people to get used to the sight of blood, and that's what they're going to do."

"Well, there's plenty of blood in there, but I'm not sure they're going to get used to it. Plenty of other stuff, too, guts and brains."

"I'll tell you when to get rid of the bodies."

"Yes, sir."

So the corpses were left lying in the sun. As the colonel had ordered, the headquarters troops were marched past the trailer to look at the dead Viet Cong.

They filed by like visitors passing before an exhibit in a museum. The sun burned down, and the bodies began to smell in the heat. The odor, at first faint because the VC had been dead only a short time, was like cooking gas escaping from an oven burner. One by one, the marines walked up to the trailer, looked into it, made some desperate jokes when they saw what was inside or said nothing at all, then walked back to their desks and typewriters. The sun burned hotter in the empty sky; the smell grew stronger. It blew into the adjutant's tent on a puff of breeze, the cooking-gas odor and a stench that reminded me of hydrogen sulfide used in high-school chemistry classes. Well, that was all the corpses were, masses of chemicals and decaying matter. Looking outside, I was pleased to see that the show was almost over; the marines at the end of the line were filing past the trailer. Because of the smell, they kept their distance. The smell was not unbearable; several hours would pass before it got that bad. It was, however, strong enough to prevent these men at the end of the line from lingering, as those at the front of the line had done, thus depriving them of the chance to look at the corpses long enough to become accustomed to the sight of blood. They just gave the bodies a brief glance, then moved quickly from the trailer and the growing stench.

The procession ended. Kazmarack and another clerk, Corporal Stasek, hitched up the trailer and drove off toward Danang. Anderson left for a staff conference that had been called in preparation for General Thompson's visit. Ten minutes later, he came lumbering back into the tent, his red, jowly face pouring sweat.

"Mister Caputo, we've got to get those bodies back here."

I looked at him incredulously.

"The Old Man wants the bodies back here so he can show them to the general when he briefs him," Anderson said.

"Stasek and Kazmarack are gone, sir. They're probably in Danang by now."

we are, sir. Home. Welcome back to dear old Dang-
Dang by the sea. How was Japan compared to this?"

I thought of the weekend I had spent in Tokyo after
the course was finished. "Kazmarack, how do you suppose Japan was compared to this?"

"Compared to this hole, I imagine Japan was number
one, sir."

"There you are."

Actually, I did not feel that bad about coming back.
I had been lonely the whole ten days in Japan, and
now, sloshing in the mud of the camp, I knew why.
My friends and my outfit were in Vietnam. I belonged
there. The regiment, in fact, was home.

I reported in to my new boss, Captain Anderson.
He was sitting heavily on a canvas chair behind a
desk made of scrap lumber, an old map board, and
ammo boxes. Across from his stood another makeshift desk, mine. Several empty shell crates, with the
words *155-mm How* painted on them served as filing
cabinets. The adjutant's, or S-1, section occupied half
the tent; the S-4 (logistics) section the other half.

I handed my orders, all thirteen copies of them, to
Anderson. He took them in a pudgy hand and signed
the endorsement. Having served for over five months
with the lean, hard-muscled Peterson, I was amazed
at the size of the adjutant's belly, bulging against his
sweaty undershirt and hanging well over his belt. He
had a large head. His face, with its weak chin, its
small eyes closely set in folds of sunburned flesh,
looked porcine.

"Welcome aboard," he grunted. "You can have the
rest of the day off to get squared away. Report in by
oh-seven-thirty tomorrow."

Lieutenant Schwartz, whom I was replacing, showed
me to the junior officer's billets. Schwartz was as happy
about my transfer to headquarters as I was unhappy
about it; he was going to take command of a rifle
company in 2nd Battalion.

He pointed to a cot over which a green mosquito
net hung like a frayed cocoon. "That's yours. You'll
like it here. It's got all the disadvantages of a line
company with none of the advantages." I dropped my

"I know they're gone. I want you to find somebody who can handle a jeep. Tell him to catch up with those two and have them bring those bodies back here ASAP."

"Captain, I don't really believe we're doing this."

"Just get moving." He turned and walked on with quick, jerky little steps.

I managed to find a driver who knew the route and told him what to do. I returned to the tent, where, in the spirit of the madness in which I was taking part, I made up a new title for myself. I wrote it on a piece of cardboard and tacked the cardboard to my desk. It read:

2LT. P. J. CAPUTO. OFFICER IN CHARGE OF THE DEAD.

The general arrived by helicopter—and what other way is there for a general?—in midafternoon. I had a glimpse of him as he walked into the headquarters next door, the colonel on one side of him, Lieutenant Colonel Brooks on the other, and a couple of nervous-looking aides trailing. He looked about the same height and build as Wheeler, but all resemblance ended there. Wheeler was wearing the drab battle dress of a field commander, Thompson a uniform that befitted a Lieutenant General in the Army of the United States. Three white stars shone on his green cap. Three more adorned each starched collar. A blue and white Combat Infantry Badge was pinned to his chest. Various patches added bits of color to his shoulder sleeves, and a name tag above his left pocket proclaimed his identity: THOMPSON.

The briefing started. Stasek and Kazmarack returned about a quarter of an hour later, both looking overwrought.

"Lieutenant, sir," Stasek said, "what the hell's going on? We had those VC buried ..."

I told them what was going on and asked where the bodies were.

"Outside, sir." Stasek started to laugh in the slightly hysterical way a man does when what he really wants to do is scream. "Christ, we had to pull them out of where we buried them. One of the VC's guts spilled out of him. Then I pulled at another one and his leg started to come off. They were just coming apart."

"Okay, that's enough," I said. "Sorry about all this. Just stand by for now, but you'll have to bring the bodies when the briefing's over."

"Yes, sir. If that general's going to look at those bodies, we'd better hose the trailer down."

"Okay, hose it down then," I said, walking out of the tent with him and Kazmarack. The trailer was parked in the same place as before.

The briefing was going on next door. I could not hear every word, just disjointed phrases: "and we're planning further operations in the Le-My area . . . that's here, general . . ." Through the screening, I saw Thompson sitting, legs crossed. He nodded while the briefing officer talked and waved a pointer at the big wall map in the colonel's tent. Wheeler was standing by his desk, a collection of captured enemy weapons hanging on a partition that divided his half of the tent from Brooks's. "One of our patrols engaged a VC force in that vicinity this morning, sir . . . activity has increased . . ." Twenty yards away, Kazmarack and another marine had connected a hose to a water carrier and were filling the trailer. The general, uncrossing his legs, said something I couldn't quite hear. "Yes, sir," replied the briefing officer. With the trailer filled, Kazmarack and the other marine disconnected the hose. They lifted the hitch from the ground, pushed the trailer back a couple of feet, pulled it forward, pushed it back, pulled it forward again, sluicing it out. There was a murmuring inside the colonel's tent. "I think I can answer that one for you, sir," someone said. Outside, Corporal Stasek said, "Okay, Kaz, tip it back a little." Kazmarack and the marine who was helping him tipped the trailer backward. They held it like that, each with both arms under the hitch, their arms straining from the weight, while Stasek squatted, reached underneath the trailer, and unscrewed the plug in the bottom. He pulled his hand back quickly when the water poured out in a heavy, red stream speckled with bits of white stuff. "Jesus Christ," Stasek said, "look at it all."

When the briefing ended, General Thompson, Colonel Wheeler, and the other officers came out of the tent. I saluted smartly as they walked past me toward my freshly washed corpses. I thought of them as mine; they were the dead and I was the officer in charge of the dead. A rivulet of blood-colored water flowed from under the trailer and soaked into the dust. The brass stepped over it carefully, to avoid ruining the shine on their boots. Someone pointed out the bodies and told the general that they were the VC who had been killed in the morning. He glanced at them, said something to the colonel, then continued on to the LZ, where his helicopter waited.

I spent the rest of the afternoon puttering over some meaningless paperwork. When I walked into the mess for the evening meal, Chaplain Ryerson and the medical officer, Milsovic, stopped eating and looked at me. Putting my tray on the plywood table, I sat down. The Chaplain, who was as thin and cheerless as the doctor was heavyset and jolly, slid along the bench to sit across from me.

"The doctor tells me we lost another marine today," he said, leaning forward slightly. He sounded accusatory, as if in recording it, I had been responsible for the boy's death.

"Yes, sir. We did."

"I just hope these boys are dying for a good reason, lieutenant. What do you think?"

"All due respect, chaplain, but we're not supposed to talk shop in the mess. Anyway, I don't want to talk about casualties. I've had enough of that today."

"Shop or no shop, I just hope these boys aren't getting killed because some officer wants a promotion."

"I wouldn't know about that."

"What do you mean, you wouldn't know about that? You saw that show that was put on for the general today, didn't you?"

"Yes, sir. But right now, I'd like to finish chow.

Maybe you ought to talk to the Old Man about it. What do you expect me to do?"

"Maybe you could explain what we're doing over here. You've been a platoon commander. When we got here, we were just supposed to defend the airfield for a while and then go back to Okinawa. Now we're in the war to stay and nobody has been able to explain to me what we're doing. I'm no tactician, but the way it looks to me, we send men out on an operation, they kill a few VC, or the VC kill them, and then pull out and the VC come right back in. So we're back where we started. That's the way it looks to me. I think these boys are getting killed for nothing."

I held up my hands. "Chaplain, what do you want me to say? Maybe you're right. I don't know, I'm just a second lieutenant. Anyway, it's not that bad a war. We've taken only eighty-four casualties since the end of April, and only twelve of those have been KIA. Hell, in World War Two an outfit like this would take eighty-four casualties in five minutes."

"What's that supposed to mean? This isn't World War Two."

"What I mean is that twelve KIAs in two months isn't bad."

Ryerson's face reddened and his voice got strident. "That's twelve wrecked homes. *Twelve wrecked homes,* lieutenant." He pointed a finger at me. "Twelve KIA is pretty bad for the families of those dead marines." I didn't say anything. My food was getting cold in the tray. A few senior officers had turned around, to see what the chaplain's outburst was all about.

"The doctor here and I think in terms of human suffering, not statistics," Ryerson said, pressing his point. "That's something you infantry types seem to forget."

I thought of Sergeant Sullivan then and remembered how deeply his death had affected the "infantry types" in C Company.

"Well, good for you and the doctor," I said. "You're real humanitarians. Do you think I liked doing what

I did today? Do you think I get a big fucking kick out of it, sky pilot?"

"Now, hold on, mister . . ."

"Hey, Phil," Milsovic said. "Watch that dago temper of yours. The chaplain didn't mean anything personal."

I cooled off, apologized to Ryerson, and finished eating.

Leaving the mess, I went back to my desk. It was difficult to work. The tent was stifling, and I felt confused. The chaplain's morally superior attitude had rankled me, but his sermon had managed to plant doubt in my mind, doubt about the war. Much of what he had said made sense: our tactical operations did seem futile and directed toward no apparent end. There were other doubts, aroused by the events of that day, which had made a mockery of all the Catholic theology the Dominican and Jesuit priests had preached to me in high school and college. Man's body is the Temple of the Holy Spirit; man is created in the image and likeness of God; have respect for the dead. Well, the four temples in that trailer had undergone considerable demolition, and it was hard to believe a Holy Spirit had ever resided in them. As for their being the image and likeness of the Deity, they were more the image and likeness of the crushed dogs seen lying at the sides of highways. And we had not showed them much respect, though they were the dead. I still believed in the cause for which we were supposed to be fighting, but what kind of men were we, and what kind of army was it that made exhibitions of the human beings it had butchered?

Twelve wrecked homes. The chaplain's words echoed. *That's twelve wrecked homes. The doctor and I think in terms of human suffering, not statistics.* I thought about Sullivan again. He was one of the statistics, just like the four enemy soldiers killed that morning. The only difference was that they were in different columns on the colonel's scoreboard. *Twelve wrecked homes.* I thought about Sullivan's young widow in Pennsylvania, and a chill passed through me. Maybe her husband had died for nothing, maybe for something. Either way, it could not make much difference to her now.

I put in a few more hours at my desk, had a beer, and went to bed early. I had the late duty-watch and knew I wouldn't get much sleep after twelve o'clock. The big guns boomed all night.

Chapter Eleven

If I were fierce and bald and short of breath,
I'd live with scarlet majors at the Base,
And speed glum heroes up the line to death.
        —Siegfried Sassoon
        "Base Details"

Lying on my cot, I heard the crackling of rifle fire, the drumming of rain against the taut canvas above my head, and a voice calling, "Stand-to. Up out of the rack, hundred-percent alert." It was very early morning, I was only half awake, and the rifle fire, the voice, and the sound of the rain seemed to come from far off. Then one of the eight-inch howitzers let go. I sat suddenly upright and knew I wasn't dreaming. The small-arms fire was loud and fairly close. Webb Harrisson—it was his voice I had heard—stood at one end of the tent, unhooking the flaps.

"Hey-ey, P.J., you're finally awake. I think we've got visitors again tonight."

Parting the flap, he went outside. I grabbed my carbine from my footlocker and followed him. Jamming a banana clip into the carbine's magazine well, pulling the bolt back to chamber a round, I ran clumsily in the mud toward the perimeter. I could not see Harrisson. The rain felt cold on my bare back. Off to the left, around 1st Battalion's section of the line, muzzle-flashes winked in the darkness. Tracers from a machine gun streaked in swift succession across the flat rice paddies beyond the wire.

Slipping in mud that had been powdery dust before

the rain, I fell and rolled into a foxhole just as a flare popped. The water in the foxhole was knee-deep and cold and silty-feeling inside my boots. Another flare went up, and another. They hung briefly in the black sky, then started to drift downward on their small parachutes, swinging back and forth, making a strange, squeaking noise as they swung in the wind. I could see the rain slanting across the wavering orange circles of the flares, the outlines of the tents, two helmeted marines in a foxhole to the left front of mine, and, across the road, the thick, wet-shining barrels on the eight-inchers. The guns kept firing at their distant targets, as if they were indifferent to the petty skirmishing only a hundred yards away.

I guessed it was another probe. The night before— the night of June 22—the VC had tried to infiltrate through headquarters company lines. Now they appeared to be looking for weak spots in One-Three's perimeter. That was only a guess—I had no idea of what was actually going on. The flares hit the ground, sputtered for a few seconds, and went out. The regimental sergeant major sloshed past me dressed only in a pair of green undershorts and carrying a Thompson submachine gun in one hand. I called him over. Big and bulky, he jumped into the foxhole with a splash.

"Jee-suz fucking Chee-rist," he bellowed, not caring who heard him. "You didn't tell me this was a goddamned swimming pool, lieutenant."

"Never mind that. What the hell's going on?"

"How the hell should I know? Probably a couple of scared kids shooting at bushes."

A spent tracer floated overhead, glowing like a spark from a campfire. There were more flares. We stared out at the landscape they dimly lighted but saw nothing that vaguely resembled a Viet Cong.

"It's just what I figured," said the RSM. "Nothing out there but bushes, fucking bushes. And here I am, up to my ass in mud. It ain't dignified."

The firing had stopped. We waited, shivering and wet, for another hour before the stand-to was secured.

The sergeant major had been wrong about marines

shooting at bushes. Shortly after reveille, two dead VC were carried into the CP. They were trussed to bamboo poles, like bagged game, and their black hair hung down in long, blood-matted shocks. They were wearing dark-blue uniforms, indicating they had been main-force regulars. Still trussed hand and foot to the poles, the bodies were tossed into a truck and carted off. I went into the colonel's tent and added two to the number in the VC-KIA column on the scoreboard.

The next seven nights were much the same. There were probes of the headquarters perimeter or of the battalions' positions, a couple of random mortar attacks on isolated outposts, a few attempted infiltrations of the airfield defenses, now manned by 1st Battalion, 9th Marines. With all the alarms, we got very little sleep.

Sometime that week, Harrisson told me that the two VC killed on the 23d had been part of a five- or six-man enemy patrol. Apparently, they had been making a reconnaissance of 1st Battalion's lines and had made the mistake of getting too close; a machine-gunner had killed them at point-blank range. That was all well and good, Harrisson said, good for the machine-gunner's cool-headedness and marksmanship, but the increase in VC activity indicated that reports of an impending enemy attack on the airfield were more than rumor. At the same time, he said, the VC were massing forces in Quang Ngai province, south of Danang, with the apparent objective of seizing the provincial capital. And finally, two North Vietnamese Army divisions were now operating in the South, one in the Central Highlands and the other somewhere in I Corps.

"I'm telling you, Charlie's going to try something soon." Harrisson looked at our sprawling tent camp, everything aboveground, uncamouflaged, laid out in tidy rows, and nothing between it and the VC but a roll of rusting concertina wire. Harrisson laughed. "Jesus, Phil, even the French dug in."

A few days later, two VC were captured while scouting a part of the regiment's positions in broad daylight. The next day, a patrol from the reconnaissance battalion sighted a battery of enemy 82-mm mortars being moved toward the airfield. The patrol, too far from the VC to attack, requested artillery fire but were turned down because another marine patrol was lost in the same area, and no one wanted to risk hitting friendly troops. The reconnaissance patrol leader reported the map coordinates of the mortars · and suggested they were being moved into position to shell the airfield. The report was duly noted and buried in a file cabinet. On the 28th, an ARVN district headquarters near us was shelled, and the VC dropped mortars on an isolated section of One-Three's lines, killing and wounding several marines.

You did not have to be Clausewitz to conclude that all those incidents added up to something: the enemy *was* planning an attack on the airfield, the defense of which was still our primary mission. But the regimental staff was not about to be panicked into hasty action. We did not spend that week feverishly analyzing the pattern of VC activity or drawing up plans for counterattacks and improving existing defenses or doing any of the things a military staff is supposed to do. No, level-headed professionals that we were, we did what staff officers usually do: nothing. Well, not exactly nothing. We played volleyball in our off-hours, and, because there wasn't enough work to keep even half the staff's twenty-odd officers busy, most of our hours were off-hours. We also read a lot—I finished *The Adventures of Augie March* that week—or pursued individual hobbies. Major Burin, the communications officer, practiced calling square-dance tunes, accompanied by the screeching fiddle music he played on his portable tape recorder. He could be heard all over camp, singing in his Kansas twang: "Allemande left with the old left hand . . . swing your partners, do-si-so, gents to the center form a Texas star." The civil affairs officer, Tim Schwartz (not the Schwartz I had replaced), discovered a new way of writing poetry: he made lists of the most esoteric words he could find in the dictionary, then strung them together in the order in which he had found them. He was quite proud of his incomprehensible verses and asked if I knew where he might publish them. I suggested the *Kenyon Review*.

When they did any work, the staff sections concentrated on daily minutiae and routine reports. The S-1 section filed its usual strength and casualty reports. S-2—intelligence—made reports on the enemy's order of battle and wrote accounts of recent enemy actions. The latter were of some historical but of little intelligence value, because S-2's main function was not to chronicle what the VC had already done but to forecast what they were likely to do. The operations section, S-3, went on logging situation reports in the unit diary, drawing up plans for operations that almost invariably sent battalions into areas where the enemy was not and compiling the number of patrols the line companies conducted each day. S-4 kept up our inventories of rations and ammunition.

The division general staff sent several messages alerting us to critical matters:

1) Marines who had nonregulation cloth name tags sewn above the left pockets of their shirts were to remove them. Henceforth, names would be stamped on in half-inch (½) block letters.

2) The practice of stripping to the waist while on working parties, patrols, etc. would no longer be tolerated by the commanding general. When outside, all personnel were to wear their shirts and/or undershirts.

3) The circulation of the *Marine Corps Gazette* was dropping. Officers who had not already done so were requested to subscribe.

And so the staffs went on, sticking to routines, which was just another way of doing nothing. They dealt with the enemy threat by ignoring it, and on July 1, the Viet Cong attacked the airfield.

It was around two o'clock in the morning, and I was just coming off duty-watch in the operations tent when the first shells hit. As a precaution against floods, the tent had been elevated on a platform of plywood and two-by-fours. A set of wooden steps led from the door to the ground. When I was about halfway down the steps, I saw a bright flash above the trees across Highway One and then heard the distinctive *crump* of a bursting mortar. The trees marked the outer edges of the airbase, which was about five hundred yards from the regimental CP. The airstrip itself, where the shell had struck, was at least another thousand yards away; so I felt no sense of immediate danger, only curiosity. Climbing back up the steps, I looked across the field beyond the CP, toward the dark, broken line of trees, and caught several more flashes. The explosions of the 82-millimeters came a few seconds later, the shells bursting rapidly one after another, like a string of firecrackers, only much louder, and the sky, which had been black above the tree line, was now a pale, flickering red. Inside the CP, marines were rolling out of their cots and grabbing their weapons.

"Did you call Conlin?" I asked through the door, talking to my relief. "Charlie's hitting the airfield."

"No shit. Conlin and the Old Man are on their way."

A recoilless rifle fired with a quick, double crack —the gun cracking first, the shell a moment afterward. A huge ball of flame rose over the trees like a mock sunrise. There was the hollow thud of exploding fuel tanks—the recoilless had hit one of the aircraft. The ball of flame boiled up, orange-crested and so brilliantly white at the center that I could clearly see the faces of the marines who were running toward the trenches on our perimeter.

I went back into the tent, feeling that I ought to be doing something but not sure what it was. Major Conlin and his assistants, Harrisson and Captain Johnson, came in wearing helmets and flak jackets. They were soon joined by the intelligence officer and his number two, Lieutenant Mora. Then Colonel Wheeler arrived, stoop-shouldered, quiet, smoking his pipe. We were all crowded in there, along with a number of radio operators and message clerks. A single shell could have wiped out half the regimental staff, and I'm sure there were some line officers who hoped one would.

The battle around the airfield had begun in earnest. The VC mortars made a steady thudding, the Marine mortars firing in return and the fuel tanks bursting. Machine guns tacked. Another bright flash was followed by a loud noise that was not a mortar shell: one of our own bombs going off or maybe an enemy satchel charge blowing up one of the aircraft. There was some confusion inside the operations tent. Radios crackled, field phones buzzed, staff officers ran from one bank of phones to another. Someone was talking to One-Nine, trying to learn where the attack was coming from and how many VC were in the assault. The colonel sat staring at the big operations map, as if, by staring at it, he could force it to reveal what was happening.

"Look, we're tripping over each other in here," Captain Johnson said. "Anybody who doesn't have to be in here, get your helmets and flak jackets on and take up your positions on the perimeter."

I started to go out. A big, bull-chested man with a deeply lined face came through the door, his heavy shoulders rolling as he walked. Seeing the two stars on his cap, I stupidly saluted and said, "Good morning, sir." Major General Lew Walt did not acknowledge the formality, making his way up to the operations map. Walt had recently taken command of the III MAF, Third Marine Amphibious Force, the headquarters for all Marine units in Vietnam. He looked angry, and he had every reason to be: the very attack the Marines were supposed to have prevented was happening.

I was in awe of Walt. I still had a strong tendency to hero-worship, and he was an authentic hero; he had won three Navy Crosses, one for single-handedly pulling an artillery piece uphill under heavy Japanese fire during a battle in the South Pacific. Beyond that, he was one of those rare general officers who believed it was his job to lead his army from up front, and not from a cushy command post so far removed from the action that it was almost desertion. He had established his forward headquarters in an amphibious tractor—a type of armored personnel carrier —parked just behind the howitzer batteries next to the regimental CP. Walt was leading his men from the cannon's mouth, where generals had positioned themselves in the days when they were fighting-men like Lee, and not business managers like Westmoreland.

It was my impression that Walt also was one of the few high-ranking officers who took the Viet Cong seriously in those confident, complacent days. And in moving his HQ so far forward and exposing himself to dangers he could have honorably avoided, he was trying to set an example of personal leadership for subordinate commanders and their staffs. It was an example few of them seemed to follow, then or later. I do know Walt was disturbed by some things he found when he took command in May. Outdoor movies were being shown at night at regimental HQ; Walt put a stop to that. Ten or twenty percent of the men in the rifle battalions were often on liberty, wandering around drunk in Danang; Walt put the city off limits. The main line of resistance around the Danang enclave showed as a solid line of men and bayonets on the staff officers' maps; Walt went out to look for himself—something few staff officers ever did—and discovered that the line was not a line, but a string of disconnected bivouacs surrounded by flimsy wire that could not have resisted a determined assault by an enemy platoon. He ordered the construction of a proper MLR, with strongpoints, forward outposts, and preregistered artillery concentrations.

But he was not able to overcome the inertia and complacency, and now the attack was progressing with destructive efficiency.

Outside, it was almost as bright as day from the flares hanging over the airfield and the fires of the burning planes. Tracer bullets scratched scarlet lines across the sky. A star cluster rocketed up, reaching higher than the white, wavering flares, then burst in a shower of sparks. It was a red star cluster, a signal that the enemy had penetrated the airfield perimeter. The one-oh-fives behind the CP had opened the counterbattery barrage. A couple of bullets hissed overhead, but I couldn't tell if we were being sniped at or if they were just stray rounds from the airfield battle.

Putting on my helmet and flak jacket, I went over to the tent where the secret-and-confidential documents were stored in a safe. The S-and-C files contained the regiment's message codes and operation plans, as well as a couple of small cryptography machines used to unscramble the codes. As the S-and-C officer, I was responsible for the security of all that James Bond stuff, and my standing orders were to burn it with thermite grenades if the camp was attacked and overrun. Sergeant Hamilton, the chief clerk, was outside the tent in his battle gear. With him was a lance corporal, a new arrival who looked tense and confused.

"Lieutenant, are the yellow hordes approaching?" Sergeant Hamilton asked. "Everything's all set. I've got the grenades out, and there's nothing I'd like better than to burn all this crap."

"The yellow hordes are through the airfield's wire. It doesn't look like they're going to hit us, but if they do, I don't want you burning this stuff unless you've got Charlies coming right at you."

"Sir, if I've got Charlies coming right at me, I'm going to throw these grenades at 'em. Then I'll throw the files on top of 'em and let 'em all burn together." A flurry of tracers went over us, and we heard the slow, throaty thumping of a heavy machine gun. Hamilton laughed. "What was that you said about them not hitting us, sir?"

"That was probably one of our own fifties. Okay, you heard what I said."

"Yes, sir. That's a great show Mr. Charles is putting on, but someone should tell him he's three days short of the Fourth." He laughed again. The joke seemed funnier than it was.

With nothing more to do, I went to my position on the perimeter. Each of the junior officers in HqCo was responsible for a section of the CP perimeter. I was in charge of a corporal and ten men, the closest thing I had to a command.

While we waited in our foxholes, a convoy carrying

a rifle company rolled past, headed toward the base. Tardily, the counterattack was getting under way. The trucks were moving fast, throwing up clouds of dust that shimmered in the orange twilight cast by the flames licking at the sky over the airfield. The convoy sped recklessly down the road, the packed marines yelling, cheering, and holding their rifles in the air. "Goddamned grunts are all crazy," said a headquarters' clerk next to me. The one-oh-five battery stepped up its fire, the guns and the gun crews silhouetted against the intermittent muzzle-flashes. The last two six-bys in the convoy went past. Each was towing an artillery piece, and I felt a flicker of excitement when I saw the howitzers, bouncing on their carriages behind the speeding trucks. A column of white flame from burning magnesium fountained up over the airfield just as the one-oh-five shells began bursting in the rice paddies south of the base.

We stayed on the perimeter until first light. Plumes of black smoke roiled the early-morning sky, but the battle was over. Later in the day, Kazmarack and I drove past the airfield. We were on our way into Danang with reports for I Corps headquarters. I expected to find the base a shambles, but it was very large and most of it had escaped serious damage. Still, the attack had had more than a minor effect. Two big transports lay at the south end of the field, both totally destroyed, bits of their wings and engines scattered about. Two fighter planes nearby looked like broken toys and a third was just a pile of ashes and twisted metal. A truck was towing another damaged plane off to the side of the runway. Stopping to look at the wreckage, we saw the holes the VC sapper teams had blown or cut in the chain link fence along the perimeter road. They had come through the sector my platoon had manned back in March and April, when we thought we were going to win the war in a few months and then march home to ticker-tape parades.

Chapter Twelve

The greatest tragedy is war, but so long as there
is mankind, there will be war.

—Jomini
The Art of War

There was no heavy fighting around Danang for the
rest of that summer. During the daytime, there did not
seem to be any war at all. The rice paddies lay quietly
in the sun. They were beautiful at that time of year, a
bright green dappled with the darker green of the
palm groves shading the villages. The peasants in the
villages in the secure areas went on living lives whose
ancient rhythms had hardly been disturbed by the war.
In the early mornings, small boys led the water buffalo
from their pens to the river wallows and farmers came
out to till the fields. They plodded for hours behind
wooden, ox-drawn plows, tilling the sunbaked hard-
ness out of the earth. In the afternoons, when it became too hot to work, they quit the fields and returned
to the cool dimness of their thatch huts. It was like a
ritual: when the heat got too intense, they unhitched
their plows and filed down the dikes toward the villages, their conical hats yellow against the green of the
paddies. A wind usually sprang up in the afternoon,
and in it the long shoots of maturing rice made a luxuriant rippling. It was a pleasant sight, that expanse
of jade-colored rice stretching out as far as the foothills and the mountains blue in the distance. At dusk,
the buffalo were driven back to the pens. With the
small boys walking beside them and whacking their
haunches with bamboo sticks, they came down the
dusty roads, their horned heads swaying and their
flanks caked with the mud of the wallows.

The war started at night. The eight-inch and one-
fifty-five-millimeter guns commenced their regular
shellings, and the VC began their sniping and mortar-

ing. Our patrols slipped down darkened trails to set ambushes or to be ambushed themselves. On the perimeter, sentries listened and looked into a blackness lighted now and then by dull flares. They waited, alternately bored and nervous, for the infiltrators who sometimes probed our lines to lob grenades over the wire or spray a position with carbine fire. They came in twos and threes, and that is how they died and how our own men died—in twos and threes. We fought no great battles. There was no massive hemorrhaging, just a slow, steady trickle of blood drawn in a series of ambushes and fire-fights. Although there was more action than in the spring, contacts with the enemy were still rare. Almost every hour of every night the same reports came in over the radios in the operations tent. They came in from outposts and patrols, and we could hear them whenever we stood watch, twenty different voices saying the same thing, like a choir reciting a chant: "Contact negative. All secure. Situation remains the same." When contacts did occur, they were violent, but nothing ever really changed. The regiment sat in the same positions it had occupied since April, and the details of the surrounding landscape became so familiar that it seemed we had been there all our lives. Men were killed and wounded, and our patrols kept going out to fight in the same places they had fought the week before and the week before that. The situation remained the same. Only the numbers on the colonel's scoreboard changed.

The numbers were not all that changed. I was twenty-four when the summer began; by the time it ended, I was much older than I am now. Chronologically, my age had advanced three months, emotionally about three decades. I was somewhere in my middle fifties, that depressing period when a man's friends begin dying off and each death reminds him of the nearness of his own.

Our men did not die in great numbers. And because they died as individuals, I remember them as individuals and not as statistics. I remember Corporal Brian Gauthier, who, as one cynical old campaigner put it, "won himself two Navy Crosses: the blue and gold one they pin on you and the white, wooden one they put over you." Gauthier, a twenty-one-year-old squad leader in A Company, was mortally wounded in an ambush on July 11. They gave him the medal because he continued to lead his men under heavy enemy fire until, to quote from the citation, "he succumbed to his wounds." Later, the regimental HQ camp was named for him. That was nice of them, but they did not give any medals to, nor name anything for, the grenadier who died in the same ambush. He did not have the chance to do anything heroic because the mine he stepped on caused the sympathetic detonation of his 40-mm grenades, killing him instantly. "Sympathetic detonation" was the phrase I used in the casualty report. It was another one of those dry, inaccurate military euphemisms. It meant that the explosion of the mine had caused his grenades to go off at the same time, and I could see nothing sympathetic about that.

I remember Frank Reasoner, who also died a hero's death, and Bill Parsons, who did not. I saw Reasoner in the operations tent the day after Gauthier was killed. I had just finished filling out reports for seven marines who had been killed or wounded by mortar fire that morning. Reasoner was sitting in the tent smoking his battered, bent pipe and looking at the map. A short, stocky man, Reasoner was twenty-nine —old for a first lieutenant—an ex–enlisted man who had worked his way up through the ranks, a husband and a father. I liked him and his air of quiet maturity. We split a beer and talked about the patrol he was taking out in the afternoon. His company was going into the paddy lands below Charlie Ridge, flat, dangerous country with a lot of tree lines and hedgerows. Reasoner finished his beer and left. A few hours later, a helicopter brought him back in; a machine gun had stitched him across the belly, and the young corporal who had pulled Reasoner's body out of the line of fire said, "He should be covered up. Will somebody get a blanket? My skipper's dead." Out on the patrol, his company had run into a couple of enemy machine-gun nests. He had charged one of the guns single-handedly, knocking it out of action. Then, having fired his carbine at the second gun, he had run to pick up one of his wounded and was killed. They gave Frank Reasoner the Congressional Medal of Honor, named a camp *and* a ship after him, and sent the medal and a letter of condolence to his widow.

Parsons, a lieutenant in E Company, 2d Battalion, was killed two nights later by one of our own 4.2-inch mortar shells. It fell on his platoon while he was briefing them in a "rear area" base camp. The marines had been crowded close together, and since a four-deuce is a fairly large shell, there were a number of casualties. At HQ, we had problems making out accurate casualty reports; no one knew exactly who had been killed and who had been wounded. Captain Anderson said I would again have to go to the division hospital to straighten things out. I begged off, saying that I had seen enough dead bodies to know that I did not want to see any more. Anderson said he would go. When he got back, he looked a little strange and said nothing except to read aloud the notes he had made at the hospital. He had made good, thorough notes: Parson's legs had been scythed off at the hip, two more men had been killed, eight others seriously wounded. I filled out the forms while he read, then filed them in the non-hostile casualties folder. Then Anderson flipped his notebook on his desk and said, "It looked like a butcher shop in there."

I also remember the night nearly two weeks later when a squad of VC sappers got through the wire of an engineer battalion's camp near the CP. A lot of flares and grenades were going off and bullets were splattering the dust around the junior officers' tent. I tore through my mosquito net, grabbed my carbine, tripped, fell against the corner of my footlocker, and knocked myself out. I lay unconscious for a few moments. Coming to, I crawled into a trench where Mora, the assistant intelligence officer, stood wearing nothing but a pistol belt. Bart Francis, another lieutenant on the staff, looked at him and said, "Really, Roland, that's hardly proper." A little giddy from the knock on the head, I laughed hysterically. An exalted Schwartz—the Prussian in Schwartz came out in combat—was meanwhile yelling orders to groups of confused enlisted men. Well, the more power to him if he could tell what was going on. I couldn't, though it was a moonlit night made brighter by the flares. Small-arms fire had broken out along our perimeter; apparently another sapper squad was trying to breach the CP's wire. The VC were shooting at the marines, the marines at the VC or at the other marines or at nothing at all. In the blanched light we saw a rifleman about twenty or thirty yards away from our trench. Crouched low, he ran into the cross fire and went down, falling as if he had slipped on a patch of ice. His legs flew out and he landed heavily on his back and lay still. When the firing died down, another officer and I climbed out of the trench and, calling for a corpsman, ran over to the marine. He did not need a corpsman. His eyes were wide but not seeing, and one of his legs, half severed at the thigh, was bent under him in what looked like a contortionist's trick.

There are other memories. Memories of Nick Pappas, a college football star who tripped a mine that put him in a wheelchair for nearly two years and ended his football-playing days for good; of the young officer in the tank battalion attached to our regiment, wounded in the leg and side by an AK-47, dying slowly of gangrene in a hospital in the Philippines, the doctors amputating the infected leg bit by bit until they reached the upper thigh and could amputate no more; of the rainy night I went to the hospital to identify three marines from my old platoon, Devlin, Lockhart, and Bryce.

They had been blown up in a listening-post bunker forward of C Company's lines. I recall that night clearly, more clearly than I care to. Kazmarack and I pulled up to the hospital, parking the jeep beside a tarpaulin that had been stretched over three tables. A light bulb hung over each of the tables. Outside, a power generator hummed steadily and the wet grass sparkled in the glare of the lights. Corporal Gunderson and another marine stood outside, their shoulders hunched against the rain. Gunderson, a squad leader in C Company, said he had found the bodies and had brought them to the hospital.

Taking my notebook from its plastic wrapper, I ducked under the tarpaulin, which was attached to the tent like an awning. A Navy doctor wearing skintight latex gloves came from the tent, accompanied by a corpsman who held a clipboard. Other corpsmen emerged, carrying the bodies on stretchers, which they lifted onto the tables. Wet, muddy ponchos covered the bodies, except for their boots. There were three corpses, but I saw only five boots. Looking at me, the doctor asked who I was and what I was doing there. I explained that I had come to verify the identities of the dead men and to make a report on the extent of their injuries.

"Okay, that's about what I have to do. I understand this might have been an accident."

"We're not sure, yet, sir," Gunderson said, stepping inside. "The comm wire into their bunker was burned. Maybe lightning hit it and the current set off their grenades. They had about ten grenades in there. Maybe a VC threw a grenade inside, through the firing slit, and set the grenades off. He could have sneaked up easy in this rain."

Nodding, the doctor pulled the poncho off of Devlin's body.

"All right, can either of you tell me who this is?" he asked.

"I think it's Devlin," I said, my jaw muscles tightening as I looked at the corpse. "Peter Devlin. He's a PFC. Was, I mean."

"I want to know who it is."

"It's Devlin," Gunderson said. "I found them."

Satisfied, the doctor began to make his examination. I guessed that he was making an autopsy. He kneaded Devlin's flesh, turned the body onto its stomach, then onto its back again, and inserted his fingers into the holes the shrapnel had made. Turning to the corpsman, he described the nature of the wounds and gave the medical terms for the injured parts of the body. The corpsman made checkmarks on a form attached to his clipboard. I tried to write it all down, but I had a difficult time understanding some of the anatomical jargon and an even harder time watching the doctor probing into the holes with his gloved hands. Finally, I asked, "Doc, how can you do that?"

"It's my job. I'm a doctor. You get used to it, and if you can't, you shouldn't be a doctor. Anyhow, he doesn't feel it."

Then he turned to the corpsman. "Penetrating fragment wound, puncture wound, right kidney." The corpsman made another checkmark. I noticed then that the waistband of Devlin's underwear was solid red, as red as if his shorts had been dipped in dye. Dye. Die. Death. Died a dyed death. I remembered the way he used to look, the way he looked when he had a face, and how he walked, and the sound of his voice. For some reason, I thought of the time Devlin had been run up for sleeping on post and I'd made a plea of leniency for him because he had always been a good marine. The captain let him off with a warning. Coming out of the captain's tent, Devlin said to me, "Sir, I know this isn't military, but I'd like to thank you for what you did for me." And I, playing the role of the stiff-lipped, stern-eyed officer, replied, "You're right, Devlin. It isn't military, so don't thank me."

Bryce was easily identified because there was hardly a mark on him from the waist up. From the waist down, he presented a challenge to the doctor's professional abilities and to my ability to emulate the doctor's air of scientific detachment. It was the nakedness of Bryce's left calfbone that bothered me. Every strip of flesh and muscle had been torn away, so that the splintered bone looked like a broken ivory stick. The doctor said something like, "Traumatic amputation, left foot and compound fracturing, left tibia with massive tissue loss," and the corpsman made more checkmarks.

"We found his boot with the foot still in it," Gunderson said. "But we left it there. We didn't know what to do with it."

The doctor waved his hand to indicate that that was all right, he didn't need Bryce's foot. He continued his examination, and when he cut off Bryce's underwear with a scissors, I turned away. I told myself that it had been quick, too quick for Bryce to have felt a thing; but I didn't believe it. The pain of a dentist's drill is quick, but you feel it. So what had that felt like? Could an incredible amount of pain be compressed into a single instant?

Lockhart had been killed by the concussion, which relieved me. I could not bear any more mutilation. Lockhart looked as if he was asleep, except for his eye sockets, bruised and swollen to the size of golf balls. "They're young men," he had said of the VC we had killed three months before. "It's always the young men who die." Lockhart was nineteen.

He was the last. Putting my notebook back in the wrapper, I got into the jeep. I felt peculiar, tense and dizzy, like a man walking a ledge on a high building. A drenched Kazmarack started the engine. Just then, another jeep pulled up.

"Yo! P.J.!" McCloy called.

"Murph. What're you doing down here?"

"Just making sure the bodies got here all right," he said, walking over to me.

I asked if he knew whether or not it had been an accident. I had to know so I could put the reports in the correct file. No, McCloy said, he didn't know. Feeley would conduct an investigation tomorrow.

"Well, it doesn't make much goddamned difference, does it?" I asked rhetorically. "Christ, that's the worst mess I've ever seen."

"Oh, it wasn't so bad."

"Are you kidding? Did you see Bryce? They were blown off."

"Don't exaggerate. They were just torn open."

"Oh, for Christ's sake, 'torn open' then. You don't think that's bad?"

McCloy held me by both shoulders. In the glow of the light bulbs, I could see him smiling. "No, I don't think it's that bad. C'mon, get a hold of yourself."

That night, I was given command of a new platoon. They stood in formation in the rain, three ranks deep. I stood front and center, facing them. Devlin, Lockhart, and Bryce were in the first rank, Bryce standing on his one good leg, next to him the faceless Devlin,

and then Lockhart with his bruised eye sockets bulging. Sullivan was there too, and Reasoner and all the
others, all of them dead except me, the officer in
charge of the dead. I was the only one alive and
whole, and when I commanded, "Platoon, rye-eet
FACE! Sliiiing HARMS! For-WARD HARCH!" they
faced right, slung their rifles, and began to march.
They marched along, my platoon of crippled corpses,
hopping along on the stumps of their legs, swinging
the stumps of their arms, keeping perfect time while I
counted cadence. I was proud of them, disciplined
soldiers to and beyond the end. They stayed in step
even in death

I woke up soaked in sweat and afraid. I wasn't
sure if I had been dreaming. It had seemed so real.
Even when I realized that it had only been a dream,
the fear remained. It was the same fear I had felt after
Sullivan's death. A mortar tube fired in the distance. I started counting: "Thousand-one, thousand-
two, thousand-three . . ." Usually, it took twenty
seconds for a mortar shell to reach its target. "Thousand nineteen, thousand twenty, thousand twenty-one,
thousand twenty-two . . ." Nothing happened. The
shell exploded away off somewhere. It was one of our
own mortars. Relieved, I smoked a cigarette, cupping
it with my hands so the burning tip would not show
through the cracks in the tent. Then, still afraid, I fell
into an uneasy sleep.

In the morning, the sun was hovering just over the
line of palm beyond Highway One and the farmers
were out working in the fields near the batteries across
the dirt road. Waking with the sight of those marching
corpses still in my mind like an after-image, I swung
off my cot. I saw the new sun and the farmers plow-
ing in the green paddies by the now silent guns, but
nothing my eyes saw could blur that persistent vision
of dead men marching. Shaving at the improvised
washstand outside the tent, I saw their faces in the
mirror that reflected my own face. I saw them when I
put on my jacket, stiff and white with dried sweat, and
when I urinated into one of the acrid-smelling piss-
tubes, and when I walked to the mess for breakfast,

hopping over the drainage ditch where the mud from
the night's rain was cracked and drying. All these
familiar things—the tube with its stench, the feel of
the salt-stiffened jacket against my back, the worn
footpath leading over the ditch to the mess—told me
I was back in the world of concrete realities, where
dead men do not rise. So why was the picture of
Bryce, Devlin, Lockhart, and the others still so clear,
and why did the dream still seem so real, and why
when there was no menace was I still afraid?

I went through the chow line and sat down across
from Mora and Harrisson. The yolks of the eggs in
my tray looked like two yellow eyes set in a slimy
white face. I mashed them with my fork and tried to
eat. Mora and Harrisson were talking about a regimental operation that was coming up in a couple of
days. It was to be a combined ARVN-Marine operation, aggressively code-named Operation Blast Out. I
ate and listened to them and felt the mental bisection
that comes from smoking the strong marijuana the
bargirls in Vietnam called Buddha Grass. Half of me
was in the mess, listening to two officers talking of
practical military matters, of axes of advance and
landing zones, and the other half was on the dream
drill field where legless, armless, eyeless men marched
to my commands. *Hut-tup-threep-fo, your lef, if you've
got a left.* Then they vanished. Suddenly. I saw them
and then I did not see them. In their place, I saw
Mora and Harrisson prefigured in death. I saw their
living faces across from me and, superimposed on
those, a vision of their faces as they would look in
death. It was a kind of double exposure. I saw their
living mouths moving in conversation and their dead
mouths grinning the taut-drawn grins of corpses. Their
living eyes I saw, and their dead eyes still-staring. Had
it not been for the fear that I was going crazy, I
would have found it an interesting experience, a trip
such as no drug could possibly produce. Asleep and
dreaming, I saw dead men living; awake, I saw
living men dead.

I did not go crazy, not in the clinical sense, but
others did. The war was beginning to take a psycho-

logical toll. Malaria and gunshot and shrapnel wounds continued to account for most of our losses, but in the late summer the phrases *acute anxiety reaction* and *acute depressive reaction* started to appear on the sick-and-injured reports sent out each morning by the division hospital. To some degree, many of us began to suffer "anxiety" and "depressive" reactions. I noticed, in myself and in other men, a tendency to fall into black, gloomy moods and then to explode out of them in fits of bitterness and rage. It was partly caused by grief, grief over the deaths of friends. I thought about my friends a lot; too much. That was the trouble with the war then: the long lulls between actions gave us too much time to think. I would brood about Sullivan, Reasoner, and the others and feel an emptiness, a sense of futility. They seemed to have died for nothing; if not for nothing, then for nothing tangible. Those men might as well have died in automobile accidents. It made me feel guilty to think about them, guilty about my own comparatively safe life on the staff, guiltier still about being the one who had translated their deaths into numbers on a scoreboard. I had acquired a hatred for the scoreboard, for the very sight of it. It symbolized everything I despised about the staff, the obsession with statistics, the indifference toward the tragedy of death; and because I was on the staff, I despised myself. It did not matter that I was there by orders, that I had made several attempts to get transferred back to a line company. I despised myself every time I went up to the board and wrote in some new numbers. Maybe it was an extreme form of the *cafard*. One of its symptoms is a hatred for everything and everyone around you; now I hated myself as well, plunging into morbid depressions and thinking about committing suicide in some socially acceptable way—say, by throwing myself on an enemy hand grenade. At other times, I felt urges to kill someone else. When in those moods, the slightest irritation was likely to set me off. Once, I asked another lieutenant a question about a message that had come into the adjutant's office. It was hot inside the tent, almost unbearable, and he was in no cheerful mood himself.

"What's troubling you?" he snapped. Leaping up, I smashed the message in his face and shouted, *"This is what's troubling me, you shithead!"* The outburst relieved some sort of inner tension, and I calmed down as quickly as I had flared up.

Some men lost their nerve. One marine took his rifle and walked off into the bush, telling his buddies that he could no longer stand waiting for an attack and was going after the VC by himself. A Navy corpsman in one of the battalions shot himself in the foot so he would not have to go on any more patrols. A company commander cracked up under a heavy mortar bombardment. In a panic, he ran away, abandoning his men and leaving his executive officer to take command.

And combat madness could be murderous. As the legal officer, I reviewed summaries of the investigations and court-martials conducted in the regiment. That was how I learned of the case of two marines in 2d Battalion. For over four months, they had been out in the bush without relief and with no more than three or four hours' sleep a night. They had seen their comrades killed and had themselves killed men. Surviving half a dozen operations and a number of combat patrols, all they had to look forward to was more of the same.

In the dry season, even the nights in Vietnam are hot, seldom any cooler than eighty or eighty-five degrees; and it was hot on the night Harris woke up Olson and told him it was his turn to go on watch.

"Screw you," Olson said. "I ain't going on post."

"Get up, Olson. You're my relief. I gotta get a little sleep."

"Screw it and screw you, Harris. I gotta get a little sleep myself."

"Olson, I hate your guts. I oughtta kill you, you shitbird."

Olson stood up and leveled his rifle at Harris. "You ain't got the balls to kill me."

"Olson, you shitbird, I gotta automatic rifle pointed at your fuckin' head. All I gotta do is give a little trigger squeeze and I'll blow your head off."

A few other marines, who were later witnesses at the court-martial, stood watching the confrontation. Perhaps they thought nothing would happen.

"Like I said, Harris, you ain't got the balls to do it." And that was the last thing Olson ever said. Harris pumped five or six rounds into Olson's skull at point-blank range.

Operation Blast Out began and ended in early August. Three thousand marines and ARVN soldiers, supported by tanks, artillery, planes, and the six-inch guns of a U.S. Navy cruiser, managed to kill two dozen Viet Cong in three days. Even those two dozen died hard. They holed up in a complex of caves and bunkers near the Song Yen River. In scenes reminiscent of the mopping-up operations against the Japanese, the marines and ARVN fought the enemy from cave to cave, bunker to bunker, blowing them out with grenades and satchel charges.

A small number of enemy soldiers and one hundred and twenty VCS were captured and brought to HQ for interrogation. VCS stood for Viet Cong suspects, a term applied to almost every unarmed male Vietnamese found in enemy-controlled areas. Ninety percent of them turned out to be innocent civilians. The suspects and the Viet Cong prisoners were brought in by helicopter. Dressed in motley uniforms, the VC looked small and ragged compared to the marine guards who herded them from the landing zone to a dusty field at the side of the road. The marines ordered them to squat, which they did with the quick compliance of men who know their lives are completely in the hands of other men who would just as soon shoot them. Blindfolded, with their hands tied behind them, the VC looked frightened. The marines were tired and edgy. As usual, it was extremely hot; the thermometer outside the operations tent registered one hundred and ten degrees, and there was no wind. The much larger group of suspects was kept at the landing zone, waiting for the VC to be questioned first.

One by one, the enemy soldiers were led into a tent, where an American staff sergeant and two

ARVN interpreters from an intelligence unit interrogated them. Outside, one of the Viet Cong, a boy of eighteen or so, started to cry when his older comrade was led away for questioning. I guess he thought the man was going to be shot. He called out the man's name, and one of the guards bent down and pinched the boy's lips together. "Now you shut up," the marine said. "You keep your goddamned mouth shut." He moved away, but the boy kept crying and calling out his friend's name. "I said, keep your goddamned mouth shut!" The marine's voice sounded brittle, and in the pressure-cooker heat, I could sense that something was going to happen if the prisoner did not quiet down. I got one of the interpreters to tell him there was nothing to fear, they were only going to be questioned. That was a half-truth: they were going to be questioned, but when that was done they would be turned over to the South Vietnamese Army, who would probably shoot them. The ARVN shot most of the prisoners we handed over to them.

Inside the tent, the VC for whom the boy had been crying was proving stubborn. He refused to look at his interrogator, the American sergeant, or to answer any questions. All he said was, "Toi khoung hieu" (I don't understand) or "Toi khoung biet" (I don't know). He was wearing shorts, sandals, and a camouflage shirt, and looked about thirty years old. He sat with his legs drawn up, his eyes fixed on the ground. "What is your name?" "Toi khoung biet." "How old are you?" "Toi khoung hieu." "How . . . old . . . are . . . you?" "Toi khoung biet." "What is your unit?" "Toi khoung hieu."

Exasperated and sweating heavily, the American leaned forward and shouted in English, "Look at me, you son of a bitch. I said you look at me when I talk to you. I want to see your eyes when I'm talking to you."

The prisoner, small but muscular and with the face of a veteran soldier, did not look up.

With one hand, the sergeant grabbed the man's face, pressing his thumb into one of the prisoner's cheeks, his fingers into the other, squeezing them together. He turned the man's head sharply from side to side. "You're real hard-core, huh? Now you look at me when I talk to you. Anh hieu? You understand me now?"

"Toi khoung hieu," the VC said through clenched teeth.

The American turned to one of the interpreters. "Tell him to look at me when I talk to him."

The interpreter translated. The sergeant let go of the prisoner's face. The man's head dropped into the position it had been in before, chin tucked in, eyes looking at the ground between his legs.

"Tell him to look at me, goddamnit!"

Grabbing the prisoner's hair, the ARVN soldier jerked the man's head up and pulled it so far back that I could see his neck muscles straining. The interpreter slapped him twice, not with his full hand, but with the backs of his fingers, flicking his fingernails across the prisoner's face. It was a quick, subtle motion, like brushing a fly away, but I could hear the sharp crack the fingernails made against the man's skin.

"Ask him if he understands now," the American said. "He looks at me when I talk to him and he answers my questions."

The ARVN spoke rapidly in Vietnamese, pulling the prisoner's head back until the latter was looking straight up at the ceiling of the tent. The VC said something. The interpreter released him, and his head fell forward; but now he was looking at the sergeant.

"I think he understands now, trung-si," the ARVN soldier said.

Outside, the suspects were being marched down the road toward the field where the last of the VC, squatting in the heat, waited to be questioned. Blindfolded, they marched in single file, each holding onto the shoulders of the man in front of him. Suspects! Looking at them, I wondered what they had done to arouse suspicion; they were all ragged, underfed men, and not one of them was under forty. I stood outside the tent and watched them marching through the dust raised by their bare or sandaled feet. I was to wait until all had been questioned and count the number,

if any, who were confirmed as Viet Cong. Then I
would add that number to the VC-POW column on the
scoreboard. They came down the road with the light,
rhythmic shuffle the peasant girls used when walking
with carrying-poles across their shoulders. Marine
guards moved along the flanks of the column, yelling
orders none of the Vietnamese understood. It was midafternoon, and I could see in the paddy fields beyond
camp other, luckier farmers filing down the dikes toward their shaded villages. On the road, an old man,
last in the file, was having trouble keeping up. He fell
behind, groped for the man in front of him, found
him, then fell behind again, groping. "Lai-dai, lai-
dai. Maulen," one of the guards said. (Get over here,
quickly.) The old man pulled his blindfold down and,
seeing where he was, caught up with the column, replaced the blindfold, and put his hands back on the
other man's shoulders. He wheezed when the guard
clubbed him in the back with the flat end of a rifle
butt. "You keep that blindfold on," the guard said,
tying it tighter. "You keep this on. Keep on. Understand?" In April, the Vietnamese officer whom Peterson had stopped from striking a villager had said we
would one day learn how things were done in Vietnam.
A lot had happened to us since April, and we were
learning. Some of our friends had been killed, others
maimed. We had survived, but in war, a man does
not have to be killed or wounded to become a casualty. His life, his sight, or limbs are not the only things
he stands to lose.

The column was halted and the suspects made to
lie on their stomachs in the field. The guards bound
their hands. They lay there, as limp and passive as
sleeping children, while the guards tied them up or
rolled them over to search for documents. The documents, placed in small piles, were later examined by
one of the ARVN interpreters, who asked each of the
Vietnamese a few questions. If everything was in order, the man was officially declared a civilian
and released; if not, he was taken into the tent for
interrogation by the sergeant and his persuasive assistants. The ARVN noticed that one of the suspects

had loosened his bonds and pointed it out to a marine guard, who went over and kicked the prone man in the ribs. Jamming a knee into the man's back, he said, "Okay, let's see you get out of this one." The man's feet were pulled up and tied to his hands, so that he lay on his belly with his body bent like a bow.

Nearby, a very old man—he must have been in his eighties—searched through one of the piles for his papers. He looked worried. Valid identification could mean the difference between freedom and a POW camp, even between life and death. In that sense, the documents were the most precious thing the old man owned. By some oversight, the guards had failed to tie him up; or perhaps they had thought him too old and frail to run away. They had also put a sheer, cheesecloth blindfold on him, which he did not have to remove to look through the papers. He continued to rummage through the pile, his dry, wrinkled hands fluttering nervously as he picked up each piece of paper and held it close to his eyes. Finally he found them, clucking happily to himself as he stuffed them in his shirt pocket. Having that sheer blindfold put on him was probably the best thing that had happened to him all day. It might have been the best thing that ever happened to him. He was lucky. He had found his papers without arousing the anger or suspicion of the guards. The ARVN soldier would now come up to him, look at his identification, ask him a few questions, and, seeing that he was a very old, harmless man, let him return to his village. For the time being, that old man had been spared becoming another casualty of the war.

Part Three

IN DEATH'S GREY LAND

Soldiers are citizens of death's
  grey land,
Drawing no dividends from time's
  tomorrows.
                    —Siegfried Sassoon
                    "Dreamers"

Chapter Thirteen

They come like sacrifices in their trim,
And to the fire-eyed maid of smoky war
All hot and bleeding will we offer them . . .
                                    —Shakespeare
                                    Henry IV, Part I

The monsoons began in mid-September. At first, the
rains fell only at night and in the early morning, heavy
rains blown by winds that came off the sea and out of
the mountains north of Danang. At dawn, the wind
dropped to a light, steady breeze, the rain to a drizzle.
Out on the line, riflemen in flooded foxholes woke to a
landscape that looked like a photographic negative,
all grays, whites, and blacks. The peaks of the Annamese Mountains were hidden by clouds, the rice
paddies and valleys by a mist called the *crachin,* and
the slopes showing between the clouds and the layers
of mist were as dark as cinder. The weather cleared by
midmorning; the fog lifted, and we could see the rim
of the mountains again. The air became still and oppressive, the paddies steaming in the sun. It stayed
like that until the late afternoon, when clouds started
to build once more over the mountains, and the wind
rose, rattling the tin cans strung on the perimeter wire.
There was an occasional peal of thunder, a flat rolling
roar indistinguishable from the sound of artillery. In
the evening, the rains began again.

Regimental headquarters was moved forward that
month, to a patch of muddy flats near the Dai-La
Pass. A battery of 155s was emplaced nearby, so we
continued to be serenaded by gunfire. There were
more guns now, and tanks and tent camps, more
barbed wire spreading steel thorns through the late-
summer rice. Also, more casualties, three to four times

as many. The splendid little war, which had long since
ceased to be splendid, was now growing up to be a
big war.

There were two hills in front of HqCo's new position, with the Dai-La Pass between them. The old
French watchtower stood in the pass, overlooking
the sodden foothills where the rifle companies were
setting up a new main line of resistance. Almost every
day, truck convoys carrying wire, sandbags, and ammunition struggled up the mired road that led through
the pass and out to the MLR. There was an atmosphere of urgency. The Viet Cong were expected to
launch a monsoon offensive, an annual rite in Vietnam, and the new line was supposed to stop them
from overrunning the airfield. So, the regiment spent
most of that month digging, and filling sandbags and
laying wire. At HQ, we started constructing a big
command bunker in response to reports that the VC
were acquiring quantities of heavy mortars and long-
range rockets. While an engineer outfit worked on the
bunker, the junior officers in HqCo were detailed to
less impressive excavations, swinging picks and entrenching tools alongside the enlisted men. Colonel
Nickerson, the regiment's new CO, had so ordered,
less in the interests of fostering a spirit of democracy
than as a way of getting the job done quickly. But the
atmosphere of urgency could be found only up front,
among the infantry battalions. The regimental staff
remained its old, relaxed self.

Digging was hard work in the rain and in mud that
turned to clay a few inches below the surface, but we
found it a welcome change from the routine of shuf-
fling papers. We were hard at it on the day the colonel
ordered us to drop what we were doing and get to
work on a priority project: his horseshoe pit. Lieutenant Nargi, Major Burin's assistant, had been put
in charge of the project two weeks earlier. Now the
colonel, his large head thrust forward, shoulders
hunched, walked over to us and asked why no work
had been done on the pit. Nargi's shrug suggested there
was a war on.

"I've been hounding you to get it done, Nargi, and

you haven't done a damned thing," said Nickerson. "I want that thing built, and now."

"Now, sir?" asked Nargi, looking up from the foxhole he had half dug.

"Now, lieutenant. I said now. You and some of these other people get to work on it now. I want to be pitching horseshoes tomorrow. Is that clear?"

"Yes, sir."

The colonel turned around and walked off, broadbacked, thick-necked, a too small helmet on his head. When he was a safe distance away, Nargi threw his entrenching tool down.

"So help me Christ," he raged, almost in tears. "I can't wait till I'm out of this fucked-up outfit. I can't take any more of this petty bullshit. Between that S.O.B. and Burin, I'm going rock-happy. So help me Christ, I'm going to slug one of them and wind up in the brig."

With that out of his system, Nargi got to work. The following evening, the colonel was happily pitching horseshoes. There weren't any horses in Vietnam, so I don't know where he found the horseshoes.

Nickerson had taken command of the regiment in late August, when Colonel Wheeler was sent back to the States because of illness. In contrast to the aloof, aristocratic Wheeler, Nickerson was a loud, profane rakehell who enjoyed mixing with the junior officers and enlisted men. He was also subject to quick, violent changes of mood. In his good moments, he was a warm, affectionate man and an energetic combat officer who worked hard at his trade. In his bad moments, he seemed to take a perverse delight in being unreasonable and often confused the petty with the important. Early on, Nickerson let it be known that he had come to Vietnam to fight a war, and he shook the staff section-heads out of their complacency by demanding a full day's work. "We ain't gonna win this war sitting on our asses in these damned enclaves," he roared on his first day with the regiment. "I'm moving this whole shebang out of here, south of that damned river." He meant he was going to move the regiment to the Viet Cong stronghold south of Danang, and someone had to remind him that our sister regiment, the 9th Marines, was already operating there. He could be forgiven that oversight. He had just arrived.

But despite the colonel's announced intent to make the staff sweat for its pay, it soon fell back into old habits. And Nickerson himself began to display strange quirks.

One evening around eight o'clock, he walked into the mess and found several officers drinking beer.

"What in the hell's going on here?" he asked.

"Nothing, sir," said a captain.

"What do you mean nothing? You're drinking. I said there would be no drinking in the mess after nineteen-thirty. It's twenty-hundred hours, gents."

"Sir," the captain reminded Nickerson, "you passed the word that there would be no hard liquor after nineteen-thirty but that we could drink beer until twenty-one-thirty. We secured the hard liquor at nineteen-thirty. We're drinking beer, sir."

"I never said that."

"Begging the colonel's pardon, but you did, sir. You said we could drink beer until twenty-one-thirty."

"*I never said that*," the colonel shouted. "No, no, I never said that. Now get your asses out of here and get to work. We're in a war zone and you should all be working. And just for being a wiseass, captain, there'll be no beer, no liquor, no nothing served in this mess after eighteen-thirty."

War zone not withstanding, the headquarters company football pool was one of the colonel's passions. The 1965 season had begun. The colonel wanted a football pool and he got it. Tim Schwartz was put in charge. I was the alternate and ran the pool in Schwartz's absence.

One drenched night, I spent several hours shivering on the perimeter with my ten-man guard detail. A stand-to had just been ordered after a sentry in HqCo was killed by a grenade, his own. (The sentry had seen, or thought he had seen, infiltrators moving toward our wire. He tried to throw a grenade at them, but his hand slipped off the spoon. The grenade went off and blew the sentry in half.) After stand-down, I sloshed back to the adjutant's tent, made out a casualty report on the sentry, then went into the colonel's tent to adjust the scoreboard. There I found a furious Nickerson. I was in charge of the pool that week, why had I failed to put out the results? I said that I hadn't had the time.

The colonel banged his fist on his desk. "Well, you get on it, Mister Caputo! You get on it first thing in the morning. I want to know who won the pool this week first thing in the morning."

"Yes, sir," I said, too wet and tired to be anything but docile.

My old battalion, One-Three, had shipped out for Camp Pendleton, where they were to be reorganized. The battalion was to return to Vietnam in November, but with none of the men who had made the March landing. Its original members were to be discharged or transferred to other units. I was sorry to see them go, but they were not sorry to be leaving. They had lost some of their friends and most of their old convictions about the reasons for the war. Oh, if someone had asked them, "Do you think you did the right thing?" they would have answered yes. But if you pointed to the casualty list and asked them why their friends had died, they would not have replied with some abstract speech about preserving democracy and stopping Communism. Their answer would have been simple and concrete: "Well, Jack was killed by a sniper and a mortar got Bill and Jim stepped on a mine." Captain Peterson summed up Charley Company's collective feelings one night shortly before the battalion shipped out. "Phil," he said to me over a beer in the HqCo mess, "we've been shot at and missed and shit on and hit, and now we're getting out of this hole."

One-Three was relieved by 1st Battalion, 1st Marines, which had been detached from its parent regiment on the West Coast and placed under our operational control. After a twenty-two-day voyage from San Diego to Danang, the new men clattered off the troopship full of restless energy. Compared to the marines in One-Three, they looked splendid, ruddy-faced and full of the raw good health that comes from getting plenty of outdoor exercise, eight hours' sleep a night, and three hot meals a day. Their rifles were as bright as their faces, their uniforms starched and creased, and they were absolutely gung-ho. Of course they were gung-ho. No dysentery cramped their bowels, no fears shrunk their hearts, no ghosts of dead comrades haunted their memories. Now that they were in Vietnam, the war was as good as won. They were going to do it all by themselves, the 1st Battalion of the 1st Regiment of the 1st Marine Division, the division that had whipped the North Koreans at Inchon and bloodied the Chinese at Chosin and kicked the Japs off Guadalcanal. Now the inheritors of that victorious tradition were in a new war—not much of a war, "but the only one we've got"—and they were going to win it, the first of the first and best of the best. The months of blank-cartridge scrimmaging were behind them; they were going to play in the Big Game. During the long trip across the Pacific, they had heard about the 7th Marines' feat at the Battle of Chu Lai, the first American engagement in Vietnam that could be called a battle. In three days of fighting in mid-August, the 7th had destroyed the Viet Cong's elite 1st Main Force Regiment. The men of the Marines' 1st Regiment were confident that they could do as well, if not better. Such confidence came not only from their ignorance, but also from their numbers. Theirs was a "fat" battalion, meaning a unit at or over its authorized strength. One-One had eleven hundred men when it came ashore.

It was a big, fine-looking battalion, and when I saw them I felt as an old man does when he sees someone who reminds him of his youth. I thought of the way we had been six months before. I was both charmed and saddened by their innocent enthusiasm, charmed because I wished I could be that way again, saddened because they didn't really know what they were getting into. I did. I was the regiment's resident statistician. I knew I would be writing a lot of their names on my mimeographed forms, because I knew they were marching into a different war than the one we had fought between March and August. It was not really a guerrilla war any longer. Our patrols were still encountering guerrillas, but we were fighting more and more actions against main-force regulars and, in some instances, against North Vietnamese Army units. I didn't know if the enemy had started his rainy-season offensive. I only knew that our battalions were holding frontages which should have been held by regiments, that the weather often grounded our planes and helicopters, that it was difficult to move supply convoys, tanks, and big guns down the muddy roads, that the enemy was fighting harder, and we were losing more men. The expedition had become a war of attrition, a drawn-out struggle in the mud and rain.

The proud, confident 1st Battalion of the 1st Marines stepped into it in September, and stayed in it until March when the monsoon campaign ended. Then they were moved up to Hue and from Hue to the Demilitarized Zone, to fight harder battles against the North Vietnamese. By that time, they were no longer a fat battalion, but a rather lean one, and their cockiness had diminished in proportion to their losses. In the six-month campaign, the battalion's total casualties would reach four hundred and seventy-five killed and wounded. More than half of those were patched up and sent out to fight again, some to be wounded again. A little less than two hundred were permanent losses —dead, invalided out, or wounded and hospitalized for long periods. That worked out to eight men a week, an attrition rate almost equal to that suffered by many British battalions—ten a week—on the Western Front in 1915 and early 1916.

It had become a different war. The casualty rate had increased enough to make death and maiming seem commonplace. In its first two months, between mid-September and mid-November, the battalion took two hundred and forty-nine casualties. Attrition. The attrition the enemy inflicted on us and that which we inflicted on ourselves. The Huey gunship that flew in to give fire support to a company pinned down in ambush and ended up giving fire support to the VC by strafing the marines. The troop-carrying helicopter that went down in a monsoon storm. The armored personnel carrier that was backing away from a mortar barrage and crushed a marine lying in the road. Altogether, I wrote an average of seventy-five or eighty reports a week. It became part of my daily routine, as monotonous as the steadily falling rain; and soon those names meant no more to me than the names in a phone book.

Except one. On September 18, I was at my desk in the adjutant's tent. It was a hot afternoon, and I was dripping sweat over the usual paperwork. The EE-8 buzzed. I picked it up: On the other end was Lieutenant Jones, the 1st Battalion adjutant. He did not announce himself as such, but spoke in our boy-scout secret code: "Crowd One? This is Bound One. Is your One Alpha there?"

"This is One Alpha."

"One Alpha, Bound Charley Two's had two storm ones and three storm twos. Can you copy?" In English, that meant 2d platoon, C Company had suffered two killed and three wounded.

"Wait one," I said. I got up and pulled some casualty report forms from the ammo-box file cabinet. Sitting down again, I said, "Okay, go ahead."

"I'll give you the storm ones first."

"Roger. Go ahead."

The first KIA was a corpsman. He had suffered a GSW, through and through, head.

"Okay, that's the first one," Jones said when he had finished with the corpsman. "Second one's last name is Levy. Lima-Echo . . ."

"Is his first name Walter?"

"Lima-Echo-Victor-Yankee. Levy."

"Bound One, is his first name Walter?" I asked, scrawling L-e-v-y beside the line headed NAME. My hand was shaking slightly and my voice sounded strange.

"One Alpha, wait one, will you? That's a roge. First name is Walter. Middle name Neville. November Echo Victor . . ."

"I can spell it."

"Okay. Rank: first lieutenant. Serial number . . ."

Some static interrupted. "Organization: you've got that. Nature of injuries: multiple fragment wounds. . . ."

"Aw, goddamnit," I said, forgetting the rules about using profanity in field communications. Writing down what Jones had just told me, I saw Levy's darkly handsome face and slow, easy grin. Everyone who knew him remarked on his smile, warm, attractive, all straight white teeth; but there was something vaguely enigmatic about it, as if he were smiling at some secret joke. "Goddamnit. Goddamn all of it."

"Did you know this guy?" Jones asked.

"We went through Quantico together. Yeah, we were pretty tight. I didn't even know he was in your outfit."

"Uh-huh. Well, let's get this done. Age: twenty-three. Circumstances: while on patrol vicinity of Danang."

"Bound One, let's drop all this roger wilco crap. Just tell me how it happened."

He told me as much as he knew. A patrol from the 9th Marines had fallen into an ambush and radioed for reinforcements. Levy's platoon was sent, but was itself ambushed before it could get to them. Levy was hit by mine shrapnel and knocked down, another marine by rifle fire. The corpsman, while treating the man with the bullet wound, was sniped. Not knowing the corpsman was dead, Levy forced himself up and half crawled, half walked to him. As he tried to pull him out of the line of fire, Levy himself was sniped.

"You're sure it's him?" I asked.

"Sure we're sure."

"All right. You might as well go ahead."

Jones went on: Levy's religion, the beneficiaries of his serviceman's life insurance policy, the address of his next of kin. That would be his parents in New York City. What would it be like when they answered the bell and saw a man in uniform standing in the doorway? Would they know instinctively why he had come? What would he say? How do you tell parents that all the years they had spent raising and educating their son were for nothing? Wasted. In that war, soldier's slang for death was "wasted." So-and-so was wasted. It was a good word.

We finished the reports. I filed them, then transmuted Levy, the corpsman, and the other casualties into numbers. The random arithmetic of war. I had been in Vietnam seven months and had not been scratched. Levy had lasted two weeks. Coming from the colonel's tent, I saw the swollen, slate-gray clouds building up over the mountains. An image of Levy smiling was in my mind. He was standing with his back against a wall, his hands in his pockets. There was a jukebox next to him. Where had that been? In Georgetown, in Mac's Pipe and Drum, a bar we went to on weekend liberties, to drink and look at girls and pretend we were still civilians. Five or six of us were there that night. We had picked up some girls, government secretaries—all the girls in Washington seemed to be government secretaries. We danced with them on the small dance floor by the front window. It must have been late autumn, because the window in my memory had steam on it. Levy had not danced. Tall and slim, he was leaning casually against the wall and smiling as we walked back to the table with the girls. There were half-empty pitchers of beer on the table and glasses with foam clinging to their sides. We sat down and filled the glasses, all of us laughing, probably at something Jack Bissell said. Was Bissell there that night? He must have been, because we were all laughing very hard and Bissell was always funny. Still standing, Levy took out his pipe, lit it, and bent down to say something to me. In my memory, I could see his lips moving, but I could not hear him. I could not remember what he said. That was in Georgetown, a long time ago, before Vietnam. I had begun to notice that in myself: I was having a hard time remembering anything that had happened before Vietnam.

I had always liked Levy and sometimes envied him. He was quietly deliberate, while I was hot-tempered and impulsive. I had a degree from a parochial commuter-college; he had gone to Columbia. His family was well-off; mine had just recently struggled out of the working class. He had had all the advantages, but he had enlisted when he could have easily done something else. I guess he had that, too: a high sense of duty. My own motives for joining the marines had been mostly personal, but Levy seemed to have no personal ambition. He was a patriot—the best sort, the kind who do not walk around with American flags in their lapels. He had volunteered because it had seemed the right thing to do, and he had done it quietly, easily, and naturally. He had one other attribute rare in this indulgent age: an inflexible fidelity to standards. At Quantico, he and I once shared a misadventure. Like me, he had not been an expert map reader. During a difficult land navigation problem, the two of us, following different compass azimuths, ended up lost in the same swamp. It was full of brambles and deep bogs, an evil-looking place where cottonmouths coiled on the branches of the stunted trees. I had been slogging through it for more than an hour, panic rising in me as I plunged out of one thicket and into another. The swamp seemed endless, and there were only a few hours of daylight left. Hacking at the brambles with my bayonet, I heard someone thrashing and cursing a few yards ahead.

Levy's face appeared through the undergrowth, thorns hanging from his helmet. He stopped yelling and cursing as soon as he saw me. I was relieved to see someone else, but Levy, who had a reputation for being unflappable, seemed embarrassed that he had been caught in a fit of temper. We decided to stick together until we had worked our way out of the swamp. There was a stream at the edge of it, and beyond the stream, a range of pine-wooded hills. We broke out our maps and tried to figure out where we were. It seemed hopeless. I forded the stream to look for a compass marker that might be tacked to one of the pine trees on the far side. Finding none, I said that I was going to cut across the hills until I came to a road. It meant failing the problem, but that was better than spending the night in those black woods. Levy, however, was not ready to quit. He said he was going to plot a course back to his last compass marker and try to figure out where he had made his mistake. I tried to talk him out

of it. To do that, he would have had to retrace his
steps through the swamp, which was bad enough in
daylight; it would be worse if he got caught in it at
night. But he was firm. He was going to do the thing
the right way, or at least give it a try. I said, all right,
go ahead. He had more grit than I. He went back in. I
forded the stream and, after running into another stray,
found my way to a road. I also failed the problem.

So did Levy. Darkness eventually forced him to
dead-reckon his way out, as I had done. The next
week, he was back in the woods with the rest of us
failures, taking the course over. But I had to admire
his determination to do the thing as it was supposed to
be done. It was typical of him. I think it was that fidelity to standards that killed him. Badly wounded in the
legs, he did not have to endanger himself by trying to
rescue the corpsman. He could have stayed under
cover without any loss of honor, but they had drilled
into our heads that a marine never left his wounded
exposed to enemy fire. We never left our wounded on
the battlefield. We brought them off, out of danger and
into safety, even if we had to risk our own lives to do
it. That was one of the standards we were expected
to uphold. I knew I could not have done what Levy
had done. Pulling himself up on his wounded legs, he
had tried to save the corpsman, not knowing that the
man was beyond saving. And he had probably done it
as he had everything else—naturally, and because he
thought it was the right thing to do.

I still could not remember what he had said to me
that night in Georgetown. It could not have been important, yet I wanted to remember. I want to remember
now, to remember what you said, you, Walter Neville
Levy, whose ghost haunts me still. No, it could not
have been anything important or profound, but that
doesn't matter. What matters is that you were alive
then, alive and speaking. And if I could remember
what you said, I could make you speak again on this
page and perhaps make you seem as alive to others as
you still seem to me.

So much was lost with you, so much talent and intelligence and decency. You were the first from our class

of 1964 to die. There were others, but you were the first and more: you embodied the best that was in us. You were a part of us, and a part of us died with you, the small part that was still young, that had not yet grown cynical, grown bitter and old with death. Your courage was an example to us, and whatever the rights or wrongs of the war, nothing can diminish the rightness of what you tried to do. Yours was the greater love. You died for the man you tried to save, and you died *pro patria*. It was not altogether sweet and fitting, your death, but I'm sure you died believing it was *pro patria*. You were faithful. Your country is not. As I write this, eleven years after your death, the country for which you died wishes to forget the war in which you died. Its very name is a curse. There are no monuments to its heroes, no statues in small-town squares and city parks, no plaques, nor public wreaths, nor memorials. For plaques and wreaths and memorials are reminders, and they would make it harder for your country to sink into the amnesia for which it longs. It wishes to forget and it has forgotten. But there are a few of us who do remember because of the small things that made us love you—your gestures, the words you spoke, and the way you looked. We loved you for what you were and what you stood for.

Colonel Nickerson said he was having trouble sleeping at night. It was the end of September, and the cause of the colonel's insomnia were the casualties a company from One-One had suffered during a week-long operation. Out of about one hundred and seventy men, they had lost nearly forty, almost all of them to booby traps and ambush-detonated mines. It would have been a tolerable price if the operation had accomplished something; it had not. The Viet Cong were still there.

I was chalking up the statistical results when Nickerson told me about his problem.

"We're taking too many casualties, lieutenant. I can't sleep half the time, thinking about those kids."

Colonels usually did not make such confessions to lieutenants, so I didn't know what to tell him. Perhaps he had begun to wonder if we were just wasting lives in

Vietnam and wanted someone to tell him otherwise. Perhaps he wanted me to say, "You rest easy, colonel. Those men died in a good cause." Well, he would have to turn to someone else for that. I had far too many doubts myself.

But the moody colonel was a completely different man two days later, when a thirty-five-man patrol from A Company was ambushed. It was a typical ambush: the VC set off a Claymore-type mine, sprayed the patrol with automatic-weapons fire, then faded back into the landscape. The action lasted no more than thirty seconds, but fifteen of those thirty-five marines were killed or wounded. Toting up the scoreboard once again, I mentioned to the new executive officer, Lieutenant Colonel Mackle, that if One-One continued taking such casualties, it would cease to exist in about four months. Nickerson walked in just then. He was splattered with mud and had an unlit cigar jammed in his mouth.

"Now whaddya mean by that, lieutenant?" he asked, and I could tell by his tone that the compassionate officer had given way to the tough, hell-for-leather commander.

"One-One's attrition rate, sir," I said. "If it keeps up, they'll have one-hundred-percent casualties by February."

"Why, I was just over at the hospital," the colonel said. "I saw those kids from that patrol. They're still fulla fight, lieutenant."

"I wasn't slandering their courage, sir. I meant they're taking too many casualties."

"Hell, there was this one kid, this Martinez kid. Know what he wants to do?"

"No, sir."

"He wants to get back out there. Get back out there at those goddamned VC. Here, I pulled this out of him." He waved a piece of shrapnel under my nose, like a second administering smelling salts to a groggy boxer.

"Hell, fifteen casualties ain't nothin'," Nickerson said, walking over to the wall map and tracing the patrol route with a stubby finger. "There's three thousand men in this regiment."

"Right you are, sir, but fifteen casualties is a lot for one platoon."

"Is it? When I landed at Guadalcanal, ninety percent of my platoon was wiped out in an hour. There were only five or six of us left, but we kept fighting."

"I'm sure you did, sir. My point was . . ."

"We kept fighting, goddamnit!" the colonel yelled, and then treated me to a long account of the battle of Guadalcanal, as it was experienced by then-Second Lieutenant Nickerson. When he paused for a breath, I said that I had to get back to work.

"Well, go ahead then. Get the hell out of here."

Chapter Fourteen

In such condition there is . . . no account of time; no arts; no letters; no society; and which is worst of all, continual fear and danger of violent death; and the life of man, solitary, poor, nasty, brutish and short.

—Hobbes
Leviathan

In late October an enemy battalion attacked one of our helicopter bases, inflicted fifty casualties on the company guarding it, and destroyed or damaged over forty aircraft. Two nights later, another Viet Cong battalion overran an outpost manned by eighty marines from A Company, killing twenty-two and wounding fifty more. The usual ambushes and booby traps claimed daily victims, and the medevac helicopters flew back and forth across the low, dripping skies.

The regiment's mood began to match the weather. We were a long way from the despair that afflicted American soldiers in the closing years of the war, but we had also traveled some emotional distance from the cheery confidence of eight months before. The mood was sardonic, fatalistic, and melancholy. I could hear it in our black jokes: "Hey, Bill, you're going on patrol today. If you get your legs blown off can I have your boots?" I could hear it in the songs we sang. Some were versions of maudlin country-and-western tunes like "Detroit City," the refrain of which expressed every rifleman's hope:

> *I wanna go home, I wanna go home,*
> *O I wanna go home.*

Other songs were full of gallows humor. One, "A Belly-full of War," was a marching song composed by an officer in A Company.

> *Oh they taught me how to kill,*
> *Then they stuck me on this hill,*
> *I don't like it anymore.*
> *For all the monsoon rains*
> *Have scrambled up my brains.*
> *I've had a belly-full of war.*
>
> *Oh the sun is much too hot,*
> *And I've caught jungle rot,*
> *I don't like it anymore.*
> *I'm tired and terrified,*
> *I just want to stay alive,*
> *I've had a belly-full of war.*
>
> *So you can march upon Hanoi,*
> *Just forget this little boy,*
> *I don't like it anymore.*
> *For as I lie here with a pout,*
> *My intestines hanging out,*
> *I've had a belly-full of war.*

There was another side to the war, about which no songs were sung, no jokes made. The fighting had not only become more intense, but more vicious. Both we and the Viet Cong began to make a habit of atrocities. One of 1st Battalion's radio operators was captured by an enemy patrol, tied up, beaten with clubs, then executed. His body was found floating in the Song Tuy Loan three days after his capture, with the ropes still around his hands and feet and a bullet hole in the back of his head. Four other marines from another regiment were captured and later discovered in a common grave, also tied up and with their skulls blasted open by an executioner's bullets. Led by a classmate from Quantico, a black officer named Adam Simpson, a twenty-eight-man patrol was ambushed by two hundred VC and almost annihilated. Only two marines, both seriously wounded, lived through it. There might have been more survivors had the Viet Cong not made a systematic massacre of the wounded. After springing the ambush, they went down the line of fallen marines, pumping bullets into any body that showed signs of life, including the body of my classmate. The two men who survived did so by crawling under the bodies of their dead comrades and feigning death.

We paid the enemy back, sometimes with interest. It was common knowledge that quite a few captured VC never made it to prison camps; they were reported as "shot and killed while attempting to escape." Some line companies did not even bother taking prisoners; they simply killed every VC they saw, and a number of Vietnamese who were only suspects. The latter were usually counted as enemy dead, under the unwritten rule "If he's dead and Vietnamese, he's VC."

Everything rotted and corroded quickly over there: bodies, boot leather, canvas, metal, morals. Scorched by the sun, wracked by the wind and rain of the monsoon, fighting in alien swamps and jungles, our humanity rubbed off of us as the protective bluing rubbed off the barrels of our rifles. We were fighting in the cruelest kind of conflict, a people's war. It was no orderly campaign, as in Europe, but a war for survival waged in a wilderness without rules or laws; a war in which each soldier fought for his own life and the lives of the men beside him, not caring who he killed in that personal cause or how many or in what manner and feeling only contempt for those who sought to impose on his savage struggle the mincing distinctions of civilized warfare—

that code of battlefield ethics that attempted to humanize an essentially inhuman war. According to those "rules of engagement," it was morally right to shoot an unarmed Vietnamese who was running, but wrong to shoot one who was standing or walking; it was wrong to shoot an enemy prisoner at close range, but right for a sniper at long range to kill an enemy soldier who was no more able than a prisoner to defend himself; it was wrong for infantrymen to destroy a village with whitephosphorus grenades, but right for a fighter pilot to drop napalm on it. Ethics seemed to be a matter of distance and technology. You could never go wrong if you killed people at long range with sophisticated weapons. And then there was that inspiring order issued by General Greene: kill VC. In the patriotic fervor of the Kennedy years, we had asked, "What can we do for our country?" and our country answered, "Kill VC." That was the strategy, the best our best military minds could come up with: organized butchery. But organized or not, butchery was butchery, so who was to speak of rules and ethics in a war that had none?

In the middle of November, at my own request, I was transferred to a line company in 1st Battalion. My convictions about the war had eroded almost to nothing; I had no illusions, but I had volunteered for a line company anyway. There were a number of reasons, of which the paramount was boredom. There was nothing for me to do but count casualties. I felt useless and a little guilty about living in relative safety while other men risked their lives. I cannot deny that the front still held a fascination for me. The rights or wrongs of the war aside, there was a magnetism about combat. You seemed to live more intensely under fire. Every sense was sharper, the mind worked clearer and faster. Perhaps it was the tension of opposites that made it so, an attraction balanced by revulsion, hope that warred with dread. You found yourself on a precarious emotional edge, experiencing a headiness that no drink or drug could match.

The fear of madness was another motive. The hallucination I had had that day in the mess, of seeing

Mora and Harrison prefigured in death, had become a constant, waking nightmare. I had begun to see almost everyone as they would look in death, including myself. Shaving in the mirror in the morning, I could see myself dead, and there were moments when I not only saw my own corpse, but other people looking at it. I saw life going on without me. The sensation of not being anymore came over me at night, just before falling asleep. Sometimes it made me laugh inside; I could not take myself seriously when I could already see my own death; nor, seeing their deaths as well, could I take others seriously. We were all the victims of a great practical joke played on us by God or Nature. Maybe that was why corpses always grinned. They saw the joke at the last moment. Sometimes it made me laugh, but most of the time it was not at all humorous, and I was sure that another few months of identifying bodies would land me in a psychiatric ward. On staff, there was too much time to brood over those corpses; there would be very little time to think in a line company. That is the secret to emotional survival in war, not thinking.

Finally, there was hatred, a hatred buried so deep that I could not then admit its existence. I can now, though it is still painful. I burned with a hatred for the Viet Cong and with an emotion that dwells in most of us, one closer to the surface than we care to admit: a desire for retribution. I did not hate the enemy for their politics, but for murdering Simpson, for executing that boy whose body had been found in the river, for blasting the life out of Walt Levy. Revenge was one of the reasons I volunteered for a line company. I wanted a chance to kill somebody.

Jim Cooney, my old roommate on Okinawa, was brought up from 3d Battalion to replace me. And it was with a sense of achievement that I gave him casualty files several times thicker than the ones that had been given to me in June.

Kazmarack drove me out to One-One's headquarters. Sergeant Hamilton saw me off. I would miss him, for his humor had helped me maintain at least an outward semblance of sanity during the previous five months: Hamilton, who suffered constantly from gastroenteritis, running into the colonel's head, then telling the officer who chewed him out, "For Christ's sake, sir, I've got Ho Chi Minh's revenge. What do you expect me to do, dump a load in my pants just because my turds don't have colonel's eagles on them? Shit and death are no respecters of rank, sir."

Battalion HQ, awash in mud, was a cluster of tents and bunkers near the French fort. There I followed the usual Stations of the Cross: to the adjutant's tent to have my orders endorsed, to the battalion aid station to drop off my health records, back to the adjutant's to have the transfer entered in my service record book, then to a meeting with the CO, a rangy lieutenant colonel named Hatch. He told me I was to be given a platoon in C Company, Walt Levy's old company. Captain Neal was the skipper and McCloy, who had extended his tour, was the executive officer. When the chat with the colonel was over, I went back to the adjutant's to wait for Charley Company's driver to pick me up. It was raining hard. It had been raining day and night for two weeks.

The driver, PFC Washington, pulled up in a mud-slathered jeep. Like all company drivers, Washington was eager, cheerful, and helpful. Drivers who were eager, cheerful, and helpful got to remain drivers, while lazy, dour, unhelpful drivers were given rifles and sent back to the line. We drove down the road that cut through the Dai-La Pass, the rain lashing our faces because there was no windshield. The road, which had been churned into a river of mud, meandered through villages stinking of buffalo dung and nuocmam. Flooded rice paddies and rows of banana trees whose broad leaves bowed in the rain lined the road. Putting the gears in low, Washington gunned the jeep up a gentle hill, the wheels spinning, the jeep fishtailing as it went over the top of the rise. From there, I could see a T-junction about half a mile ahead, a clump of dark trees shading a hamlet, then the rice paddies and foot-hills, which rose in tiers toward the black mountains. The plumes of mist rising through the jungle canopy made the mountains look menacing and mysterious.

We went down the hill, and the road became like reddish-brown pudding two feet deep. Several farmers stood by a village well, washing their legs and feet. Far away, a machine gun was firing in measured bursts. Washington turned onto a side road just short of the T-junction, passing a cement house whose walls were pocked with bullet and shrapnel holes. A section of 81-mm mortars, emplaced in a field near the house, was shelling a hill in the distance. The shells made gray puffs on the crest of the hill, which was also gray, as gray as slag in the rain. Running along the edge of an overgrown ravine, the side road led into a stretch of low, worn-looking hills. C Company's base camp lay just ahead. The tents were pitched randomly beside a one-oh-five battery, whose candy-stripe aiming stakes looked strangely festive against the background of tents, guns, mud, and rain-swept hills. A squad of marines slogged up the track that led from the base camp to the front line. They walked slowly and in single file, heads down, long, hooded ponchos billowing in the wind. The stocks of their rifles, slung muzzle-down against the rain, bulged under the backs of the ponchos; hooded and bowed, the marines resembled a column of hunchbacked, penitent monks.

Captain Neal was sitting behind his desk in the headquarters tent. A wirily built man with bleak eyes and taut, thin lips, he resembled one of those stern schoolmasters seen in sketches of old New England classrooms. I handed him my orders. He looked up from his paperwork and all I could see in his eyes was their color, pale blue.

"Lieutenant Caputa, been expecting you," he said.

"Caputo, sir."

"Welcome aboard." He attempted to smile, and failed.

"I'm giving you second platoon, Mister Caputa. They've been without an officer since Mister Levy was killed."

"I was at Quantico with Mister Levy, skipper."

"Third and weapons platoon don't have officers, either."

He stood up, unfolded a map, and briefed me on

the situation. The battalion, the whole division in fact, was now on the defensive. Our job was to prevent another VC attack on the airfield by holding the main line of resistance. No offensive operations of any kind were being conducted, except squad- and platoon-sized patrols, and even those were not to venture farther than two thousand yards from the MLR.

The company's frontage extended from the T-Junction south along the road to the Song Tuy Loan River, a distance of nearly a mile; that is, three times the distance a full-strength company could defend adequately, and this company was considerably understrength. The gaps in the line were covered by artillery barrages. The company followed a set routine: two platoons, less the squads on ambush patrol, manned the MLR at night. A third platoon held Charley Hill, a combat outpost about seven hundred yards forward. In the morning, a twenty-five-percent alert was maintained on the line, while the rest of the men hiked the half-mile back to base camp to eat a hot meal, clean their rifles, and rest. In the afternoon, they relieved the morning watch, worked on their positions, or went out on daylight patrols. In the evening, the routine began again.

Mines and booby traps accounted for almost all of the company's casualties. There was some sniping and, rarely, a mortar shelling. I was to keep a sharp lookout for immersion foot in my platoon. The men were constantly wet. They were also tired, and sometimes hungry because they subsisted almost exclusively on cold C rations. *But I was not to give them any slack.* Give 'em slack and they'd start thinking about home, and the worst thing an infantryman could do was think. Did I understand all that? Yes. Did I have any questions? No.

"Good. You're going up to the line tonight, so draw your gear now, Mister Caputa."

"Caputo, sir. As in *toe.*"

"Whatever. You'll be going up tonight."

"Yes, sir," I said, thinking that he was absolutely the most humorless man I had ever met.

Evening vespers began about seven o'clock, when the

howitzers and mortars started firing their routine
harassment missions. With my new platoon, I sloshed
up to the line. The shells ripped the air over our heads
and the rain, slanting before a high monsoon wind,
pelted our faces. The platoon moved up the track at
the steady, plodding pace that is one of the signs of
veteran infantry. And they were veterans if they were
anything. Looking at them, it was hard to believe that
most of them were only nineteen or twenty. For their
faces were not those of children, and their eyes had
the cold, dull expression of men who are chained to
an existence of ruthless practicalities. They struggled
each day to keep dry, to keep their skin from boiling
up with jungle rot, and to stay alive. In the sodden
world they inhabited, the mere act of walking, an act
almost as unconscious as breathing, could bring death.
The trails they had to patrol were sown with mines.
One misstep, and you were blasted to bits or crippled
for life. One misstep or a lax moment where your
eyes wandered and failed to notice the thin strand of
wire stretched across the trail.

We reached the road that marked the front line. I
crawled into the platoon command post—a foxhole
ringed with sandbags and covered by a leaky poncho.
Jones, the radioman, Brewer, the platoon runner, and
a corpsman crawled in with me. The CP was on a
grassy hillock just behind the road. A pool of cold
water lay at the bottom of the foxhole. We bailed it
out with our helmets and, spreading a poncho over
the mud, sat down to smoke a last cigarette before
darkness fell. Jones slipped the heavy, ancient
PRC-10 radio from his back, propping it against one
side of the hole.

"Charley Six, this is Charley Two. Radio check," he
said into the handset. "How do you read me, Six?"

"Two, this is Six. Read you loud and clear. Six
Actual says to advise your actual that Alpha Company taking some mortar fire."

"Roger, Six. If no further traffic, this is Two out."

"Six out."

"Did you hear that, sir?" Jones said.

I said that I had.

The wind was blowing hard, and the rain came sweeping horizontally across the paddies to strike the hooch like buckshot. I listened for the mortars, but could not hear anything over the wind, the rain, and the dry-rattling branches of the bamboo trees around us. The last of my platoon were filing through the gray dusk toward their positions. Heavy-legged, they walked along the line—which was not a line, but a string of isolated positions dug wherever there was solid ground—and dropped off by twos into the foxholes. The coils of concertina wire in front of the positions writhed in the wind.

I had the first radio watch. Jones and the others lay down to sleep, curling up into the fetal position. Looking out, I tried to familiarize myself with the landscape. Second platoon's part of the line followed the course of the road, skirted a hamlet that was guarded by some Popular Forces—village militia—and ended at the river. Altogether, we held a frontage of seven hundred yards, normally the frontage for a company, and there were dangerously wide gaps between positions. One such position, called the "school-house" because of the cement-walled school that stood there, was separated from the next, a knoll near the river, by about two hundred yards of flooded rice paddy. The two positions were like islands in an archipelago. Out front were more paddies, a stream with jungle-covered banks, then the gray-green foothills. Charley Hill stood there, a muddy, red little knob that stuck out of the surrounding hills like an inflamed sore. In the dimming light, I could just see the olive-drab patches of the hooches and the small figures of our men. There was nothing in front of the outpost but more hills, then the mountains, rising into the clouds. Compared to that place, the front line was the center of civilization. Charley Hill was at the ragged edge of the earth.

It was soon dark. I still could not hear anything but the wind and crackling branches, and now I could see nothing except varying shades of black. The village was a pitch-colored pool in the gray-black paddies. Beyond the inky line of the jungle bordering the stream, the Cordillera was so black that it looked like a vast hole in the sky. Even after my eyes adjusted, I could not see the slightest variation in color. It was absolutely black. It was a void, and, staring at it, I felt that I was looking into the sun's opposite, the source and center of all the darkness in the world.

The wind kept blowing, relentless and numbing. Soaked through, I started to shiver. It was difficult to hold the hand-set steady, and I stammered when I called in the hourly situation report. I could not remember having been so cold. A flare went up, revealing the silhouettes of palm trees tossing in the wind and sheets of rain falling from scudding clouds. A strong gust knifed into the foxhole, tugged at the hooch, and tore one side of it from its moorings. Rubbery and wet, the poncho slapped against my face, and Brewer said "Goddamn" as the rain sluiced into the now exposed hole. Then a stream of water guttered down from the hilltop and seeped through cracks in the sandbags, almost flooding us out. The poncho was still flapping like a sail loosed from its sheets. "Goddamn motherfuckin' Nam."

"Jones, Brewer, get that thing pegged down," I said, bailing again with my helmet. The rain fell into my collar and poured out the sleeves of my jacket as if they were drainpipes.

"Yes, sir," said Jones. He and Brewer climbed out, got hold of the poncho and pegged it down, pounding the metal stakes with the butt ends of their bayonets. The corpsman and I bailed, and the work warmed us a little. There was still an inch of water in the foxhole when we settled down again. I turned the radio over to Jones. It was his watch. Lying on my side, knees drawn up, I tried to sleep, but the puddles and chilling wind made it impossible.

Around midnight, automatic-rifle fire spattered into one of the positions near the hamlet. The squad leader called me on the field phone and said that twenty rounds had been fired into his right flank, but without causing any casualties. There was another burst.

"He's at it again, Two Actual," said the voice on

the phone. "I think he's in the tree line along that stream."

"Roger. Give him a couple of M-79s. I'll be right down."

Taking a rifleman along for security, I went down the road and through the village. Two M-79 grenades exploded in the tree line. The mud on the road was ankle deep. We could not see anything except a lamp burning in one of the huts. Staying close to the culvert at the roadside in case we had to take cover quickly, we reached the position that had taken the fire. There were a couple of bullet holes in the marines' hooch. It began to rain harder, although that did not seem possible. Huddling down next to the riflemen, I tried to see something in the black tree line a hundred yards across the rice paddies. The paddies had been turned into a miniature lake, and wind-driven waves lapped the dike in front of us. Then a white-orange light winked in the gloom. Bullets streamed past us with that vicious, sucking sound, and I went down on my belly in the mud.

"See you now, you cocksucker," one of the riflemen said, pumping rapid fire at the sniper's muzzle-flash. Three or four more grenades, flashing brightly, crashed into the trees.

"That should give him something to think about, if it didn't blow his shit away," said the rifleman who had done the firing.

We waited for perhaps half an hour. When nothing more happened, my guard and I headed back toward the CP. The wind had let up finally, and in the quiet air mosquitoes hummed. Two mortar shells hit far behind us, where the road climbed and curved around a bend in the river. They exploded near D Company's lines, bursting in showers of lovely red sparks. In the opposite direction, One-Three, newly returned to Vietnam with all unseasoned troops, was having a fire-fight with figments of its imagination. We passed the hut where the lamp was burning. "Hey, GI," someone whispered. "GI, you come." A middle-aged farmer stood in the doorway, waving us inside. The marine brought his rifle up, just in case, and we went into the hut. It reeked of garlic, woodsmoke, and rotten fish-sauce, but it was dry and we were grateful for even a few moments out of the rain. I lit a cigarette, grateful for that, too. I drew the smoke deep into my lungs, feeling it calm my nerves.

The farmer had meanwhile taken some photographs out of an oilskin packet. They were photos of Vietnamese whores and American soldiers making love in various positions. The farmer hissed and chuckled as he showed us each a picture. "Good, huh?" he said. "Number one, no? Want buy? You buy. Number one."

"Jesus Christ, you old pervert, no," I said. "Khoung. No buy."

"No buy?" the farmer asked in the surprised tone of all salesmen when met by a customer's refusal.

"Khoung. Chao Ong."

"Chao Ong, dai-uy." (Good night, captain.)

"No dai-uy. Trung-uy." (Lieutenant.)

"Ah. Ah. Trung-uy. Hokay. Chao trung-uy."

"How do you like that shit, lieutenant," said the rifleman when we were outside. "We're supposed to be fighting for these people. We're getting soaked and our asses shot at and he's in there whacking off at dirty pictures."

"Life is full of injustices."

"If you're a grunt, that's no lie, sir."

We slept fitfully for the rest of the night and woke up to a drizzling dawn. Dazed, the platoon hiked back to base camp, leaving one squad behind to guard the line. The rice paddies were underwater and filled with snakes. We could see the wakes they made as they slithered just beneath the surface. One fireteam, marooned on an island of high ground, had to borrow sampans from the villagers to get back to the road. Like prisoners in a labor gang, the marines marched toward camp joylessly and without expectation that the new day would bring anything different or better. Shivering myself warm, I felt more tired than I had ever felt before. I was worn out after only one night on the line, and I wondered how the platoon felt,

after months on the line. I found out soon enough:
they felt nothing, except occasional stabs of fear.

It went like that for the rest of the month. It was a
time of little action and endless misery. I was given
command of 1st platoon for a week, while its officer
was absent. Our sole casualty that week was a squad
leader who ended up hospitalized with a centipede
bite. The real fighting had shifted to the Ia Drang
Valley in the Central Highlands, where the Seventh
Cavalry, of Little Bighorn fame, was fighting the
North Vietnamese in what was then the biggest battle
of the war. But it was quiet at Danang. Almost every
hour of every night, the radio operators chanted, "All
secure. Situation remains the same." I took out two or
three patrols, but there was no contact except for the
usual snipers. All secure. Situation remains the same.
The company lost two machine-gunners to a mine. All
secure. Situation remains the same. We trudged up to
the line and back again, patrolled the booby-trapped
trails, dug foxholes and redug them when they were
collapsed by the rain. It rained all the time. We slept,
when we slept, in the mud. We shivered through our
nervous night watches, calling in reports every hour:
All secure. Situation remains the same. A sentry
from B Company was killed one morning by infiltrators. And still it rained. The Viet Cong lobbed a few
shells at us, but they fell short, exploding in the paddies a long way from our wire, gray smoke blossoming,
water and clods of mud geysering. Charley Six observed six enemy mortar rounds six-oh millimeters two
hundred meters from this position. No casualties. All
secure. Situation remains the same.

At the end of the month, the Viet Cong staged a
small attack on the village. The rain that night was
falling lightly. It leaked from the swollen sky like pus
from a festering wound. The second squad leader,
Sergeant Coffell, who had been transferred to One-
One from another battalion, and I were on watch in a
murky foxhole, talking to each other to keep awake.
We talked about home, women, and our fears. A
heavy mist lay in the jungle along the stream in front

of us. The trees appeared to be standing in a bank of deep snow. Coffell was whispering to me about his dread of Bouncing Betties: mines that sprang out of the ground and exploded at waist level. He was going to take a patrol out in the morning and said he hoped they did not trip any Bouncing Betties. His last company commander had been hit by one.

"It tore one of his legs off at the thigh, sir. His femur artery was cut and the blood was pouring out of it like out of a hose. We couldn't stop it. We didn't know what the hell to do, so we just started packing mud into it, from out of the rice paddy. We kept slapping mud into the stump, but it didn't do any good. No, sir, those Bouncing Betties, goddamn, I hate those things."

An automatic rifle thumped in the village behind us. One of the Popular Force militiamen fired a burst from his carbine.

"Goddamn PFs shooting at shadows again," Coffell said.

"Shadows don't carry automatic rifles. That sounded like an AK to me."

Then came a crackling as of a dry brush pile set alight. Hand grenades exploded and tracers were glowing redly above our heads. A couple of rounds whacked into the sandbags of a nearby position, narrowly missing a machine-gunner. Crouching low, I picked up the field phone and called Dodge, the platoon sergeant. He was with another squad at the schoolhouse position, on the opposite side of the village. I asked if he could see where the fire was coming from.

"No, sir. We're pinned down here. Can't even lift our heads. We got automatic-weapons fire hitting the schoolhouse. It's coming from near the ville, but I can't say exactly."

"Then Charlie's behind us. Anyone hit?"

"No, sir, but old watash almost got it between the running lights. Four, five rounds hit the wall next to me. Got sprayed with a lot of plaster . . ."

The line went dead as two more grenades burst.

"Dodge, are you reading me?" I asked, clicking the

receiver button several times. There was no answer.
The grenades had cut the landline; so now I had one
squad pinned down and no communications with them.

Rolling over the parapet of the foxhole, I crawled
up to the road embankment to see if I could spot the
enemy's muzzle-flashes. I could. The Viet Cong were
in the village, shooting in every direction. A line of
red light appeared above the road. It was moving
rapidly toward me, and one of the tracers cracked
past my ear, close enough for me to feel the shock
wave. With the sick feeling that comes when you are
receiving fire from your rear, I rolled back down the
embankment.

"Coffell, they're behind us. Face your people about.
Face 'em toward the road and tell 'em to drop anything that moves on that road."

"Yes, sir."

Sliding on my belly toward the radio, I heard my
heart drumming against the wet earth. "Charley Six,
this is Charley Two Actual," I said, trying to reach
Neal. "Do you read me?" I was answered by static.
"Six, this is Two requesting illumination on concentration one. Are you reading me, Six?" The static hissed
in the receiver. A rifleman was lying next to me,
his M-14 pointed at the road. He had turned his head
to face me. I could not tell who he was. In the darkness, I could only see his hollow, haggard eyes staring
from beneath his helmet's brim. "Six, this is Two. If
you are receiving me, I have Victor Charlies in
the ville behind me. One squad pinned down by
automatic-weapons fire and landlines cut by grenades.
Request illumination on concentration one." Mock-
ingly, the static hissed. I hit the radio with my fist.
Discards from World War II, the PRC-10s could always be relied on to break down in a crisis.

After trying for nearly fifteen minutes, I got through
to company HQ. Neal said he knew nothing about a
fire-fight.

"It's going on right behind me. Or was. It's just
about over now."

"I don't hear anything," he said.

"Six, that's because it's almost over. They were really going at it before. Can you give me some illumination on concentration one? Maybe we can spot the VC pulling out."

"I didn't hear anything before, Charley Two."

"In the village, Six! The Victor Charlies are in the ville behind me, engaged with the PFs. My first squad pinned down."

I knew why Captain Neal had not heard anything: he was in the company's base camp, half a mile behind the line. He slept there, or in the command bunker, most every night. "I really felt bad about sleeping in my tent while you guys were out there," he told me after one particularly wretched night. "Yes, sir," I said. "We felt pretty bad about it, too."

"Charley Two, have you got any casualties?"

"Negative."

"Do you think you can handle the situation?"

"Roger. A little illumination would help."

"Keep me informed. This is Six Actual out."

"Two out."

So, I would get no illumination. I was not to be illuminated.

The skirmish had ended by the time I finished talking with Neal. We made contact with the PF commander, who said, "Now, hokay. VC di-di."

I called Neal again. "Victor Charlies have pulled out, Six. No casualties. We searched area with negative results."

"Roger. How's your situation now?"

"All secure," I said. "Situation remains the same."

In the company mess the next morning, I sat with my numbed hands wrapped around a mug of coffee. I had not slept after the fire-fight. None of us had slept. We had been put on full alert because an enemy battalion was reported to be moving in our direction. We waited, and, waiting, fought off sleep. A sniper teased us now and then, the rain fell incessantly, but nothing happened. At dawn, we moved back to base camp, except for those who had to stay on the line or go on patrol.

It was still raining while I sat in the mess across from Captain Neal. Outside, a line of marines shuffled past the immersion burners, each dipping his mess kit into the boiling water. I wanted to sleep. I wanted four or five hours of dry, unbroken sleep, but I had to lay communications wire to a new position. That would take most of the day. I also had to inspect the police of my platoon's sector. Neal had found a pile of empty C-ration tins near the schoolhouse, which upset him. He liked to keep a tidy battlefield. So I would have to make sure the men buried the tin cans. I mustn't forget to do that, I thought. It's important to the war effort to pick up our garbage. A voice inside my head told me I was being overly bitter. I was feeling sorry for myself. No one had forced me to join the Marines or to volunteer for a line company. I had asked for it. That was true, but recognizing the truth of it did not solve my immediate problem: I was very tired and wanted to get some sleep.

Neal said he had been looking at my service record and noticed that I had been in Vietnam for nine months without an R-and-R. There was an opening on a flight to Saigon the next morning. Would I like to go to Saigon for three days' R-and-R? Yes, I said without hesitating. Oh yes yes yes.

The green and brown camouflage C-130 landed at Tan Son Nhut airport in the early evening. We rode into Saigon on a bus that had wire screens on its windows, to deflect terrorist grenades. It pulled up in front of the Meyercourt, a hotel reserved for soldiers on R-and-R. The high wall surrounding the hotel was topped with barbed wire, and an MP armed with a shotgun stood by the door in a sand-bagged sentry booth. Out on the balcony of my eighth-floor room, I watched a flare-ship dropping flares over the marsh-lands south of the city. Shellfire flickered on the horizon, the guns booming rhythmically. So, even in Saigon there was no escape from the war. But the room was clean and cheap. It had a shower and a bed, a real bed with a mattress and clean sheets. I took a hot shower, which felt wonderful, lay down, and slept for fifteen hours.

I found escape from the war the next morning. It

was in a quiet quarter of the city, where tall trees shaded the streets and I could walk for a long way without seeing soldiers, whores, or bars; just quiet, shady streets and whitewashed villas with red tile roofs. There was a sidewalk café on one of the side streets. I went inside for breakfast. The café was cool and fresh-smelling in the early morning, and the only other customers were two lovely Vietnamese girls wearing orange ao-dais. The waiter handed me a menu. A *menu*. I had a choice of what to eat, something I had not had in months. I ordered juice, café au lait, and hot croissants with jam and butter. After eating, I sat back in the chair and read a collection of Dylan Thomas. The book, a gift from my sister, took me a long way from Vietnam, to the peaceful hills of Wales, to the rocky Welsh coasts where herons flew. I liked "Fern Hill" and "Poem in October," but I could not read "And Death Shall Have No Dominion." I didn't know much about Dylan Thomas's life, but I guessed that he had never been in a war. No one who had seen war could ever doubt that death had dominion.

As I was leaving, an old woman with one arm came up to me begging. She handed me a note which read, "I am fifty years old and lost my left arm in an artillery bombardment. My husband died in a battle with the Viet Cong in 1962. Please give me 20 piasters." I gave her a hundred; she bowed and said, "Cam Ong." Tell her, Dylan, that death has no dominion.

On my second day in Saigon, I met an Indian silk-merchant in one of the city's noisy, enclosed market places, and he asked how I liked Saigon. I said that I liked it very much. It was a beautiful city, a magnificent city when you compared it to the mess in the countryside. "Yes, you are right," he said sadly. "There is something wrong with this country. I think it is the war."

In the evening, I had dinner on the terrace of the Continental Palace Hotel. The Palace was a very old French hotel, where waiters behaved with a politeness that was not fawning and with a dignity that was not haughtiness. I sat at one of the linen-covered tables on the terrace, beside an archway that looked out on the street. A few French plantation owners, old colonials who had stayed on in Indochina, were sitting across from me. Suntanned men dressed in cotton shirts and khaki shorts, they were drinking cold white wine, and eating and gesturing as if they were on the Champs Elysées or the Left Bank. They were enjoying themselves. It occurred to me that it had been a long time since I had seen anyone enjoying himself.

A waiter came up and asked for my order.

"Chateaubriand avec pommes frites, s'il vous plaît."

The waiter, an old Vietnamese man with the bearing of a village elder, winced at my accent. "Pardonnez-moi monsieur. Le chateaubriand est pour deux."

"I know, I want it anyway." I said switching back to English.

"Bien. Vin Rouge?"

"Oui, rouge. A bottle."

"But there is only you."

"I'll drink it. Don't worry."

He wrote on his pad and walked off.

Waiting for the wine, I looked at the Frenchmen talking, gesturing, and laughing at some joke or other, and I began to feel light-headed. It had something to do with the relaxed manner of those men, with their laughter and the sound their forks made against the plates. The wine heightened the sensation. Later, after finishing the chateaubriand and half the bottle of red wine, I realized what the feeling was: normality. I had had two nights of solid sleep, a bath, an excellent dinner, and I felt normal—I mean, I did not feel afraid. For the first time in a very long time, I did not feel afraid. I had been released from that cramped land of death, the front, that land of suffering peasants, worn soldiers, mud, rain, and fear. I felt alive again and in love with life. The Frenchmen across from me were living, not just surviving. And for the time being, I was a part of their world. I had temporarily renewed my citizenship in the human race.

I drank more of the wine, loving the way the sweating bottle looked on the white linen tablecloth. The thought of deserting crossed my mind. It was a deli-

ciously exciting thought. I would stay in Saigon and
live life. Of course, I knew it was impossible. Physically, it was impossible. I was white, several inches
taller and about seventy pounds heavier than the biggest Vietnamese. The MPs could not miss me. But I
was also constrained by the obligation I had toward
my platoon. I would be deserting them, my friends.
That was the real crime a deserter committed: he ran
out on his friends. And perhaps that was why, in spite
of everything, we fought as hard as we did. We had no
other choice. Desertion was unthinkable. Each of us
fought for himself and for the men beside him. The
only way out of Vietnam, besides death or wounds,
was to fight your way out. We fought to live. But it was
pleasant to toy with the idea of desertion, to pretend
I had a choice.

Twenty or thirty of us were standing on the tarmac
when the C-130 taxied to a stop. Our three days of
freedom were over. An old gunnery sergeant stood
next to me, entertaining the crowd with jokes. He
knew more jokes than a stage comedian, and he told
them one after another. He had fought on Iwo Jima
and in Korea and had been in Vietnam for seven
months. He was a veteran, and with his brown, lined
face, he looked it. His rapid-fire jokes kept us laughing, kept us from thinking about where we were
going. Perhaps he was trying to keep himself from
thinking. But the jokes and laughter stopped when the
hatch of the C-130 opened and they brought the bodies off. The corpses were in green rubber body-bags.
We knew what they were by the humps the boots
made in the bags—and why was that always such a
painful sight, the sight of a dead man's boots?
The mood changed. No one spoke. Silently we
watched the crewmen carry the dead down the ramp
and into an ambulance parked near the aircraft. And
I felt it come back again, that old, familiar, cold,
cramping fear. The humorous gunnery sergeant, veteran of three wars, shook his head. "Goddamn this
war," he said. "Goddamn this war."

Chapter Fifteen

. . . We are but warriors for the working day.
Our gayness and our gilt are all besmirched
With rainy marching in the painful field.
                                              —Shakespeare
                                              Henry V

Poised like high-wire artists, we crossed the narrow bamboo bridge that spanned the stream. The monsoons had turned the stream into a river, and the deep, brown water rushed swiftly beneath us. From their foxholes on Charley Hill a short distance ahead, 3d platoon mocked our balancing act. "Don't fall in and get your feet wet, dears."

"Up yours, shit-for-brains," one of my marines called back.

A drizzling rain fell. The platoon filed across the rice paddy on the other side of the stream, slipping on the muddy dike, then climbed the hill. At the top, they waited for Jones and me to pick up a spare radio. They sat down to rest and smoke a last cigarette before the patrol got under way. Dull green, broken by islands of palm trees, the foothills stretched away from the outpost toward the mountains. We could not see the mountains; they were hidden behind a solid, lead-colored wall of clouds. Third platoon had been on Charley Hill a long time, a little too long. Ragged and filthy, they stared at us with fatigued eyes and made a few more tired jokes.

"Watch those nasty booby traps out there," one said. "We don't want you to get killed, Allen."

"Ain't nobody gonna get killed," said Lance Corporal Allen, a fire-team leader in my platoon.

"If you do get killed, can I have your boots? We're about the same size."

"You'll get my boots in your balls. Listen, you sit

tight here, asshole. We'll drive a whole friggin' regiment into you."

"Friggin'? *Friggin'*. Wooah, they're gonna drive a friggin' regiment into us. Allen, you are a baaaaad motherfucker."

"Don't you know it, asshole. It's your mother."

"Then I'm your son, and if you get dinged, I'll be an orphan. So let me have your boots, Daddy."

"Like I said, in the balls. In the balls."

I went into the dugout to pick up the radio. It was almost as muddy inside as out. Water seeped through the bunker's clay walls and dripped from the rotted canvas curtain hanging over the doorway. I checked the radio.

"It works, believe it or not," said McKenna, the 3d platoon leader. He had joined C Company recently, a dark-haired, jive-talking Bronx Irishman who was known as Black Mac and who conceived of the war as a street gangfight on a grand scale.

The radio did work. That was unusual. Little Jones—for some reason, all radio operators are small men—hoisted the PRC-10 onto his back. I lit a cigarette, reluctant to leave the dugout and spend all day out in the rain. I could hear it pattering against the bunker's sandbagged roof. I did not want the rain and the long hours of walking and the waiting for a booby trap to blast someone into fragments. Two weeks had passed since Saigon, but I was as tired now as I had been before the R-and-R. No, more tired. It was as if I had had no rest at all, as if no amount of rest could overcome my fatigue. The same was true of the others. The company had run nearly two hundred patrols in the month I had been with it, and then there had been all those nights on the line. The men were in a permanent state of exhaustion. They were in a shaft, plunging daily from one level of fatigue to the next, and the squad leaders kept pleading for a break. "They're tired, lieutenant. They're so tired that half of 'em are half asleep on patrol. They've got to get some slack." But there was no slack. There was no rotating back to the rear, as in previous wars, because there was no rear to rotate to.

Jones adjusted the radio's pack straps and walked out.

"Did your boys pass Captain Bligh's rifle inspection the other day?" McKenna asked.

"Yeah, we passed. A rifle inspection! The son of a bitch must think we're in garrison."

"You should've seen the shit he pulled out here. He came out and the first thing he does is line everyone up in platoon formation. That was cool. One fuckin' mortar round would've wasted everybody. Then he finds a rifleman with a dusty chamber, reams him out and reams the whole platoon out. He went on down and found another rifleman with a speck of rust on his magazine, and he took the magazine and threw it in the mud. Just like that. The platoon was ready to kill him. After he left, Sergeant Horne told everybody to get back to work, and we almost had a mutiny. This one kid tells Horne to get laid, so Horne decks him. I mean, you just don't tell that big son of a bitch to get laid. The kid got his rifle then and told Horne he was going to kill him. The kid probably wanted to kill Neal, but Horne'd do. Horne tells him, 'Go ahead, it'll only get you a rope or life,' and then grabs the weapon away before the kid can fire it. The kid just broke down. 'I can't take it no more,' he said. That's all he kept saying, 'I can't take it no more and all this petty harassment on the front lines.' You know, I think the skipper's nuts. Somebody's going to put a bullet in the back of his head one of these days."

"Well, whoever does, I hope they give him the Congressional Medal of Honor. Jesus, Mac, the war's bad enough without having to put up with that goddamned tyrant."

"We're in the Corps, P.J. The Crotch. Semper fi and fuck your buddy."

"El Crotcho endalay. I'm going and get this little walk over with."

I crushed my cigarette and went out to where the platoon waited, patiently enduring their misery.

"Saddle up, Second," said Sergeant Bittner, the new platoon sergeant. Dodge, suffering from old leg injuries, had been transferred to battalion HQ. "Saddle up, Second. Movin' out."

The platoon rose as one, like a congregation at a Mass.

"Point fire-team out twenty-five meters. Smoking lamp is out. No talking or smoking once we're off this hill. Pick up your interval and maintain it. Ten paces between each man. Stagger the column."

The commands were not really necessary. They were just part of the ritual. The platoon knew what to do, having done it often enough.

We slid over the edge. That was what it was like every time we moved off the outpost and into the enemy-controlled country beyond, like sliding over an edge.

The platoon followed the traces of an old road for a short distance, stumbled down into a watery ravine, toiled up a hill, went down into another ravine, then up another hill. The words to a half-remembered nursery rhyme went through my head: "Oh, the grand old Duke of York, he had ten thousand men; he marched them up the hill, then marched them down again." We wound through the foothills for an hour, fighting off the wet caresses of the high elephant grass. Scaling a low, razor-backed ridge, the column started down toward the paddy lands that bordered the river, moving across the paddies with veteran skill. The point fire-team crossed first, covered by the rest of the patrol and a machine-gun team. When the point reached the tree line on the far side, the main body went across, the machine-gun team still covering; then they crossed. Our tactical maneuvering did not even draw a glance from the farmer who was working in one of the fields. He rode over the mud on a sledlike plow, whipping the steaming flanks of his water buffalo with a long, bamboo rod. We went across, cursing the ankle-deep ooze that hobbled us. It was as black as tar and almost as thick. The rain never stopped.

After three hours of walking, the platoon reached the river trail. It was the same one I had patrolled with One-Three months before, but it had a new name: Purple Heart Trail. The Tuy Loan River was in full flood. Racing between its crumbling clay banks, it eddied around the deep pools and made riffles over the sunken bushes that had been on dry ground before the monsoon. Pangee traps and spider holes began to appear alongside the trail. We did not see anyone in the villages or in the fields, some of which were pocked with shell craters. There was no sound but the infrequent cries of birds and the hissing of rain through the trees. At point, Lance Corporal Crowe walked delicately—like a man walking through a minefield. And that's what the trail was, a long, narrow minefield. The blackened stump of a tree testified to that; a booby trap had exploded there two days before, seriously wounding two marines from another platoon. Purple Heart Trail usually lived up to its name. Crowe's head was turning from side to side, his eyes flicking from side to side, lizardlike, looking for the shining thinness of a trip wire, for the length of electric detonating cord snaking off into the underbrush. Behind him, Allen and PFC Lonehill searched the trees for snipers. I followed them, with Jones behind me and then the rest of the patrol. We walked with muscles tensed and senses awakened, walked on feet sore from constant dampness. Ahead, there was a clearing, and, on its far side, the village we were to search. Crowe, Allen, and Lonehill started out into the clearing, quickening their pace as they moved across the exposed ground. Jones and I came next. The bullet sounded like a bullwhip cracking. It struck a branch just overhead. Jones and I slid over the edge of the riverbank, Jones bending the radio antenna down to conceal it from the sniper.

"Allen. Sniper, right flank. Probably in the tree line. Can you reach him with the M-79?"

"Think so, lieutenant," said Allen, who was crouched with the other two marines behind a hump in the ground.

The grenade launcher popped once, twice, three times. The sniper fired again. Low, the bullet sang through the grass and sent chunks of mud flying as it struck the trail. The first 40-millimeter burst, and I yelled, "Second, double-time across the clearing, on the double!" Lonehill sprayed the tree line with his automatic rifle. The sniper, panicked by the return fire, loosed five or six wildly aimed rounds. The platoon came running up the trail, helmets and equipment clattering, as the last two grenades went off.

Safely across the clearing, we approached the village. Crowe checked its bamboo gate for booby traps. The gate was clear. Coffell's squad cordoned off the village while Corporal Aiker's squad searched it. The search turned up the usual stuff: a small food cache, a couple of tunnels, and a few clips of small-arms ammunition, so old they might have been there since the French Indochina War.

There were only four people in the village, two old women, a girl, and a small boy.

"Chao-Ba," I said to one of the women.

She smiled, baring her red teeth. "Chao-anh."

"Manh gioi khoung?"

"Toi manh." (I am well.)

"Ba gap Viet Cong khoung?" (Woman, have you seen the Viet Cong?)

Fumbling beneath her blouse, revealing for a moment a pair of sagging, desiccated breasts, she handed me her identification card. It was the regulation, plastic-laminated I.D. card issued by the government. If it had not been issued by the government, it had been issued by the VC, who often forged I.D. cards.

"Woman, this tells me nothing. I ask you, have you seen the Viet Cong?"

"Khoung." (No.)

I gestured toward the clearing and, not knowing the Vietnamese word for sniper, said in English, "VC. VC. Ten minutes ago. Bang. Bang."

"Toi khoung hieu." (I don't understand.)

I mimicked the motions of a man firing a rifle, then pointed at myself. "VC. Bang. Bang. At me. Toi. Ten minutes ago."

"Ah, toi hieu."

"Where are the Viet Cong?"

"Toi khoung biet." (I don't know.)

I had been through the same routine a dozen times in a dozen other villages, and it was beginning to exasperate me—that mulish peasant stubbornness.

"Woman, you know." I showed her a clip of .30-caliber ammunition. "You know. VC here. How many?"

"I don't know."

"Mot? Hai? Lam?" (One? Two? Five?)

"I know nothing about the Viet Cong."

I had my first violence fantasy then, a hint that I was breaking down under the strains and frustrations peculiar to that war. In my mind, the red liquid in the woman's mouth was blood, not betel-nut juice. In my mind, I had slapped her across the mouth with the back of my hand, and blood was pouring out from between her lips as she told me all I wanted to know. I had beaten the truth out of her. With one slap of my hand, I had ended her litany of "no" and "I don't know." There was no one out there to stop me from actually doing it, no one and nothing except that inner system of moral checks called conscience. That was still operating, so I did not touch the old woman. I merely asked, again, "Where are the Viet Cong?"

"I don't know."

My right arm tensed. "You old bitch, tell me where they are," I said in English.

"I don't understand."

"Ba gap Viet Cong khoung?"

"No. I know nothing about the Viet Cong. There are many VC in the mountains."

"I know, buku VC in the mountains. How many here?"

"No VC are here."

"VC here," I said, holding up the ammo clip.

"No VC here."

"Yeah, right, you old bitch, and we'll probably walk out of here and get sniped again."

"I don't understand."

"That's because I'm speaking English. You don't understand a goddamned thing, do you?"

"Toi khoung hieu."

"Cam anh ba. Di-di." (Thank you, woman. Go now.)

She nodded and, with the others, shuffled into a hut. I sat down next to Coffell and pulled a ration tin out of the baggy side-pocket in my uniform. Coffell asked if I had learned anything. No, I said, of course not.

"Pass the word to break for chow. We'll move out in fifteen minutes."

"Yes, sir," he said, rising like an old man with arthritic joints. Coffell was twenty-four. "You know, I sure don't like the idea of that long walk back."

"Well, we could always stay out here."

"I like that idea even less."

The platoon ate cold C rations in the rain, then headed back toward friendly lines. Cutting cross-country to avoid retracing our steps over the trail, we slashed through elephant grass as sharp and thick as the spines on a hedgehog's back. The weather turned strange. Spells of total calm and intense heat were broken by brief, heavy squalls that seemed to blow in out of nowhere. All the way back, we were alternately soaked, chilled, and scorched. At dusk, we reached the front line, or what, in that war, passed for a front line. Sergeant Pryor's squad, left behind to guard the platoon's section of the line, were blackening their faces with charcoal and shoe polish before they went out on ambush. Coffell's and Aiker's squads trudged off to their positions, with nothing before them but one more damp night of nervous waiting.

Waiting was about all we did for the next week. We were sniped at and rained on every night. The platoon's new command post, an abandoned one-story barn whose stone walls had been chipped in some long-forgotten battle, acquired a few more scars. Meanwhile, C Company was alerted to be ready to be flown into an operation code-named Harvest Moon. It was a large operation for that stage of the war. Night after night, flickering artillery rumbled. We waited, numbed by the ceaseless rain and wind. It was always worse than combat itself, waiting to go into combat.

The action was taking place near Hoi-An, a small city south of Danang. One afternoon, we learned that the enemy unit involved in the battle was the 1st Regiment.

"Jesus Christ, that's the outfit we wiped out at Chu

Lai," said Coursey, the 1st platoon leader. He had
fought in the Battle of Chu Lai before being transferred
to One-One.

"Guess you forgot to wipe out their recruiting de-
partment," I said.

"Well, I hope we don't go in. I don't want any part
of it. One of those is enough."

"I'd like to get down there," said Captain Neal.
"You guys aren't very adventurous." Neal was writing
the name of his hometown on a piece of stationery. He
did that often, wrote the name of the Tennessee town
over and over on bits of paper, on C-ration boxes and
acetate map covers; wherever he could find something
to write on, he wrote the name of his hometown.

Hudson, the artillery officer attached to C Company,
rolled over and sat up on his cot. "Go right ahead,
skipper. You go right ahead down there if you think
it's an adventure. This damned war doesn't seem like
an adventure to me."

"I just don't want any part of it," Coursey repeated,
his face rucked by months of exposure. "I had just
about all the adventure I'll ever want at Chu Lai.
They're all inconclusive, these goddamned operations. We wiped out that regiment at Chu Lai, now
we're fighting 'em again and we'll probably wipe 'em
out again and then have to fight 'em again in a few
months. Bullshit."

"Well, I'd still like to get down there."

"So would I. I'm ready for the Cong. Me and my
boys are ready to rumble with Charlie." It was Mc-
Kenna, showing off a jungle hammock he had acquired
in a barter with the Special Forces detachment at
Danang. He was wearing his helmet and flak jacket
and had the rolled-up hammock strapped to his cartridge belt. "We'll wipe their ass. Can you dig it? Old
fuckin' Luke the Gook's gonna die." In a crouch, with
his carbine at port, he crept up and down the aisle between the cots like a stalking hunter. "Can you dig it?
With my brand-new, nylon, camouflaged super fuckin'
Special Forces jungle hammock, I'm ready for anything."

"The only thing you're ready for is the goddamned psycho ward," said Hudson.

"Oh, man, *man*. I'm cool and outfitted for the boonies. With this jungle hammock and my platoon of bad-asses, *I am the greatest jungle-fighter in the world*. Look at me, look, I'm the world's greatest jungle-fighter." He crept around grinning maniacally.

"You're the world's greatest asshole, Mac," Hudson said.

McKenna whirled and sprayed the artillery officer with imaginary bullets. "Ta-da. Ta-da. Tatatatata. You're zapped, you cannon-cockin' Texas shitkicker, zapped by the world's greatest jungle-fighter. I'm a killer, man, a fuckin' killer.

"Can you dig it? I'm a killer and I've got a platoon full of the baddest badasses in the Nam. We're bad, baaaad fuckin' killers." He turned to Neal, who was writing the name of the town in the margins of the letter paper. He had filled the rest of the sheet. "Look at me, skipper," McKenna said, creeping and grinning. "I'm the world's greatest jungle-fighter. You send us down there, me and my badasses. I'm invincible with my Special Forces hammock."

Without looking up from his scribbling, Neal said, "Take that silly thing off, Mister McKenna."

"But skipper, it's my jungle-fighter's hammock. It's got everything, waterproofing, mosquito netting . . ."

"I said to take it off."

"Yes, sir."

"And when you've got that done, go over to the comm bunker and check on the landline communications to Charley Hill."

Crestfallen, the world's greatest jungle-fighter said, "Yes, sir."

Operation Harvest Moon ended during the third week of December. Flights of helicopters, unrejoicing, came bringing in the sheaves to the division hospital. There were so many wounded, a corpsman told us, that the hospital would take only emergency cases. "They were putting the dead in cold-storage reefers," he said, "but they ran out of room, so now they're putting the bodies in ammo crates and stacking 'em four-high in a squad tent." Because the enemy had lost the equivalent of a battalion, all our generals agreed that the operation had been a great success.

My platoon received a Christmas present on the 23d: we were attached to Captain Miller's D Company, which was going to conduct a three-day operation to clear the Viet Cong out of Hoi-Vuc. That village, which had been cleared many times before, was still in enemy hands. The plan of attack was as dangerous as it was simple. My platoon was to create a diversion to cover D Company's movement on the village, which we would do by marching down the trail on the north bank of the river, drawing as much attention as possible. Meanwhile, D Company would advance on Hoi-Vuc from the south and hit the VC from the rear. The danger lay in the fact that my platoon would have to walk five miles down that elongated minefield called Purple Heart Trail. In all likelihood, we would hit at least one big mine or fall into an ambush, and because the platoon had been reduced to just slightly more than half its original strength, we could not afford to suffer even moderate casualties.

Nevertheless, we were all in a cheerful mood when we trudged off Charley Hill that morning. The weather had finally broken, and we welcomed the sun, whose heat we had cursed in the dry season. We also rejoiced in our temporary liberation from Captain Neal. Most of all, we were going to do something besides wait.

The platoon crossed the rice paddy south of the outpost, snaking along its dike in what looked like a tribal dance. The river lay just ahead, winding, yellow-brown, fringed by palm and bamboo jungle. We turned onto the trail, instinctively increasing our interval to ten paces. "Line of departure. Lock and load." The squad leaders passed the word back. "Lock and load." There was a ragged, metallic clicking as rifle bolts slammed shut. The marines walked slowly through the jungle's silent green twilight, some limping from the boils that covered the soles of their feet. We forded the narrow stream marking the frontier of Indian country. Allen, Lonehill, and Crowe jogged out ahead of the column, Crowe's head turning from side to side, its movements as mechanical as the sweeps of a radar antenna.

I tightened the shoulder straps of my pack, heavily loaded with signal flares, smoke grenades, dry socks, a poncho, and three days' rations. An entrenching tool and machete were lashed to its sides. In my pockets, I carried a map, compass, hand grenades, more flares, halizone tablets, malaria pills, and a spare magazine for my carbine. A pistol, two clips of ammunition, knife, first-aid kit, and two full canteens hung from my belt. My steel helmet and flak jacket added twenty pounds to the load. The gear probably weighed over forty pounds altogether, but I felt a wonderful, soaring lightness in my limbs. I felt good all over, better than I had felt in months. Even Neal, who was not inclined to hand out compliments, had praised my gung-ho enthusiasm before the platoon left base camp. A sudden and mysterious recovery from the virus of fear had caused the change in mood. I didn't know why. I only knew I had ceased to be afraid of dying. It was not a feeling of invincibility; indifference, rather. I had ceased to fear death because I had ceased to care about it. Certainly I had no illusions that my death, if it came, would be a sacrifice. It would merely be a death, and not a good one either. A good death involved a certain amount of choice, ritual, and style. There were no good deaths in the war.

But the manner of dying no longer mattered. I didn't care how death came so long as it came quickly and painlessly. I would die as casually as a beetle is crushed under a boot heel, and perhaps it was the recognition of my insectlike pettiness that had made me stop caring. I was a beetle. We were all beetles, scratching for survival in the wilderness. Those who had lost the struggle had not changed anything by dying. The deaths of Levy, Simpson, Sullivan, and the others had not made any difference. Thousands of people died each week in the war, and the sum of all their deaths did not make any difference. The war went on without them, and as it went on without them, so would it go on without me. My death would not alter a thing.

Walking down the trail, I could not remember having
felt an emotion more sublime or liberating than that
indifference toward my own death.

The platoon marched all morning and into the afternoon. Gently, almost imperceptibly, the trail climbed
toward the high country. The Song Tuy Loan had become narrower. Twigs and debris sailed on its surging
current. For a distance nearly as straight as a canal,
the river curved sharply, eddying where it curved, then
vanished into the scrub jungle ahead. A quarter-mile
short of our objective, Hoi-Vuc, we turned onto a track
that circled through dense jungle and rejoined the main
trail where the river made a horseshoe-bend around
the village. It took a long time to hack our way through
the bush. Crowe and I took turns with the machete.
Leeches dropped off the dripping leaves and fastened
on our necks. We splashed across another stream. Underbrush had dammed it into a series of stagnant
pools. But the jungle was not as dense on the other
side, and we had easy walking through a deep-shaded
bamboo forest. Strands of sunlight fell through the still,
delicate leaves of the bamboo. Allen's fire-team moved
out well ahead of the column. They were probably the
three best scouts in the business. Months in the bush
had changed them from fairly ordinary young men
into skilled manhunters; Allen, a gaunt midwesterner
who smiled, when he smiled, with all the humor of a
skull; Crowe, short and stocky, an expert with the
sawed-off twelve-gauge he carried; Lonehill, a full-
blooded Comanche from Oklahoma, a crack shot who
stood six feet two and looked at you with a stare that
made you choose your words carefully when you spoke
to him. They padded soundlessly down the muddy
track. We could hear only the slim, deadly kraits slithering in the brush, the bumping of distant shellfire
and the querulous rushing of the river ahead.

The rifleman in front of me dropped suddenly to
one knee, holding up his right hand to signal a halt.
He pointed to his collar (platoon leader up) then
joined the palm of his left hand to the fingertips of his
right, forming a T (enemy ahead). I relayed the signals to the marine behind me and moved up the trail

in a crouch. In the hush, my waterlogged boots seemed to make a great deal of noise. The woods ended in a small clearing. Coming out of the woods, I blinked in the hard, bright light of the clearing. Allen's fire-team was across it, squatting in a thicket at the river's edge. Crowe and Lonehill had their weapons aimed at something on the far side of the river, where the huts of the village showed as dun-colored patches through the trees and hedgerows. Allen was facing me, his face smudged by sweat-streaked camouflage paint and wreathed by the green sprigs stuck in the band of his mottled helmet-cover. He signaled me to get down and come forward. I did, crawling on my elbows and belly with the carbine cradled in my crooked arms. Crawling, I could see the river shining in the light of the late-afternoon sun, the hedgerows on the opposite bank, the gray walls and tile roof of a wrecked shrine several yards behind them, and, near the shrine, part of the figure of a man wearing a khaki uniform. Allen motioned for me to stop, and crawled out to meet me in the middle of the clearing. Crowe and Lonehill remained in the thicket. They crouched, as fixed as statues, Crowe with his shotgun poised, Lonehill sighting down the length of his automatic M-14.

"Lieutenant, there's three of 'em, three regulars standin' by that pagoda," Allen whispered hurriedly. "No more'n fifty yards away, standin' at sling arms. There's maybe ten, fifteen more around the bend in the river. They're takin' baths or somethin'. We could hear 'em talkin' and splashin' around. If you can get the platoon up, we can waste all of 'em. Fish in a barrel, sir."

"All right. You people hold your fire unless they spot you. I'll try to get the platoon on line, but it's going to take a long time to move quietly in that bush back there. Just make sure you hold your fire unless they spot you."

"Yes, sir." He started back.

Still on my belly, I turned around as slowly as I could, afraid the Viet Cong could hear the beating of my heart.

Chapter Sixteen

The worn white soldiers in Khaki dress,
Who tramped through the jungle and camped in
 the byre,
Who died in the swamp and were tombed in the
 mire.
                    —Rudyard Kipling
                    "The Ballad of Boh Da Thone"

Creeping through the stunted grass, I seemed to be
making as much racket as a man stumbling through
piles of dry leaves. Please don't let them hear me or
see me, I prayed silently. Please let everything go
right. Let me get them, all of them. Guilt washed over
me because I was asking God to help me kill. I felt
guilty, but I prayed anyway. Let me get them, all of
them. I want all of them. The edge of the clearing was
less than ten yards away, but it seemed I would never
get there. It kept receding, like a mirage. My heartbeat
sounded like a kettle-drum pounding in a tunnel. I
was certain the Viet Cong could hear it or the sound
of my breathing.

The rifle shot was deafening compared to the dead
silence that had preceded it. The bullet kicked up dust
a few yards from my face, and I whirled around on
my stomach like a crab. Crowe and Allen were down
and rolling over—the round had passed right between
them—rolling over to fire while Lonehill, on one knee,
sent a long, ecstatic burst into the hedgerows across
the river. One of the Viet Cong threw up his arms and
seemed to rise several inches off the ground before he
fell heavily on his back, his rifle twirling through the
air like a majorette's baton. It was as if an invisible
giant had picked him up, then slammed him to the
earth. I could not see the VC's body; one of his comrades must have pulled him into the underbrush as
I was getting to my feet. The third Viet Cong had

taken cover behind the shrine. I hadn't seen him, but instinct told me he was there. Lonehill was firing into the hedgerows, Crowe blasting away with his twelve-gauge, although the shot-pattern was too wide to be lethal at that range. I began running toward them, realized I still had to get the rest of the platoon, pivoted to run back into the woods, and went down when a line of bullets chewed the earth beside me. Staggering to my feet, I went down again as the VC behind the shrine fired a second time with his BAR or machine gun—I couldn't tell which. Lying in a shallow dip in the ground, I made love to the earth. The Viet Cong around the river bend had opened up, so that, on the peninsula of land formed by the horseshoe bend, the four of us were caught in a cross fire. I tried once more to make it to the edge of the clearing but was struck in the face by spraying dust as soon as I lifted my head to run. The experience of being under heavy fire is like suffocating; air suddenly becomes as lethal as a poison gas, its very molecules seem to be composed of pieces of lead flying at two thousand miles an hour. The bullets hissed and cracked over my head, and I yelled—no, screamed—"Allen! I'm pinned down. Pour it on 'em, goddamnit. Your right front, around the bend. POUR IT ON 'EM GODDAMNIT." The three marines managed to sound like a small army, with Crowe's shotgun roaring loudly. Then came the flat, dull blasts of 40-millimeters as Allen laid down a barrage with his grenade launcher.

An eerie sense of calm came over me. My mind was working with a speed and clarity I would have found remarkable if I had had the time to reflect upon it. I knew what I was going to do. The platoon could not assault across the deep, fast river, but it could pour a withering fire into the Viet Cong. If that did not kill all of them, it would at least kill some and drive the rest out of the village. But first, I had to bring up a machine gun to suppress the fire coming from around the river bend, and a rocket launcher to knock out the enemy automatic weapon in place behind the cement-walled shrine. That had to be done before the platoon could be deployed safely. They would bunch up in the small clearing and a lot of them would be hit if the enemy fire wasn't suppressed first. And it had to be done quickly, before the Viet Cong recovered from their surprise and started to fire more accurately. The whole plan of attack flashed through my mind in a matter of seconds. At the same time, my body was tensing itself to spring. Quite separate from my thoughts or will, it was concentrating itself to make a rush for the tree line. And that intense concentration of physical energy was born of fear. I could not remain in the hollow for longer than a few more seconds. After that, the Viet Cong would range in on me, a stationery target in an exposed position. I had to move, to face and overcome the danger. I understood then why a cornered animal is so dangerous; he is terrified and every instinct in him focuses on a single end: destroying the thing that frightens him.

Without a command from my conscious mind, I lunged into the woods and crashed down the trail, calling for a machine gun and a 3.5-inch rocket team. They came up, stumbling beneath their heavy weapons, and sprinted across the clearing to where Allen's men were still firing. The three-five's backblast made an ear-splitting crack an instant before its armor-piercing shell slammed into the shrine and bits of concrete and tile spiraled up out of the smoke. The machine gun sprayed the hedgerows, the casings of the long, slim 7.62-mm bullets clanging as they flew rapidly out of the gun's ejection port. Elated, I emptied my carbine into the hole the rocket launcher had made in the shrine's wall. Then a second three-five shell went off and there was no more firing from the enemy gun.

"First and third squads up!" I shouted, running back toward the woods. "First and third up, on line. Second watch our rear."

Led by big Sergeant Wehr, the platoon guide, the marines broke out of the jungle at a run. Wehr, who had just arrived in Vietnam, seemed a little bewildered by the invisible things crackling in the air.

"On line, I said! On line here. First on the left, third squad on the right. On line and start putting rapid fire into the ville."

Bent low beneath the enemy fire, the marines quickly shook themselves into a skirmish line, wheeling like skaters playing crack-the-whip, extending their front along one leg of the river bend. Then the line surged across the clearing, the men firing short, spasmodic bursts from the hip and the whole line going down when it reached the riverbank, going down and opening up with an unrestrained rapid fire. I could not hear any individual shots, just a loud, continuous tearing noise. The hedgerows fifty yards away shook as if struck by a violent wind, and a hut flew apart when it was hit by a three-five shell. Pieces of bamboo and thatch were tossed up by the blast and then tumbled down, the thatch flaming as it fell.

I scrambled along the line on my hands and knees, shouting myself hoarse to control the platoon's fire. The marines were in a frenzy, pouring volley after volley into the village, some yelling unintelligibly, some screaming obscenities. Allen ran up to me. His blue eyes looked crazed. He said he had seen some of the Viet Cong pulling out and one of them falling, hit by machine-gun fire. A bullet smacked into the earth between us and we went rolling over and came rolling back up again, me laughing hysterically, Allen looking even more crazed as he pumped 40-millimeters into the village. A few moments later, Miller called on the radio and confirmed that we had driven the VC out of Hoi-Vuc; a sniper in his company had seen a squad of them fleeing down a trail, and had killed two.

There was still some enemy fire coming at us, but it was ragged and badly aimed. I passed the word that the Viet Cong were on the run and that D Company had killed two more. The platoon became as excited as a predator that sees the back of its fleeing prey; a few marines slid down the bank and started shooting from the water's edge. I could feel the whole line wanting to charge across the river. The platoon was one thing, one being poised to spring and smash the life out of whatever stood in its way. I could feel it, and, feeling it, sent Lance Corporal Labiak's fireteam downstream to look for a ford. If we could get across the river, we could finish the job. I wanted to get across the river in the worst way. I wanted to level the village and kill the rest of the Viet Cong in close combat. I wanted us to tear their guts out with bayonets.

We took some sniper fire and silenced it with M-79 grenades. Labiak came back, soaked up to his chest. The river could not be crossed, he said. The bottom dropped off sharply and the current had almost swept him off his feet. Well, all right, there would be no pursuit, no final, climactic bayonet charge. Still, I felt a drunken elation. Not only did the sudden release from danger made me feel it, but the thrill of having seen the platoon perform perfectly under heavy fire and under my command. I had never experienced anything like it before. When the line wheeled and charged across the clearing, the enemy bullets whining past them, wheeled and charged almost with drill-field precision, an ache as profound as the ache of orgasm passed through me. And perhaps that is why some officers make careers of the infantry, why they endure the petty regulations, the discomforts and degradations, the dull years of peacetime duty in dreary posts: just to experience a single moment when a group of soldiers under your command and in the extreme stress of combat do exactly what you want them to do, as if they are extensions of yourself.

I could not come down from the high produced by the action. The fire-fight was over, except for a few desultory exchanges, but I did not want it to be over. So, when a sniper opened up from a tree line beyond the village, I did something slightly mad. Ordering the platoon to train their rifles on the tree line, I walked up and down the clearing, trying to draw the sniper's fire.

"When he opens up, every man put five rounds rapid into the tree line," I said, walking back and forth and feeling as invulnerable as an Indian wearing his ghost shirt.

Nothing happened.

I stopped walking and, facing the tree line, waved my arms. "C'mon, Charlie, hit me, you son of a bitch," I yelled at the top of my lungs. "HO CHI MINH

SUCKS. FUCK COMMUNISM. HIT ME, CHAR-
LIE."

Some of the marines started laughing, and when I
heard one of them mutter, "That stocky little fucker's
crazy," I started laughing too. I was crazy. I was soaring high, very high in a delirium of violence.

"C'mon and hit me, Charlie," I yelled again, firing
a burst into the tree line with my carbine. "YOU
SON OF A BITCH, TRY AND HIT ME. FUCK
UNCLE HO. HANOI BY CHRISTMAS."

I was John Wayne in *Sands of Iwo Jima*. I was
Aldo Ray in *Battle Cry*. No, I was a young, somewhat
immature officer flying on an overdose of adrenalin because I had just won a close-quarters fight without
suffering a single casualty.

The sniper declined my offer, and I gradually calmed
down. A call from Captain Miller brought me back to
the real world. The platoon had done a fine job, he
said. It was a diversionary force, and by God, it had
certainly provided the VC with plenty of diversion. He
ordered us to remain in position for the night. I did not
particularly like that idea; the enemy knew where we
were and would probably mortar us. On the other
hand, that's what we were supposed to do, divert the
enemy's attention away from Miller's company.

The platoon formed a perimeter and started to dig
in. Knowing we would probably be shelled, we dug
the holes deep, or as deeply as we could in the gummy,
resistant soil. When Jones and I finished, we stuck our
entrenching tools in the parapet and slid into the hole
for a cigarette. A cigarette had never tasted quite so
good. I was still elevated. Smoking, I cleaned my carbine, running the rag lovingly over the varnished
stock, the barrel, and the long, curved banana clip,
enjoying the feel and the sound of the bolt mechanism
as I worked it back and forth. I had not killed anyone with it, but I had caused a few deaths, and a
part of me had enjoyed that, too, enjoyed watching
the first Viet Cong die.

The reprieve from the monsoons ended that night.
Our foxholes were turned into miniature swimming

pools. Sniper fire cracked over us most of the night. Although it had only a slim chance of hitting its mark, it kept us on edge. Every fifteen or twenty minutes there was a *crack-crack-crack* and nothing visible but a swirling blackness and the white mists rising over the river. In the early hours before dawn, it stopped raining. With neither rain nor wind to keep them down, swarms of mosquitoes rose from the damp earth to feed on us. The leeches had a banquet too.

Lying in a half-sleep in six inches of water, I heard a shrill wailing and someone yelling "INNNCOMM-IIING!" and then a sound as of lightning striking a tree, a splitting sound. The earth shuddered.

"Jesus Christ, what was that?" asked Jones, next to me on radio watch.

"Whatever it was, it wasn't a sixty or an eighty-two. Get D Company. It might be our own stuff."

Reaching back over his shoulder, Jones unhooked the handset of the PRC-10 and intoned, "Delta Six, this is Charley Two, over . . . Delta Six, Delta Six, this is Charley Two. Charley Two, over . . . Delta Six, this is Charley Two, do you read me, over . . . This is Bound Charley Two calling Bound Delta Six, do you read me, Six, over . . ."

There was another high-pitched whistling, growing louder. The ground shook again as the shell smashed into the riverbank less than fifty yards away. A shower of earth, twigs, and hot shrapnel struck the river with a hiss.

"Delta Six, this is Charley Two," Jones said, lying with one arm over the back of his neck. "Do you read me Delta Six, over." He turned to me. I rolled onto my side and felt the cold shock of water pouring down my shirt and into the crotch of my trousers. "Sir, I can't reach D Company. The batteries must've gotten wet."

"Goddamn radios. Goddamn junk shit they send us. Well keep trying. If that's our own stuff, we can get them to cease firing."

"What if it ain't our own stuff?"

"Then maybe we'll get our asses blown away. Keep trying."

"Delta Six, Delta Six, this is Bound Charley Two calling Bound Delta Six, over."

A faint voice, broken by static, crackled in the receiver.

". . . two . . . position . . . over."

"Delta Six. You're breaking up. Say again."

"This is Delta Six . . . your position . . . over."

I grabbed the handset and gave our map coordinates, hoping the voice on the other end was not one of the VC, who sometimes monitored our radio traffic. "Listen, Delta Six, we have impacting rounds less than five-zero meters from this position. Could be Victor Charlie one-twenties or rockets. Interrogatory: is our own arty firing now? If our arty firing now, tell them to cease fire."

"Two, read you . . . say again all over . . ."

"Say again Delta Six." Another shell came in. "Delta Six, say again."

". . . say again all after impacting, Charley Two, over."

"I say again, impacting rounds . . ." A fourth shell crashed into the riverbank and I thought of Lance Corporal Smith's fire-team, who were on a listening post near there. "Delta Six, you probably could hear that last one. Could be Victor Charlie one-twenty mike-mike mortars. Interrogatory: is our own arty firing a mission near this position? Over."

"Reading you weak and garbled, Two. Say again all after mortars."

"Aw, Jesus fucking Christ. . . ." I started to repeat the message, then rolled over, burying my head in my hands, holding it up just far enough to keep my mouth out of the water. It had become academic as to whether the shells were our own or the enemy's. For the full concentration was coming in with a crazed howling and someone was again yelling "INNCOMMIIING!" The shells seemed to take forever to fall. For what seemed a long time, we heard the lunatic chorus wailing in the sky, our bodies braced for the coming shock, hearts constricted, all thoughts suspended.

Then the storm struck. The shells, impacting about twenty-five yards from the perimeter, exploded one right after another, creating one enormous blast that went on for five minutes. Shrapnel flew overhead with a sound like that of taut steel wires snapping. Jones and I, huddled beside each other like two frightened children, pressed ourselves against the earth. I tried to become part of the quaking earth and wished we had dug the foxhole deeper than three feet. I wanted God to shut that roaring out of my ears. Make it stop. Please God, *make it stop*. One shell struck very close. I could not tell exactly where. It seemed to explode just outside the platoon's small perimeter, and I thought we were going to be blown out of the hole, out and up into that lethal space where the shrapnel scythed the air. The ground slammed against my chest, bouncing me up an inch or so, and a part of me kept going up. I felt myself floating up out of myself, up to the tops of the trees. Hovering there, I felt an ineffable calm. I could see the flashing shells, but they no longer frightened me, because I was a spirit. I saw myself lying face down in the foxhole, my arms wrapped around the back of my neck. I felt no fear, just a great calm and a genial contempt for the puny creature cringing in the foxhole below me. I wondered if I was dying. Well, if I am, I thought, it is not so bad. Dying is actually pleasant. It is painless. Death is an end to pain. Rich the treasure, sweet the pleasure, sweet is pleasure after pain. Death is a pleasure. The Big D is the world's most powerful narcotic, the ultimate anesthetic.

Then the shelling stopped, and my spirit, reluctantly leaving the peace of its elevated plane, slipped back into my body. I was whole again. I was a whole man. The Jesuits at college had stressed that: the purpose of a Jesuit education is to create a whole man. And I was a whole man again in my foxhole; a whole in a hole.

I crawled out to the edge of the perimeter and called to Smith's fire-team.

"Yes, sir," Smith said in a whisper.

"You guys all right?"

"Outside of being cold, wet, miserable, hungry, and scared shitless, we're just fine, sir."

"No casualties?"

"No, sir. Because I'm black, the shells couldn't see me."

I laughed to myself, thinking, They're all right, the best you could ask for. They've been through a fire-fight and a shelling and they're making jokes about it.

The platoon survived the shelling. There was a brief period of total quiet, then the sniping started again. *Crack-crack-crack.* In the wet dawn, we brewed tins of C-ration coffee and shivered ourselves warm while Jones worked on the radio. I sat sipping the coffee on the parapet of the foxhole. Sergeant Pryor walked over and slumped down next to me, a sweat-yellowed cigarette hanging from his lips. He looked like the others, his sunken eyes rimmed with the blackness of fatigue, his face and hands lumpy masses of insect bites.

"Well, sir, I don't mind saying that yesterday and today were the longest day and night of my life. Especially last night. That was the longest night of my life."

"How long've you got to go?" I asked, as one convict to another.

"Seven, eight months. Seven, eight more months of this shit. I'm so goddamned tired. Is the radio working yet, sir?"

"No. We're still out of contact."

"Shit."

"Without that radio, we might as well be on the dark side of the moon."

Pryor laughed mirthlessly. "Might as well be?" He field-stripped his cigarette, scattering the paper and tobacco as an old man might scatter birdseed in a park. "Might as well be? Where do you think we are, lieutenant?"

After trying for half an hour, Jones reached D Company. Miller ordered the platoon to move northward to Hill 92, in the foothills, and set up a patrol base.

It took us six or seven hours to get there. The column wound through a labyrinth of draws and ravines, through the knee-deep muck of the marshes, and over narrow jungle tracks. We walked always in the rain and were constantly harassed by snipers. Halfway to the hill, the platoon was held up by a brush and log barricade the Viet Cong had thrown across the trail. The barricade was in a gully where the trail was hemmed by two steep hills, both covered with jungle so thick we could not have gone through it with a bulldozer. Unable to go around the barricade, we would have to blast through it with grenades. Walking up to it with Lance Corporal Crowe, I saw a strand of spider's silk glistening in the mass of brush and leaves. Only a few inches of it showed, and it was straight and taut and did not move in the wind blowing through the gully. Fear shot through me like a jet of liquefied gas.

"Crowe," I said, "move real careful around that barricade. It's booby-trapped. I can see part of the trip wire."

"Yes, sir."

I did some quick, basic arithmetic: the hand grenades would go off four to five seconds after we released the spoons. There was a culvert thirty, perhaps forty, feet behind us, where the trail started to curve around one of the hills. We would have to pull the pins, place the grenades where they would have the most effect, being careful not to put the slightest pressure on the trip wire, then run and take cover in the culvert. I spelled it out to Crowe and asked him if he thought we could make it.

"We'll have five seconds max."

"I think we can do it, sir. If we don't, they'll mail us home in envelopes."

Each of us took out a fragmentation grenade. Smooth-surfaced, egg-shaped, and about the size of pears, they did not look capable of blowing a man in half.

"Crowe, we're going to do it by the numbers. When I say pull the pin, we'll pull the pins, keep the spoons down, and then set the grenades down. You set yours under that log on the left. I'll put mine on the right. Don't touch a thing. Set it down real easy. Then you take off first, so we don't bump into each other. Got it?"

"Yes, sir."

I wiped the slick film of sweat off my palm and straightened the pin so it could be pulled quickly. (No, you do not pull grenade pins with your teeth, the way it's done in the movies. If you did, the only thing to come out would be your teeth.)

"Pull the pin."

We pulled them and, keeping the spoons depressed in the web of our hands, set the grenades down. I tried not to look at the thin, shining strand of spider's silk. Crowe took off running, with me behind him. We dove into the culvert, covering our heads with our hands. I counted: "Thousand-one, thousand-two, thousand-three . . ." Silence. ". . . Thousand-four, thousand-five, thousand-six."

"Son of a goddamned bitch, they're both duds. Nothing works, Crowe. Radios, grenades, nothing. Goddamnit."

"We'll have to do it over, sir." It was more a question than a statement.

"Yes, we will."

Walking back up the trail, my legs felt semiparalyzed, the way they feel in nightmares of pursuit and helpless flight. There was no guarantee that the grenades would not blow up in our faces. Perhaps they had defective, slow-burning fuses. My legs kept getting heavier and heavier, and then I felt the worst fear of all: the fear of fear. For I seemed very near the point of total paralysis, and that terrified me more than anything. *Hey, didja hear about Lieutenant Caputo? He froze out on that patrol. Dude just froze up because of a booby trap. Sheee-hit, fuckin' worthless officers.* I talked myself into covering the last twenty feet to the barricade, as a father might talk to a toddler taking its first steps. First the right foot. Now the left. Now the right again. That's it. Almost there, little fella.

"Pull the pin, Crowe."

We set the grenades down. The four of them looked like a nest of olive-green eggs.

"Okay, take off!"

We pounded down the trail and made swan dives

into the culvert. The grenades and the booby trap went off with a shattering boom. Debris sifted down on us. Crowe smiled victoriously.

The platoon reached Hill 92 in the midafternoon. The men were worn out by that time, their shoulders aching from the weight of rifles, packs, and flak jackets. They had been under one kind of fire or another for twenty-four hours and were dazed with fatigue. Rigging shelters against the drumming rain, they lay down to rest. Some did not bother to build shelters. They had ceased to care even for themselves. I walked around, checking their feet. A few had serious cases of immersion foot, their shriveled skin covered with red pustules and blisters. It amazed me that they could walk at all. We ate lunch. Our rations were the same as the Viet Cong's: cooked rice rolled into a ball and stuffed with raisins. The riceballs were easier to carry than the heavy C-ration tins and alleviated the diarrhea from which we all suffered. Eating the rice on that desolate hill, it occurred to me that we were becoming more and more like our enemy. We ate what they ate. We could now move through the jungle as stealthily as they. We endured common miseries. In fact, we had more in common with the Viet Cong than we did with that army of clerks and staff officers in the rear.

I was putting on dry socks when Captain Neal called on the radio. A Christmas cease-fire had gone into effect. The operation had been secured. My platoon was to return to friendly lines as quickly as possible. Why not lift us out with helicopters? I asked. No, Neal said, that was out of the question. I passed the word and the troops cheered. "Hey-hey. We're gonna get some slack. Merry fuckin' Christmas."

"No, no. I want to stay out here," said PFC Baum. "I just love it out here in the mud and the rain and the shit."

Shouldering our packs, we tramped down to Purple Heart Trail, the quickest route back. The trail forked near Dieu Phoung, a hamlet several hundred yards west of Charley Hill. The right fork led along the river, the left over the foothills toward the outpost. We took the latter because it was shorter and less likely to be mined or ambushed.

Outside the hamlet was a flooded rice paddy with a steep embankment at its far end. A barbed wire fence, anchored at one end to a dead tree, ran along the length of the embankment. The trail climbed through a hole in the fence near the tree. The lead squad, Sergeant Pryor's, Jones, and I crossed the rice paddy. The water was cold and chest-deep in places, and the rain dimpled the water in a way that reminded me of an evening rise on a trout stream. That was how the Ontonogan River looked in the evenings, in the place where it made a slow, wide bend around a wooded bluff upstream from the rocky, white-water narrows at the Burned Dam. There, the river had been deep and smooth where it curved, and the big trout rising made rings in the copper-colored water. Bill, my fishing buddy, and I used to cast for browns in the deep pool at sunset. We never caught many, but we had a fine time, casting and talking about the things we were going to do when we left school, about all that awaited us in the great outside world, which seemed so full of promise. We were boys and thought everything was possible. The memory sent a momentary pang through me: not so much a feeling of homesickness as one of separation—a distancing from the hopeful boy I had been, a longing to be like that again.

Pryor's squad climbed the embankment, the men slipping on the muddy trail, slipping and falling into each other until they were bunched in a knot. The rest of the platoon waded through the rice paddy behind us, holding their rifles in the air. A snake made a series of S's in the black water as it slithered between two men in the column. On dry ground again, Pryor's marines picked up their interval and hiked up the ridgeline that rose above the embankment. The Cordillera loomed in the distance, high and indomitable. The last two squads started to struggle up the bank, bunching up as one man after another slipped and slid into the man behind him.

Standing by the dead tree, I helped pull a few marines up the trail. "Pass it back not to bunch up," I said. To my left, a stream whispered through a brushy ravine. "Don't bunch up," a marine said. "Pass it back." On the other side of the paddy, the rear of the column was filing past a hut at the edge of the hamlet. Smoke started to roll from the hut and a woman ran out yelling.

"Bittner," I called to the platoon sergeant, who was bringing up the rear, "what the hell's going on?"

"Can't hear you, sir."

"The hut. Who the hell set fire to the hut?"

"Somebody said you passed the word to burn the hut, sir."

"What?"

"The word came back to burn the hut, sir."

"Jesus Christ. I said, 'Don't bunch up.' DON'T BUNCH UP. Put that fire out."

"Yes, sir."

I stood by the leafless tree, watching the marines douse the fire with helmets full of water. Fortunately, the thatch had been wet to begin with and did not burn quickly. Turning to walk back toward the point squad, I saw Allen stumbling on the trail.

"Allen, how're you doing?" I asked, extending my arm. Taking hold of it, he hauled himself over the lip of the embankment.

"Hackin' it, lieutenant. I'm hackin' it okay," Allen said, walking beside me. Ahead, I could see Pryor's squad trudging up the ridge and the point man briefly silhouetted on the ridgeline before he went down the other side. "But this here cease-fire's come along at the right time," Allen was saying. "Could use a little slack. This here cease-fire's the first slack . . ."

There was a roaring and a hot, hard slap of wind and a needle pricking my thigh and something clubbed me in the small of the back. I fell face down into the mud, my ears ringing. Lying on my belly, I heard an automatic carbine rattle for a few seconds, then someone calling "Corpsman! Corpsman!" Because of the ringing in my ears, the shots and voice sounded far away. "Corpsman! Corpsman!" Someone else yelled "Incoming!" I got to my hands and knees, wondering what fool had yelled "incoming." That had not been a shell, but a mine, a big mine. Who the hell had yelled "incoming"? You did, you idiot. It was your voice. Why did you say that? The fence. The barbed wire fence was the last thing you saw as you fell. You had fallen toward the fence, and it was like that time when you were six and walking in the woods with your friend Stanley. Stanley was nine, and he had been frightening you with stories about bears in the woods. Then you had heard a roaring, growling sound in the distance and, thinking it was a bear, you had run to the highway, tried to climb the barbed wire fence at the roadside, and caught your trousers on the barbs. Hanging there, you had cried, "Stanley, it's a bear! A bear, Stanley!" And Stan had come up laughing because the growling noise you had heard was a road-grader coming up the highway. It had not been a bear, but a machine. And this roaring had not been a shell, but a mine.

I stood, trying to clear my head. I was a little wobbly, but unmarked except for a sliver of shrapnel stuck in one of my trouser legs. I pulled it out. It was still hot, but it had not even broken my skin. Allen was next to me on all fours, mumbling, "What happened? I don't believe it. My God, oh my God." Some thirty to forty feet behind us, there was a patch of scorched, cratered earth, a drifting pall of smoke, and the dead tree, its trunk charred and cracked. Sergeant Wehr was lying near the crater. He rose to his feet, then fell when one leg collapsed beneath him. Wehr stood up again and the leg crumpled again, and, squatting on his good leg, holding the wounded one straight out in front of him, he spun around like a man doing a cossack dance, then fell onto his back, waving one arm back and forth across his chest. "Boom. Boom," he said, the arm flopping back and forth. "Mah fust patrol, an' boom."

Allen got to his feet, his eyes glassy and a dazed grin on his face. He staggered toward me. "What happened, sir?" he asked, toppling against me and sliding down my chest, his hands clutching at my shirt. Before I could get a grip on him, he fell again to all fours, then collapsed onto his stomach. "My God what hap-

pened?" he said. "I don't believe it. My head hurts."
Then I saw the blood oozing from the wound in the
back of his head and neck. "Dear God my head hurts.
Oh it hurts. I don't believe it."

Still slightly stunned, I had only a vague idea of
what had happened. A mine, yes. It must have been
an ambush-detonated mine. All of Pryor's squad had
passed by that spot before the mine exploded. I had
been standing on that very spot, near the tree, not ten
seconds before the blast. If it had been a booby trap
or a pressure mine, it would have gone off then. And
then the carbine fire. Yes, an electrically detonated
mine set off from ambush, a routine occurrence for the
rear-echelon boys who looked at the "overall picture,"
a personal cataclysm for those who experienced it.

Kneeling beside Allen, I reached behind for my
first-aid kit and went numb when I felt the big,
shredded hole in the back of my flak jacket. I pulled
out a couple of pieces of shrapnel. They were cylindri-
cal and about the size of double-0 buckshot. A Claymore, probably homemade, judging from the black
smoke. They had used black powder. The rotten-egg
stink of it was in the air. Well, that shrapnel would
have done a fine job on my spine if it had not been
for the flak jacket. *My spine*. Oh God—if I had
remained on that spot another ten seconds, they would
have been picking pieces of me out of the trees.
Chance. Pure chance. Allen, right beside me, had been
wounded in the head. I had not been hurt. Chance.
The one true god of modern war is blind chance.

Taking out a compress, I tried to staunch Allen's
bleeding. "My God, it hurts," he said. "My head
hurts."

"Listen, Allen. You'll be okay. I don't think it broke
any bones. You'll be all right." My hands reeked from
his blood. "You're going to get plenty of slack now.
Lotsa slack in division med. We'll have you evacked
in no time."

"My God it hurts. I don't believe it. It hurts."

"I know, Bill. It hurts. It's good that you can feel
it," I said, remembering the sharp sting of that tiny
sliver in my thigh. And it had done nothing more than

raise a bump the size of a beesting. Oh yes, I'll bet your wounds hurt, Lance Corporal Bill Allen.

My head had cleared, and the ringing in my ears quieted to a faint buzz. I told Pryor and Aiker to form their squads into a perimeter around the paddy field. Casualty parties started to carry the wounded out of the paddy and up to the level stretch of ground between the embankment and the base of the ridgeline. It was a small space, but it would have to do as a landing zone.

A rifleman and I picked up Sergeant Wehr, each of us taking one of the big man's arms. "Boom. Boom," he said, hobbling with his arms around our necks. "Mah fust patrol, lieutenant, an' boom, ah got hit. Gawd-damn." A corpsman cut Wehr's trouser leg open with a knife and started to dress his wounds. There was a lot of blood. Two marines dragged Sanchez up from the paddy. His face had been so peppered with shrapnel that I hardly recognized him. Except for his eyes. The fragments had somehow missed his eyes. He was unconscious and his eyes were half closed; two white slits in a mass of raspberry red. Sanchez looked as if he had been clawed by some invisible beast. The marines fanned him with their hands.

"He keeps going out, sir," said one of the riflemen. "If he don't get evacked pretty quick, we're afraid he'll go out for good."

"Okay, okay, as soon as we get the others up."

"Rodella, sir. Get Rodella up. Think he's got a sucking chest wound."

I slid down the embankment and splashed over to where the corpsman, Doc Kaiser, was working to save Corporal Rodella. There were gauze and compresses all over his chest and abdomen. One dressing, covering the hole the shrapnel had torn in one of his lungs, was soaked in blood. With each breath he took, pink bubbles of blood formed and burst around the hole. He made a wheezing sound. I tried talking to him, but he could not say anything because his windpipe would fill with blood. Rodella, who had been twice wounded before, was now in danger of drowning in his own blood. It was his eyes that troubled me most. They were the hurt, dumb eyes of a child who has been severely beaten and does not know why. It was his eyes and his silence and the foamy blood and the gurgling, wheezing sound in his chest that aroused in me a sorrow so deep and a rage so strong that I could not distinguish the one emotion from the other.

I helped the corpsman carry Rodella to the landing zone. His comrades were around him, but he was alone. We could see the look of separation in his eyes. He was alone in the world of the badly wounded, isolated by a pain none could share with him and by the terror of the darkness that was threatening to envelop him.

Then we got the last one, Corporal Greeley, a machine-gunner whose left arm was hanging by a few strands of muscle; all the rest was a scarlet mush. Greeley was conscious and angry. "Fuck it," he said over and over. "Fuck it. Fuck it. Fuck the cease-fire. Ain't no fuckin' cease-fire, but they can't kill me. Ain't no fuckin' booby trap gonna kill me." Carrying him, I felt my own anger, a very cold, very deep anger that had no specific object. It was just an icy, abiding fury; a hatred for everything in existence except those men. Yes, except those men of mine, any one of whom was better than all the men who had sent them to war.

I radioed for a medevac. The usual complications followed. How many wounded were there? Nine; four walking wounded, five needing evacuation. *Nine?* Nine casualties from a single mine? What kind of mine was it? Electrically detonated, black-powder, a homemade Claymore probably. But what happened? Goddamnit, I'll tell you later. Get me a medevac. I've got at least one, maybe two who'll be DOW if we don't get them out of here. How big was the mine? Four to five pounds of explosive, plenty of shrapnel. It was placed on an embankment and the platoon was down in a rice paddy below it. Most of the shrapnel went over their heads. Otherwise, I'd have several KIAs. Okay? Now get me those birds. "Boom. Boom," said Sergeant Wehr. "Mah fust patrol an' boom, ah get hit." Charley Two, I need the first letter of the last names and the serial numbers of the WIAs needing evac. Now? Yes, now. Rodella and Sanchez had lapsed into unconsciousness. The corpsmen and some marines were fanning them. Doc Kaiser looked at me pleadingly.

"Hang loose, doc," I said. "The birds'll be here, but the assholes in the puzzle-palace have to do their paperwork first. Bittner! Sergeant Bittner, get me the dog tags of the evacs, and hustle."

"Yes, sir," said Bittner, who was one of the walking wounded. A green battle dressing was wrapped around his forehead. One of the walking wounded. We were all walking wounded.

Bittner gave me the dog tags. I tore off the green masking tape that kept the tags from rattling and gave Captain Neal the required information. Then the radio broke down. Jones changed batteries and started giving long test-counts: "Ten-niner-eight-seven . . ." I heard Neal's voice again. Did I have any serious casualties? For Christ's sake, yes, why do you think I'm asking for a medevac?

"Charley Two," said Neal, "you must have not been supervising your men properly. They must have been awfully bunched up to take nine casualties from one mine."

"Charley Six," I said, my voice cracking with rage. "You get me those birds now. If one of these kids dies because of this petty bullshit I'm going to raise some-kinda hell. I want those birds."

There was a long pause. At last the word came: "Birds on the way."

The helicopters swooped in out of the somber sky, landing in the green smoke billowing from the smoke grenade I had thrown to mark the LZ. The crew chiefs pushed stretchers out of the hatches. We laid the casualties on the stretchers and lifted them into the Hueys, the rain falling on us all the time. The aircraft took off, and watching the wounded soaring out of that miserable patch of jungle, we almost envied them.

Just before the platoon resumed its march, someone found a length of electrical detonating cord lying in the grass near the village. The village would have been as likely an ambush site as any: the VC only had to press the detonator and then blend in with the civilians, if indeed there were any true civilians in the village. Or they could have hidden in one of the tunnels under the houses. All right, I thought, tit for tat. No cease-fire for us, none for you, either. I ordered both rocket launcher teams to fire white-phosphorus shells into the hamlet. They fired four altogether. The shells, flashing orange, burst into pure white clouds, the chunks of flaming phosphorus arcing over the trees. About half the village went up in flames. I could hear people yelling, and I saw several figures running through the white smoke. I did not feel a sense of vengeance, any more than I felt remorse or regret. I did not even feel angry. Listening to the shouts and watching the people running out of their burning homes, I did not feel anything at all.

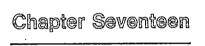

Chapter Seventeen

. . . for, as I am a soldier . . .
I will not leave the half-achieved Harfleur
Till in her ashes she lie buried.
The gates of mercy shall be all shut up,
And the fleshed soldier, rough and hard of
    heart,
In liberty of bloody hand shall range
With conscience wide as hell . . .
                              —Shakespeare
                                Henry V

Eleven days after the patrol, while Greeley, Rodella, and Sanchez lay recovering in the hospital—Greeley and Rodella waiting to be evacuated out of Vietnam, Sanchez to be returned to duty, as Wehr and Allen had been earlier, Wehr still limping when they discharged him with a slap on the back and a cheery bid to "go back out there and get 'em, tiger"—the battalion clustered nervously, waiting to be flown into an operation against a North Vietnamese regiment.

In the assembly area at C Company's base camp, men were sitting on their packs or standing in small, restless groups. A one-oh-five from the battery nearby fired a round, and the shell flew out with a diminishing hiss to burst against a far-off hill. Otherwise, it was quiet. Voices murmured in the black of the moonless night and cigarettes glowed, furtively inhaled behind cupped hands. McCloy and I, leaning against a jeep, could not see individual marines, only the dark mass of men and the round silhouettes of their helmets. On the road behind us, a convoy stood idle. Parked close together, with only their square outlines visible in the darkness, the big six-bys looked like a line of freight cars. Sometimes a flare went up in the distance, and we would see a few faces, drawn and worn with waiting, bulging packs with blanket rolls strapped to them, the olive-drab cabs of the trucks, the barrels of the howitzers pointing skyward, a rifle propped against a pack, its polished stock shining until the flare went out and plunged everything back into darkness.

This night, January 5, was our third night of waiting for Operation Long Lance to get under way. The battalion was to make a night helicopter assault at a point about twenty-five miles southwest of Danang. This was the Vu Gia Valley, named after the river that flowed through it. An NVA regiment, supported by a local battalion of Viet Cong, was supposed to be using it as a base for operations against Danang. At a briefing, the company officers had been told the attack would be the second night helicopter assault in history. Perhaps that was intended to inspire us, but the reason the assault had to be made at night was anything but inspirational: the North Vietnamese regiment reportedly had a battery of 37-mm anti-aircraft cannon—the same guns they were using against our jet fighter-bombers in the North. In daylight, helicopters would be defenseless against them. As one of my riflemen put it, "If they've got those thirty-sevens, we might just go down like ducks on opening day."

Preparations for Long Lance had been thorough, since a night assault is an extremely tricky maneuver. But we were going into an area where no American or South Vietnamese units had been before, and, as usual, intelligence could not say definitely how many enemy units were in the valley. Intelligence was not even sure if any were there at all. The NVA regiment might be there; then again, it might not. It might have flak guns, then again, it might not. That was one of the things that made the war such a nerve-jangling experience: the constant and total uncertainty. Whether we were going out on a squad patrol or into a battalion-sized attack, we never knew what we were going to run into. We were always tense with the feeling that anything could happen at any moment.

The officers had celebrated New Year's Day by attending a series of briefings. We spent the next two days briefing and rehearsing our men, checking and rechecking their equipment, then briefing and rehearsing them again, until every private knew exactly what he was supposed to do. Like the other two companies that were to make the attack, C Company was substantially understrength; but by making riflemen out of our clerks and cooks, by placing our light-duty cases back on full duty, and by refusing to allow anyone with anything less than terminal cancer from going on the sick list, we were able to muster about one hundred and forty effectives. That was a respectable number, though still seventy men short of a marine rifle company's usual combat strength.

The assault had been scheduled for the night of January 3. The men were up for it, on a keen edge. The last days of December had been grueling for Charley Company, a succession of patrols down Purple Heart Trail, with more casualties from mines and booby traps. We *were* making history: the first American soldiers to fight an enemy whose principal weapons were the mine and the booby trap. That kind of warfare has its own peculiar terrors. It turns an infantryman's world upside down. The foot soldier has a special feeling for the ground. He walks on it, fights on it, sleeps and eats on it; the ground shelters him under fire; he digs his home in it. But mines and booby traps transform that friendly, familiar earth into a thing of menace, a thing to be feared as much as

machine guns or mortar shells. The infantryman knows
that any moment the ground he is walking on can
erupt and kill him; kill him if he's lucky. If he's un-
lucky, he will be turned into a blind, deaf, emasculated,
legless shell. It was not warfare. It was murder. We
could not fight back against the Viet Cong mines or
take cover from them or anticipate when they would
go off. Walking down the trails, waiting for those things
to explode, we had begun to feel more like victims
than soldiers. So we were ready for a battle, a traditional, set-piece battle against regular soldiers like
ourselves.

But Long Lance was postponed on the 3d because
the *crachin* had socked in the landing zone. The next
day, we were again trucked to the airfield, made to
wait by the helicopters all night, and then driven back
to base camp to wait some more. Now, on the 5th, we
were still waiting for the weather to clear. We were
exhausted with waiting. Our edge had begun to dull.
We had begun to think. It was becoming more and
more difficult to maintain that suspension of imagination which makes waiting for an attack emotionally
bearable.

For a few, one way out was to feign illness. They
were uniformly unsuccessful. One marine broke down,
and it was not a pleasant thing to see. A veteran of
the Battle of Chu Lai and of countless patrol actions
since, he let out a cry, collapsed, and rolled in the
mud, sobbing that he could stand no more. The rest of
the company stood rigidly at attention, many near the
breaking point themselves. Then Sergeant Horne bulled
up to the marine, kicked him in the ribs, and pulled
him to his feet. "You yellow son of a bitch," Horne
bellowed. "You worthless yellow scumbag, you'll stand
it, you hear me?" Horne's face was scarlet and fierce
beneath its flaring moustache. He shook the marine
violently. "You're a fucking coward, but you're going and you'll take it. You'll take it as long as I do."
Holding the man by the front of the shirt, he shook
him like a rag doll. "YOU HEAR THAT, YOU
FUCKING COWARD? YOU'LL TAKE IT AS LONG
AS I DO." And none of us did a thing to stop Horne

because we felt the same terror. And we knew that that kind of fear was a contagion and the marine a carrier. So, shake the hell out of him, Sergeant Horne. Beat him, kick him, beat that virus out of him before it spreads.

The medicine worked. The marine recovered, his fear of battle overcome by a greater fear of the big, bull-chested Horne.

We heard Gunnery Sergeant Strong's voice: "Charley Company, fall in. Saddle up and get on the trucks. Let's go, hustle it up."

"Yeah, right, gunny," someone said. "Hurry up and wait."

"Knock off the chatter, girls, and get your asses on the trucks."

The dark mass of men moved with a creaking of canvas web gear and a rattling of rifle slings, flowing toward the convoy, their boots sloshing in the mud. The truck engines coughed to life, then swelled to a steady roar. McCloy put his arm around me as I shouldered my pack.

"Well, I think we'll be going in this time, P.J. 'Once more dear friends, into the breach!' "

I laughed. It seemed nothing could dampen Mc-Cloy's romantic spirit. The slender, straw-blond Kentuckian had a mechanism in his head, a shock-proof prism that turned the starkest realities of the war into the colorful stuff of romance. He never saw mangled, festering corpses, only heroes bravely fallen in battle. And now that we were going into a potentially disastrous attack, he saw himself as Prince Hal, going once more into the breach.

The convoy started to bump down the road, the wheels of the trucks spinning as they sought a purchase in the soft mud. We rode without lights, except when the drivers flashed the headlamps to avoid collisions. The six-bys plowed slowly through the muck, the drivers running through the gears and the noise of the engines rising from a deep roar to a high whine, then falling back to a roar, then up to a whine again. We passed through a village whose groves of sheltering trees made a vaultlike blackness over the road. The

drivers turned their lights on and off, on and off. In the
flickering beams we could see the misty rain that
chilled us. Men's faces, rifles, and the glistening leaves
of the trees at the roadside appeared for an instant,
then vanished. In the shadows, where we could not
see them, water buffalo bawled at the machines. The
convoy turned onto the road that curved around Hill
327 and ran toward the airfield. On the higher ground,
the road was drier, and the trucks picked up speed. A
shell flashed on the horizon. A few seconds later, we
heard the long, mournful echo of the explosion. Coming around a sharp bend, the drivers again flicked
their lights, and I saw the men in the truck ahead.
The marines sat braced against the wooden guardrails.
A few were sleeping, their limp bodies jostled by the
rocking motion of the truck. A machine-gunner
slouched behind his M-60 on the bed of the truck, the
gun resting on its bipods and the belt of cartridges
gleaming like a row of long, sharp teeth. Allen was
sitting by the tailgate, a rifle held vertically between
his knees. His face looked determined, angry and sad
at the same time. It was the expression of a veteran, a
man going to the place where he has been too many
times before. Then the lights went off and I could see
only outlines and the slim profiles of rifle barrels.
They were just a mass of faceless men again.

Charley Company reached the airfield sometime in
the very early morning. D Company and the battalion
headquarters group arrived as we were dismounting
from the trucks. There was a mystery and drama about
it: the rumbling trucks, voices commanding "Fall in,"
tailgates banging open, and large numbers of men,
half-visible as they formed ranks. The helicopters
squatted on the tarmac, their outstretched, drooping
rotor blades resembling the wings of gliding hawks.

C Company fell in, stood at attention for a few minutes, then was put at rest. We waited, were called to
attention again, and told to form helicopter teams. The
company shifted from its regular formation into eight-
man teams with the precision of a school band performing a movement at halftime. We waited again; then the
teams were marched to the helicopter loading points,

marched back to the assembly area, then back to the loading points again. It was the same routine we had gone through on the previous two nights. Neal ordered the company to lie down and rest in formation. Chilled by the rain, we rolled up in our ponchos and slept, or tried to. Looking at the helicopters, my imagination started to work. I saw black flak clouds in the sky, falling, flaming helicopters, bodies tumbling out of them into space. Well, you could not escape fear before an action. All you could do was to control it and keep your head clear. So, I thought about my platoon's mission, which was to secure the high ground at the southern edge of the landing zone and hold it until the rest of the battalion was in. Forcing myself to think of nothing but that, I felt calmer inside and fell asleep.

Dawn broke, the light of the rising sun seeping through the gray clouds like blood through a dirty battle dressing. Wet and bone-tired, we waited all morning. The weather began to clear. It grew very hot, but the sun was a balm to joints and muscles stiffened by the monsoon damp. Shortly after noon, the decision came down: we were to risk a daylight assault. The helicopter engines revved to a steady, pulsating roar, and with mixed feelings of relief and dread, we climbed on board.

The aircraft covered the twenty-five miles in a quarter of an hour. The valley lay below, a band of bright green rice paddies lying between two gloomy mountain ranges. I could see the Vu Gia River, light-brown in the sun, the ribbon of jungle growing along its banks, the roofs of villages showing through the jungle, a red road running past the villages, a couple of creased, barren hills in the surrounding rice fields, and the rib of muddy high ground, like a miniature ridgeline, which my platoon was to hold. The helicopters started to make a tight circling descent, and the mountains on the south side of the valley came into view, then the mountains on the north, flashing in the square frame of the open hatch like photographs on a screen. The force of the turn pressed us against the webbed jump seats. The flight leveled off. I searched the sky for the dark puffs of flak but saw none. There was a squeezing in my guts as the aircraft, dropping rapidly, went in for an assault landing. Coffell cupped his hands around his mouth and hollered, "Line of departure, lock and load." The marines loaded their rifles, but we could not hear the bolts locking over the engine noise and the buffeting wind. We had once again crossed that line between a world of relative stability and one that was wholly unstable; the world where anything could happen at any moment.

Sitting near the hatch and looking down at the up-rushing green, I heard the muffled popping of small-arms fire and saw a puff of smoke expanding at one end of the landing zone. Another puff appeared at the opposite end. From our altitude, the mortar shells looked like gray, blossoming flowers. The helicopter went on down, the small arms cracking and popping. There was no more mortar fire, but that was small comfort: the first two shells were probably registration rounds. The Viet Cong would wait until we were all in. The rifle fire continued, sounding like the old Rice Krispies commercials. Snap. Crackle. Pop. The aircraft was in level flight now, racing about a hundred feet over the ground. Some distance away, I saw two or three Viet Cong in black uniforms running for the cover of a tree line. Unbuckling their chin straps, the marines knelt in a row behind me. Tight-lipped, they waited for the lurch of the flare-up and the instant when they would lunge out of the hatch.

A helicopter assault on a hot landing zone creates emotional pressures far more intense than a conventional ground assault. It is the enclosed space, the noise, the speed, and, above all, the sense of total help-lessness. There is a certain excitement to it the first time, but after that it is one of the more unpleasant experiences offered by modern war. On the ground, an infantryman has some control over his destiny, or at least the illusion of it. In a helicopter under fire, he hasn't even the illusion. Confronted by the indifferent forces of gravity, ballistics, and machinery, he is himself pulled in several directions at once by a range of extreme, conflicting emotions. Claustrophobia plagues him in the small space: the sense of being trapped and

powerless in a machine is unbearable, and yet he has
to bear it. Bearing it, he begins to feel a blind fury toward the forces that have made him powerless, but he
has to control his fury until he is out of the helicopter
and on the ground again. He yearns to be on the
ground, but the desire is countered by the danger he
knows is there. Yet, he is also attracted by the danger,
for he knows he can overcome his fear only by facing
it. His blind rage then begins to focus on the men who
are the source of the danger—and of his fear. It concentrates inside him, and through some chemistry is
transformed into a fierce resolve to fight until the danger ceases to exist. But this resolve, which is sometimes
called courage, cannot be separated from the fear that
has aroused it. Its very measure is the measure of that
fear. It is, in fact, a powerful urge not to be afraid anymore, to rid himself of fear by eliminating the source
of it. This inner, emotional war produces a tension almost sexual in its intensity. It is too painful to endure
for long. All a soldier can think about is the moment
when he can escape his impotent confinement and release this tension. All other considerations, the rights
and wrongs of what he is doing, the chances for victory
or defeat in the battle, the battle's purpose or lack of it,
become so absurd as to be less than irrelevant. Nothing matters except the final, critical instant when he
leaps out into the violent catharsis he both seeks and
dreads.

The platoon, or most of it, lay against the slope of
the crescent-shaped ridge, firing into the tree line from
which the Viet Cong were shooting at the helicopters
landing the rest of the battalion. The tree line was
about two hundred yards in front of us, across some
rice paddies, the landing zone an equal distance behind. I could not remember how we had gotten to
where we were, only jumping out of the helicopter into
muddy water up to our waists, stumbling, heavy-legged
and clumsy, with bullets lashing the air over our heads;
then we had scrambled up the slippery ridge, wet and
cold from the waist down, hot and sweating from the
waist up. A few of my men had become disoriented in

the confusion of the landing. I could see them, bunched up as they awkwardly staggered down a dike at the edge of an irrigation canal. I yelled at them to spread out, but they could not hear me. Two mortar shells gestured in the field in front of us. Two more went off behind, bursting with that ugly, crumping sound. I climbed off the high ground and ran down the dike toward the stragglers. "Spread it out, people," I yelled. "Goddamnit, spread it out. C'mon, this way. Move move *move!*" I grabbed one bewildered rifleman by the collar and shoved him off the dike into the paddy. "This way, I said. C'mon, move. We've got incoming." Staggering like drunks, they followed me to the ridge. We climbed its reverse slope hand over hand, slipping in the sticky, drying mud. A dozen shells, crashing against the forward slope, sent up a spray of mud and singing steel splinters. We hit the deck hard. Smoke from the mortar shells rolled over the ridge, the air stinking of high-explosive. Several more rounds struck behind us. Jones, lying beside me, said, "They've got us bracketed, sir. We might just die on this fuckin' tit of a hill."

But we did not die, because the enemy did not have us bracketed. Instead, he walked the shells into the landing zone. The scene there was almost a battle portrait. The last helicopters were taking off, climbing nose down, banking sharply as they climbed, with the dark-green mountains in the background. Marines were fanning out across the rice paddies, some in extended skirmish lines, some in serried, staggered ranks, the mortar shells bursting among them. An enemy automatic rifle tack-tacked from a row of grassy mounds west of the landing zone. The bullets spurted in the light-green paddies, and one of our white-phosphorus shells flashed near a clump of palms atop one of the mounds, the orange-white streamers arcing over the graceful trees. A line of riflemen were breasting a flooded field, weapons held over their heads; they had just begun to climb onto a dike when they vanished in a cloud of shell smoke. One of the marines flew into the air, dropping sideways as he fell, the tiny stick that was his rifle sailing off in the opposite direction.

A heavy shell banged into the paddies between my platoon and the tree line. Behind us, a knot of marines were running in the crouched position men adopt under fire. Several were carrying radios, and the tall, waving antennae made an obvious target. As loudly as I could, I yelled at them to spread it out. They kept moving in a closely packed crowd, and one of my marines said, "That's battalion headquarters. Fuckin' pogues don't know enough to stay out of the rain." I hollered at them again, but they could not hear or simply ignored me. I was about to yell a third time, when they were all engulfed in smoke and clouds of pulverized earth, the shells going *crump-crump-crump* and bodies falling or flying out of the smoke. Faint with distance, the cry "Corpsman! corpsman!" drifted across the field. It was battalion headquarters, and it had almost been wiped out. The operations chief, a master sergeant with three wars behind him, lay in the muck with one of his legs blown off. The operations officer had been hit in the groin. The artillery officer had been badly wounded in the face and head. Altogether, HQ lost eight officers and a number of enlisted men. Only Colonel Hatch escaped serious injury. And the mortars kept coming in and the small arms crackling.

We heard a hollow cough, then another. Several seconds later, two 60-millimeters exploded nearby. "I heard 'em that time," a corporal said. "I heard 'em."

"Are they in the tree line? It sounded like the tree line to me."

"Good a place as any to put mortars, lieutenant, but I dunno."

I was drenched with sweat and my mouth felt as if it were full of steel wool. Battalion HQ had been nearly wiped out. D Company was suffering casualties, and ours was pinned down. My platoon was supposed to hold the ridge until ordered to do otherwise, but I felt compelled to take some sort of action. I called Neal on the radio and asked if the 4.2-inch mortar battery supporting the battalion could shell the tree line. I wasn't sure if the enemy mortars were in there

—the Viet Cong were maintaining their usual invisibility—but the four-deuces would at least suppress the VC rifle fire. Neal replied that our mortars were unable to fire, and, because we were far out of range of the artillery at Danang, he had decided to call in an air strike.

The planes came in several minutes later. Three Skyhawks, flying low, streaked over us. "Bound Charley Two," the flight leader said over the radio, "this is Playboy. Mark your positions with air panels, target with willy-peter." We set out the orange, iridescent panels and fired a white-phosphorus round into the tree line. The first of the squat, dull-gray planes banked around and knifed toward that column of white smoke, Viet Cong machine-gunners firing at it wildly. Two bombs tumbled end over end from its wings. The first was a dud, but the second exploded with a blast that made the earth lurch beneath us. The platoon cheered, but the enemy mortars continued to fall in the landing zone. The second Skyhawk made a pass, dropping two more bombs into the pillar of black smoke rising from where the first had struck. One of the two-hundred-and-fifty-pounders fell on the village behind the tree line. There was a tremendous eruption of smoke, dirt, roof tiles, chunks of concrete, burning thatch, and tree branches. "Playboy, Playboy," I said, "this is Bound Charley Two. You were over on that last one. Put it in the tree line."

"Roger," the pilot answered, and I felt a giddy sense of power. I was controlling those machines.

The third plane came in, skimming the treetops, engine screeching. Two napalm canisters spun down from the Skyhawk's bomb rack into the tree line, and the plane pulled into a barrel-rolling climb as the red-orange napalm bloomed like an enormous poppy.

"Beautiful! Beautiful!" I said excitedly. "They were right on 'em."

The napalm rolled and boiled up out of the trees, dirty smoke cresting the ball of flame. The enemy mortar fire stopped. Just then, three Viet Cong broke out of the tree line. They ran one behind another down a dike, making for the cover of another tree line

nearby. "Get 'em! Get those people.. Kill 'em!" I
yelled at my machine-gunners, firing my carbine at the
running, dark-uniformed figures two hundred yards
away. The gunners opened up, walking their fire toward the VC. The bullets made a line of spurts in the
rice paddy, then were splattering all around the first
enemy soldier, who fell to his knees. Letting out a war
whoop, I swung my carbine toward the second man
just as a stream of machine-gun tracers slammed into
him. I saw him crumple as the first Viet Cong, still on
his knees, toppled stiffly over the dike, behind which
the third man had taken cover. We could see only the
top of his back as he crawled behind the dike. What
happened next happened very quickly, but in memory
I see it happening with an agonizing slowness. It is a
ballet of death between a lone, naked man and a remorseless machine. We are ranging in on the enemy
soldier, but cease firing when one of the Skyhawks
comes in to strafe the tree line. The nose of the plane
is pointing down at a slight angle and there is an orange twinkling as it fires its mini-gun, an aerial cannon
that fires explosive 20-mm bullets so rapidly that it
sounds like a buzz saw. The rounds, smashing into the
tree line and the rice paddy at the incredible rate of
one hundred per second, raise a translucent curtain
of smoke and spraying water. Through this curtain, we
see the Viet Cong behind the dike sitting up with his
arms outstretched, in the pose of a man beseeching
God. He seems to be pleading for mercy from the
screaming mass of technology that is flying no more
than one hundred feet above him. But the plane
swoops down on him, fires its cannon once more, and
blasts him to shreds. As the plane climbs away, I look
at the dead men through my binoculars. All that remains of the third Viet Cong are a few scattered piles
of bloody rags.

After the fight in the landing zone, C and D Companies started to advance through the valley, driving
on the blocking position B Company had set up several
miles away. We slogged across the paddies beneath an
unforgiving sun. There was no enemy resistance, but

that did not last for long. In the midafternoon, Charley
Company was ordered to search Ha Na, one of the
large villages that fronted the Vu Gia River. It proved
a hellish task because the village was crisscrossed by
thorny hedgerows as cruel and unyielding as barbed
wire fences. We had to hack through them with machetes or blow holes in them with grenades, and when
we couldn't cut or blast our way through, we would
circle around them, only to run into more. The result
was the division of the company into small groups of
confused men who bumped into each other, cursing
each other as they cursed the thorns that slashed their
skin and tore their uniforms.

Sergeant Pryor's squad uncovered a large cache of
rice, medical supplies, and uniforms. It was stored in a
poorly camouflaged pit, the rice in tins, the medical
supplies in metal chests, the uniforms tied in bundles.
Altogether, the food and equipment amounted to a
ton. Calling Neal on the radio, I asked if we could get
a helicopter to haul it out. No, he said, there wasn't
time for that. The operation was running behind schedule. The company had to be at its first objective, Hill
52, by such and such a time. Get moving.

"Get moving," I said to Pryor, "we can't get a
chopper."

The sergeant, his trousers in tatters, turned to me
with rage on his sunburned face. "You mean leave this
stuff? No way I'm going to leave this stuff for Charlie,
sir. What the fuck'd they make us search this ville
for?"

"All right. Destroy it in place and then get your
people moving." I handed him two white-phosphorus
grenades.

He threw them into the cache, which began to burn.
So did a nearby house, as the chunks of bursting phosphorus landed on its thatch roof. Flames engulfed the
house in a matter of seconds, and the sparks from the
blaze flew into a neighboring hut, setting it afire. Four
women ran out, screaming. Above their cries, I heard
the team of engineers attached to the company yelling
"Fire in the hole!" They had found a complex of concrete bunkers at the edge of the village and were about

to blow it with TNT charges. Terrified, the women
threw themselves on the ground and covered their
ears as the charges went off. They screamed again
when a second charge shook the ground and brought
a cascade of dirt and powdered concrete down on their
heads.

Sniper fire started to lash at us from the cane fields
flanking the village, the crack of bullets almost indistinguishable from the sound made by the bursting
bamboo frames of the burning huts. Six or seven
houses were blazing now, and flames were licking at
the tops of the trees. Coursey's and McKenna's platoons pushed ahead. Mine went on with the search. A
corporal, his face blackened with soot, came up to me.
He was holding a Vietnamese man at gunpoint.

"We found this son of a bitch trying to get away,"
the corporal said. "What should we do with him?"

The man, who looked to be about forty, was dressed
in a khaki shirt and dark trousers. "Teach school. No
VC," he said.

"I'll bet you do. Tie him up and bring him to the
skipper," I said to the corporal. I did not like the look
in the marine's eyes and added: "Alive. You get him
to the skipper alive."

"Yes, sir," the corporal said. He pulled the man's
shirt down and tied his hands with the sleeves. The
schoolteacher, who turned out to be the political officer for the local Viet Cong battalion, was built like a
flyweight wrestler.

"No VC. Teach school," he repeated as the marine
led him away, both of them choking in the smoke.

The heat inside the village was terrific, a blast-
furnace heat that seared our lungs. Pryor shoved two
hysterical young women toward me.

"Lieutenant, let's take these two in. I felt their
hands. They're soft. Not a callus on 'em. They sure as
hell aren't peasant girls."

Before I could answer, the engineers again yelled
"Fire in the hole!" We ducked down. There was another jarring blast. The girls fell, screaming and rolling
in the dust. Pryor pulled them up, grabbing one in
each hand, and shook them roughly. "Stop that," he

said. "Stop that goddamned screaming." Then to me: "What should we do with 'em, lieutenant?"

"Let them go, for Chrissake."

"But sir . . ."

"I said to let them go, sergeant."

He pushed the two girls away. "Yes, *sir*," he sneered. "Yes, *sir*." I could feel myself losing control of him and the platoon. The marines were still overwrought from the earlier fighting, and with the heat, the hedgerows, the sniping, the wailing villagers, and the noise of the spreading fire they were on the verge of losing what little emotional balance they had left.

Machine-gun and rifle fire broke out up front. Bullets were smacking into the trees around us. I learned from Neal that Coursey's platoon had opened up on a squad of Viet Cong attempting to cross the river in a boat, and enemy riflemen on the opposite side of the river, covering their comrades in the boat, had opened up on the platoon.

Several minutes later, a fighter-bomber came in to strafe the Viet Cong positions on the far side of the Vu Gia. It dove down firing rockets and cannon. Maddened by the noise, several water buffalo broke out of their pen, stampeding through the village, red-eyed and bellowing, hooking with their curved horns. One of the infuriated beasts gored a marine in Coursey's platoon and was then cut down with an automatic rifle.

Half of Ha Na was in flames by this time, the flames leaping from house to house, the fire creating its own wind. Gagging, I ran through the smoke trying to reorganize the platoon. The hedgerows and the blaze had broken it up into bands of two or three men each. "Get your people together and move on Hill 52," I said whenever I found an NCO. "Get your people together." The marines stumbled half blind through the black clouds, trying to get away from the fire. Sergeants and corporals bawled "Get on line! Tie in on your right and left. Where's Smith's fire-team? Tie in on your right. Guide is right. Where's Baum? Baum! Where the fuck are you?" Sniper bullets whined in from the cane field.

Then D Company, three hundred yards away on our

left flank, met heavy resistance. We could hear it above the sniping and the exploding bamboo, a sound like that of a huge piece of canvas being torn in half. Heavy mortars started crashing somewhere in front of us. Neal called me on the radio: Miller's company had run into a nest of enemy machine guns and had lost thirteen men. They were now pinned down and shelling the Viet Cong positions with four-deuces. C Company *had* to get to Hill 52 quickly. Get your people moving. Yes, sir. Right away, sir. "SECOND PLATOON ON LINE! MOVE!" After shouting ourselves hoarse and filling our lungs with smoke, the NCOs and I managed to form something that resembled a line. It was still a mess. Some of McKenna's men were mixed in with mine, mine with his. The platoon drove toward the hill, pressed by the fire roaring behind them, pressed by the NCOs' constant cries of "stay on line, tie in your right, guide is right." The village was a long one, sprawling beside the riverbank for a quarter of a mile. There seemed to be a hedgerow every ten yards, or a pangee trap or a ditch with crisscrossed bamboo stakes in it. There was another tearing-canvas noise in the fields beyond the canebrake. Neal again called me on the radio: D Company had advanced on the machine guns behind the mortar barrage, but the four-deuces had had no effect on the heavily reinforced VC bunkers. Miller had lost seventeen men in the assault and fallen back to call in air strikes. My platoon was not moving fast enough. We were not keeping abreast of Coursey's men.

I handed the receiver back to Jones. Yelling at the men and kicking them, I pushed them forward. Jets came in to bomb and strafe the enemy machine-gun bunkers. The planes shrieked directly over our heads, deafening us. The two-hundred-and-fifty-pound bombs made the ground tremble, and the trees and houses shimmied in front of our eyes. More planes came over, strafing with their cannon, the cannon making that buzz-saw sound. Then the first flight, circling around, flew over again and dropped more bombs. Huge columns of brown smoke jetted upward, but the VC machine guns kept hammering. "Move it out, people," the squad leaders yelled, trying to make themselves heard above the noise. "Guide is right. Don't bunch up in the center." Behind us was the advancing wall of flame from the burning village. We smashed through another hedgerow, flushed a Viet Cong from a concrete building, captured him, and then blew up the building with a satchel charge. Lunging through the sulfur-stinking smoke of the blast, dust and bits of cement raining down on them, the marines leaped into a traversed trench line. I tried to reform them there, but it was enfiladed by a sniper in the cane field. *Crack-crack-crack*. The rounds narrowly missed us, and we clambered out of the trench to pour rifle fire into the field. A Viet Cong came running out of the yellow-green cane. At a range of nearly four hundred yards, Lonehill put a bullet at the man's feet, adjusted the elevation knob of his rifle, and coolly fired again, the enemy soldier falling hard. The planes came in for another bombing run. There was a great roar, and the forms of the men in front of me blurred for an instant, as if a filmy, wavering curtain had dropped between us. While the planes bombed, we clawed our way through hedgerows and smoke toward the hill whose serene, pale-green crest we could see rising from the trees ahead. We had advanced a few hundred yards, but the hill did not look any closer. The noise of the battle was constant and maddening, as maddening as the barbed hedges and the heat of the fire raging just behind us.

Then it happened. The platoon exploded. It was a collective emotional detonation of men who had been pushed to the extremity of endurance. I lost control of them and even of myself. Desperate to get to the hill, we rampaged through the rest of the village, whooping like savages, torching thatch huts, tossing grenades into the cement houses we could not burn. In our frenzy, we crashed through the hedgerows without feeling the stabs of the thorns. We did not feel anything. We were past feeling anything for ourselves, let alone for others. We shut our ears to the cries and pleas of the villagers. One elderly man ran up to me, and, grabbing me by

the front of my shirt, asked, "Tai Sao? Tai Sao?" Why?
Why?

"Get out of my goddamned way," I said, pulling his
hands off. I took hold of his shirt and flung him down
hard, feeling as if I were watching myself in a movie.
The man lay where he fell, crying, "Tai Sao? Tai
Sao?" I plunged on toward the foot of the hill, now
only a short distance away.

Most of the platoon had no idea of what they were
doing. One marine ran up to a hut, set it ablaze, ran
on, turned around, dashed through the flames and
rescued a civilian inside, then ran on to set fire to the
next hut. We passed through the village like a wind; by
the time we started up Hill 52, there was nothing left
of Ha Na but a long swath of smoldering ashes,
charred tree trunks, their leaves burned off, and heaps
of shattered concrete. Of all the ugly sights I saw in
Vietnam, that was one of the ugliest: the sudden dis-
integration of my platoon from a group of disciplined
soldiers into an incendiary mob.

The platoon snapped out of its madness almost immediately. Our heads cleared as soon as we escaped
from the village into the clear air at the top of the hill.
Miller's company, we learned, had overrun the enemy
machine guns after the air strikes, but had lost a lot of
men. C Company was ordered to remain on Hill 52
for the night. We started to dig in. The still-flaming
rubble of Ha Na lay behind us. In the opposite direction, smoke was rising from the place where D Company had fought its battle and from the tree line the
planes had bombed in the first hour of fighting.

It was quiet as we dug our foxholes, strangely quiet
after five hours of combat. My platoon was a platoon
again. The calm of the outer world was matched by
the calm we felt inside ourselves, a calm as deep as
our rage had been. There was a sweetness in that inner
quietude, but the feeling would not have been possible
if the village had not been destroyed. It was as though
the burning of Ha Na had arisen out of some emotional necessity. It had been a catharsis, a purging of
months of fear, frustration, and tension. We had relieved our own pain by inflicting it on others. But that

sense of relief was inextricably mingled with guilt and shame. Being men again, we again felt human emotions. We were ashamed of what we had done and yet wondered if we had really done it. The change in us, from disciplined soldiers to unrestrained savages and back to soldiers, had been so swift and profound as to lend a dreamlike quality to the last part of the battle. Despite the evidence to the contrary, some of us had a difficult time believing that we were the ones who had caused all that destruction.

Captain Neal had no difficulty believing it. He was rightfully furious at me, and warned that I would be summarily relieved of command if anything like it happened again. I did not need the warning. I felt sick enough about it all, sick of war, sick of what the war was doing to us, sick of myself. Looking at the embers below, at the skeletons of the houses, a guilt weighed down on me as heavily as the heaviest pack I had ever carried. It was not only the senseless obliteration of Ha Na that disturbed me, but the dark, destructive emotions I had felt throughout the battle, almost from the moment the enemy mortars started to fall: urges to destroy that seemed to rise from the fear of being destroyed myself. I had enjoyed the killing of the Viet Cong who had run out of the tree line. Strangest of all had been that sensation of watching myself in a movie. One part of me was doing something while the other part watched from a distance, shocked by the things it saw, yet powerless to stop them from happening.

I could analyze myself all I wanted, but the fact was we had needlessly destroyed the homes of perhaps two hundred people. All the analysis in the world would not make a new village rise from the ashes. It could not answer the question that kept repeating itself in my mind nor lighten the burden of my guilt. The usual arguments and rationalizations did not help, either. Yes, the village had obviously been under enemy control; it had been a VC supply dump as much as it had been a village. Yes, burning the cache was a legitimate act of war and the fire resulting from it had been accidental. Yes, the later deliberate destruction had been committed by men *in extremis;* war was a state of extremes, and men often did extreme things in it. But none of that conventional wisdom relieved my guilt or answered the question: "Tai Sao?" Why?

We passed a quiet night: it was noisier for D Company. Treating the many wounded, Miller's corpsmen had run out of morphine, and helicopters were unavailable to evacuate the casualties. So, the dead and wounded lay out there all night, the dead bloating, the wounded moaning because there was no morphine.

The Viet Cong made a feeble attack against the battalion's lines just before dawn, but were driven off with mortar fire. Later, helicopters flew in to evacuate the casualties and resupply us with rations and ammunition. Hovering over Hill 52 while the crew chiefs kicked the supplies out of the hatches, the aircraft drew a hail of automatic-weapons fire from the Viet Cong positions across the river. We answered with a few bursts from our machine guns, the short rounds geysering in the river that was bright gold in the early morning light.

The war went on.

Chapter Eighteen

Merry it was to laugh there—
Where death becomes absurd and life absurder.
For power was on us as we slashed bones bare
Not to feel sickness or remorse of murder.
                    —Wilfred Owen
                       "Apologia Pro Poemate Meo"

Filing up the trail that weaved through the stunted scrub jungle surrounding the outpost, the six men in the patrol walked on their bruised and rotted feet as if they were walking barefoot over broken glass. The patrol was waved in, and the marines climbed over the rusty perimeter wire one by one. The foothills where they had been all morning stretched behind them, toward the moss-green mountains wavering in the heat-shimmer.

The heat was suffocating, as it always was between monsoon storms. The air seemed about to explode. Sun-dazed, half the platoon were dozing beneath their hooches. Others cleaned their rifles, which would start to corrode in a few hours and have to be cleaned again. A few men squatted in a circle around a tin of cheese which had been brought to Charley Hill with the twice-weekly ration resupply. The cheese was a special treat: a change from the dreary diet of C rations, and it eased the diarrhea that gripped us. Squatting around the tin, the men ate with their fingers, grunting their approval.

"Hey, we got some cheese," one of them said to Crowe's patrol. "Good cheese. You guys want some cheese?"

Too tired to eat, the men in the patrol shook their heads and hobbled toward their foxholes. Their skin was pallid except for their faces and necks, their hands, and a V-shaped spot on their chests, which were tanned. One rifleman's bicep bore a tattoo: a skull and crossbones underscored by the words USMC —*Death before Dishonor*. I laughed to myself. With the way things had been going since Operation Long Lance, I was confident that the marine would not have to worry about facing the choice. Page and Navarro, killed a few days before, had faced no choice. The booby-trapped artillery shell had not given them any time to choose, or to take cover, or to do anything but die instantly. Both had had only four days left of their Vietnam tours, thus confirming the truth in the proverb, "You're never a short-timer until you're home."

I was sitting on the roof of the outpost's command bunker, sunning my legs. The corpsmen said that sun and air would help dry the running sores on feet and lower legs. The disease had been diagnosed as tropical impetigo. I had probably contracted it on our last patrol—three days in a monsoon rain that would have impressed Noah; three days of slogging through the slime of drowned swamps. The corpsmen had given me penicillin shots, but even antibiotics were not effective in that climate. Pus continued to ooze from the ulcers, so that whenever I took off my boots to change socks I had to hold my breath against the stench of my own rotting flesh. Well, I could have caught something a lot worse than a skin disease.

Holding a map in one hand, Crowe walked up to me to make his report. Crowe, called Pappy by the teen-age platoon because he had reached the advanced age of twenty-three—growing older than twenty-one was an achievement for most combat riflemen—had a face that made his nickname seem appropriate. The months of wincing at snipers' bullets, the sleepless nights, and the constant strain of looking for trip wires had aged him. Behind his glasses, Crowe's eyes were as dull as an old man's.

He said his patrol had picked up some intelligence information. Spreading the map over the bunker's sandbagged roof, he pointed to a village called "Giao-Tri (2)."

"You remember those three VCs we found in this ville two weeks ago, sir?"

I said that I did. He was referring to an earlier patrol and the three young men we had brought in for questioning. Since Giao-Tri was a village usually controlled by the Viet Cong, it was unusual to find young men there. The three youths, moreover, had been carrying papers that were obvious forgeries, and their ages had been falsified. McCloy, who by this time spoke fluent Vietnamese, and an ARVN militia sergeant gave them a perfunctory interrogation. They were released when the sergeant determined that their papers had been forged and their ages falsified so they could stay in school and out of the army. They were draft-dodgers, not Viet Cong.

"Well, sir," Crowe went on, "it looks like two of 'em are Charlies after all, the two older ones."

"How'd you find that out?"

"The younger one told me, Le Dung I think his name is. We found him in the ville again and I started to question him. You know, a little English, a little Vietnamese, a little sign language. He said the other two was VC, sappers who was makin' mines and booby traps. I think he's tellin' the truth because one of the other two walked by when we was talkin' and the kid shut up. He looked scared as hell and shut up. So, when the other dude's out of sight, I ask the kid, 'VC? Him VC?' And the kid nods his head and says 'VC.' The third guy is standin' over by a house, buildin' a gate or somethin'. I pointed at the guy and said, 'VC there?' The kid nods again and says that both the Charlies live in that house. Then I broke out my map and the kid said there were five Cong in Binh Thai, sappers too, and armed with automatic rifles. He drew me a picture of the weapons. Here." Crowe handed me a piece of paper with a crude drawing of a top-loading automatic rifle that resembled a British Bren. "Then he says there's a platoon—fifteen VC— in Hoi-Vuc and they've got a mortar and a machine gun."

Angry, I swung off the bunker. "Crowe, why in hell didn't you capture those two and bring 'em in?"

"Well, I don't know, sir. I mean, Mister McCloy cleared 'em. He said they was okay before."

"Goddamnit, we didn't know this before. Crowe, this company's lost thirty-five men in the last month. All of them to mines and booby traps, and you get a guy who shows you two sappers and you leave them there."

"Sorry, sir. It's just that they were cleared. Hell, we never know who's the guerrilla and who ain't around here."

"No shit. Listen, the info's good. You did all right. Shove off and take a break."

"Yes, sir."

I went down into the bunker, where Jones was cleaning his rifle. It was stifling inside, the air stale with the smells of sweat, rifle oil, and the canvas haversacks hanging from pegs driven into the mud walls. Cranking the handle of the field phone, I called company HQ with Crowe's report, dreading the lecture I would get from Captain Neal. *Why didn't he capture them? What's the matter with that platoon of yours, lieutenant? Aren't your people thinking?*

Having lost about thirty percent of his command in

the past month alone, Neal had become almost intolerable. I assumed battalion was putting a great deal of
pressure on him; since Operation Long Lance ended,
the company had killed only three guerrillas and captured two more, while suffering six times as many
casualties itself. C Company's kill ratio was below
standard. Bodies. Bodies. Bodies. Battalion wanted
bodies. Neal wanted bodies. He lectured his officers on
the importance of aggressiveness and made implied
threats when he thought we lacked that attribute.
"Your people aren't being aggressive enough," he told
me when one of my squads failed to pursue two VC
who had fired on them one night. I argued that the
squad leader had done the sensible thing: with only
eight men, at night, and a mile from friendly lines, he
had no idea if those two guerrillas were alone or the
point men for a whole battalion. Had he pursued, his
squad might have fallen into a trap. "Mister Caputo,
when we make contact with the enemy, we maintain it,
not break it," said Neal. "You had best get those people
of yours in shape." Meekly, so meekly that I despised
myself as much as I despised him, I said, "Yes, sir. I'll
get them in shape." A few days later, Neal told me
and the other officers that he was adopting a new policy: from now on, any marine in the company who
killed a confirmed Viet Cong would be given an extra
beer ration and the time to drink it. Because our men
were so exhausted, we knew the promise of time off
would be as great an inducement as the extra ration of
beer. So we went along with the captain's policy, without reflecting on its moral implications. That is the
level to which we had sunk from the lofty idealism of
a year before. We were going to kill people for a few
cans of beer and the time to drink them.

McCloy answered the phone. Neal was busy else-
where, so I was spared another chewing out. I read
Crowe's report to McCloy, who of course asked, "Why
didn't they bring them in?" I explained. Murph said he
would pass the information on to battalion S-2. Yes, I
thought, putting the receiver back in its canvas-covered
case, and they'll pass it on to regimental S-2, who'll
pass it on to division G-2, who'll bury it in a file cabi-

net, and the sappers will go on blowing up Charley Company. An immense weariness came over me. I was fed up with it, with the futile patrols and inconclusive operations, with the mines and the mud and the diseases. Only a month remained to my Vietnam tour, and my one hope was to leave on my own feet and not on a stretcher or in a box. Only a month. What was a month? In Vietnam, a month was an eternity. Page and Navarro had had only four days left. I was much haunted by their deaths.

Jones, leaning against a wall of the bunker, was still cleaning his rifle. There was a sheen of sweat on his face. His cleaning rod, drawn back and forth through the rifle bore, made a monotonous, scraping sound. I lay down on the poncho that was spread across the floor. Sleep. I had to get some sleep. Taking one of the haversacks off its peg, I propped it against my helmet to make a pillow and rolled onto my side, grimacing when my trousers, which had been glued to the pussy sores, pulled loose and tore away bits of flesh. To sleep, to sleep, perchance not to dream. I had again begun to have some very bad dreams.

The month that followed the attack in the Vu Gia valley had itself been a bad dream. I can recall only snatches of that time; fragmentary scenes flicker on my mental screen like excerpts from a film: There is a shot of the company marching near a tree line that was napalmed during the assault. Through my field glasses, I see pigs rooting around forms which resemble black logs, but which are charred corpses. *Click.* The next scene. A crazy, running fire-fight on the last day of the operation, the Viet Cong dashing down one side of a wide river, firing as they run, my platoon running down a dike on the other side, firing back. Bullets dance in the rice paddy between the river and the dike, then spurt toward Jones and me. As the rounds strike at our feet the two of us dive over backward into a heap of buffalo dung from which we leap up laughing insanely, the offal dripping from our faces. Then the company's mortar crew is dropping sixties on the enemy and my platoon pours rifle fire into the pall of shell smoke. An artillery observer, flying over in a spotter plane, calls on the radio to say that he sees seven enemy bodies lying on a trail near the river bank.

Click. The next scenes take place at the company's operation area near Danang. They are all of a piece, shots of patrols coming back diminished by two or three or half a dozen men. The soundtrack is monotonous: the thud of exploding mines, the quick rattle of small-arms fire, the thrashing of marines pursuing enemy ambush parties, almost never finding them, men crying "Corpsman!" and the *wap-wap-wap* noise of the medevac helicopters. *Click.* There is one piece of time-lapse footage, but instead of showing flowers blooming, it shows our company slowly dissolving. With each frame, the ranks get shorter and shorter, and the faces of the men are the faces of men who feel doomed, who are just waiting their turn to be blown up by a mine. *Click.* A shot of my platoon on a night patrol, slogging through a blackness so deep that each man must hold onto the handle of the entrenching tool on the back of the man in front of him. A driving rain whips us as we stumble blindly through the dark. Holding onto an E-tool handle with one hand, I am holding a compass in the other. I cannot see the marine who is an arm's length in front of me, only the pale, luminous dial of the compass. *Click.* There is a scene of PFC Arnett, who has been hit by a mine. He is lying on his back in the rain, wrapped in scarlet ribbons of his own blood. He looks up at me with the dreamy, far-off expression of a saint in a Renaissance painting and says, "This is my third Purple Heart and they ain't gettin' no more chances. I'm goin' home."

Other episodes reflect what the war has done to us. A corporal is chasing a wounded Viet Cong after a fire-fight. He follows the man's blood trail until he finds him crawling toward the entrance to a tunnel. The enemy soldier turns his face toward his pursuer, perhaps to surrender, perhaps to beg for mercy. The corporal walks up to him and casually shoots him in the head. *Click.* Sergeant Horne is standing in front of me with a nervous smile on his face. He says, "Sir,

Mister McKenna's gone crazy." I ask how he has arrived at this diagnosis. "We were set in in a daylight ambush near Hoi-Vuc," Horne says. "An old woman came by and spotted us, so we held her so she wouldn't warn the VC that we were around. She was chewing betel-nut and just by accident spit some of it in Mister McKenna's face. The next thing I knew, he took out his pistol and shot her in the chest. Then he told one of the corpsmen to patch her up, like he didn't realize that he'd killed her." There is a quick-cut to the officer's tent that night. In the soft light of a kerosene lamp, McKenna and I are talking about the murder. He says, "Phil, the gun just went off by itself. You know, it really bothers me." I reply that it should. "No, that isn't what I mean," McKenna says. "I mean the thing that bothers me about killing her is that it doesn't bother me."

I slept briefly and fitfully in the bunker and woke up agitated. Psychologically, I had never felt worse. I had been awake for no more than a few seconds when I was seized by the same feeling that had gripped me after my nightmare about the mutilated men in my old platoon: a feeling of being afraid when there was no reason to be. And this unreasoning fear quickly produced the sensation I had often had in action: of watching myself in a movie. Although I have had a decade to think about it, I am still unable to explain why I woke up in that condition. I had not dreamed. It was a quiet day, one of those days when it was difficult to believe a war was on. Yet, my sensations were those of a man actually under fire. Perhaps I was suffering a delayed reaction to some previous experience. Perhaps it was simply battle fatigue. I had been in Vietnam for nearly a year, and was probably more worn-out than I realized at the time. Months of accumulated pressures might have chosen just that moment to burst, suddenly and for no apparent reason. Whatever the cause, I was outwardly normal, if a little edgier than usual; but inside, I was full of turbulent emotions and disordered thoughts, and I could not shake that weird sensation of being split in two.

Thinking fresh air might help, I climbed out of the musty bunker. I only felt worse, irritated by the pain that came each time my trousers tore loose from the ulcers. The sores itched unbearably, but I couldn't scratch them because scratching would spread the disease. The late-afternoon air was oppressive. Heat came up from the baked earth and pressed down from the sky. Clouds were beginning to build in gray towers over the mountains, threatening more rain. Rain. Rain. Rain. When would it stop raining? From the heads rose the stench of feces, the soupy deposits of our diseased bowels. My need for physical activity overcame my discomfort and I set out to walk the perimeter. Around and around I walked, sometimes chatting with the men, sometimes sitting and staring into the distance. A few yards outside the perimeter, the walls of a half-ruined building shone bright white in the sun's glare. It made me squint to look at them, but I did anyway. I looked at them for a long time. I don't know why. I just remember staring at them, feeling the heat grow more oppressive as the clouds piled up and advanced across the sky. The building had been a temple of some kind, but it was now little more than a pile of stones. Vines were growing over the stones and over the jagged, bullet-scarred walls, which turned from white to hot-pink as the sun dropped into the clouds. Behind the building lay the scrub jungle that covered the slopes of the hill. It smelled of decaying wood and leaves, and the low trees encircled the outpost like the disorderly ranks of a besieging army. Staring at the jungle and at the ruined temple, hatred welled up in me; a hatred for this green, moldy, alien world in which we fought and died.

My thoughts and feelings over the next few hours are irretrievably jumbled now, but at some point in the early evening, I was seized by an irresistible compulsion to do something. "Something's got to be done" was about the clearest thought that passed through my brain. I was fixated on the company's intolerable predicament. We could now muster only half of our original strength, and half of our effectives had been wounded at least once. If we suffered as many casual-

ties in the next month as we had in the one past, we
would be down to fifty or sixty men, little more than a
reinforced platoon. It was madness for us to go on
walking down those trails and tripping booby traps
without any chance to retaliate. *Retaliate.* The word
rang in my head. *I will retaliate.* It was then that my
chaotic thoughts began to focus on the two men whom
Le Dung, Crowe's informant, had identified as Viet
Cong. My mind did more than focus on them; it fixed
on them like a heat-seeking missile fixing on the tail-
pipe of a jet. They became an obsession. I would get
them. I would get them before they got any more of
us; before they got me. I'm going to get those bastards,
I said to myself, suddenly feeling giddy.

"I'm going to get those bastards," I said aloud, rushing down into the bunker. Jones looked at me quizzi-
cally. "The VC, Jones, I'm going to get them." I was
laughing. From my map case, I took out an overlay of
the patrol route which 2d squad was to follow that
night. It took them to a trail junction just outside the
village of Giao-Tri. It was perfect. If the two VC
walked out of the village, they would fall into the ambush. I almost laughed out loud at the idea of their
deaths. If the VC did not leave the village, then the
squad would infiltrate into it, Crowe guiding them to
the house Le Dung had pointed out, and capture them
—"snatch," in the argot. Yes, that's what I would do.
A snatch patrol. The squad would capture the two
VC and bring them to the outpost. I would interrogate
them, beat the hell out of them if I had to, learn the
locations of other enemy cells and units, then kill or
capture those. I would get all of them. But suppose
the two guerrillas resisted? The patrol would kill them,
then. Kill VC. That's what we were supposed to do.
Bodies. Neal wanted bodies. Well, I would give him
bodies, and then my platoon would be rewarded instead of reproved. I did not have the authority to send
the squad into the village. The patrol order called only
for an ambush at the trail junction. But who was the
real authority out on that isolated outpost? *I* was. I
would take matters into my own hands. Out there, I
could do what I damned well pleased. And I would.

The idea of taking independent action made me giddier still. I went out to brief the patrol.

In the twilight, Allen, Crowe, Lonehill, and two other riflemen huddled around me. Wearing bush hats, their hands and faces blackened with shoe polish, they looked appropriately ferocious. I told them what they were to do, but, in my addled state of mind, I was almost incoherent at times. I laughed frequently and made several bloodthirsty jokes that probably left them with the impression I wouldn't mind if they summarily executed both Viet Cong. All the time, I had that feeling of watching myself in a film. I could hear myself laughing, but it did not sound like my laugh.

"Okay, you know what to do," I said to Allen, the patrol leader. "You set in ambush for a while. If nobody comes by, you go into the ville and you get them. *You get those goddamned VC.* Snatch 'em up and bring 'em back here, but if they give you any problems, kill 'em."

"Sir, since we ain't supposed to be in the ville, what do we say if we have to kill 'em?"

"We'll just say they walked into your ambush. Don't sweat that. All the higher-ups want is bodies."

"Yes, sir," Allen said, and I saw the look in his eyes. It was a look of distilled hatred and anger, and when he grinned his skull-like grin, I knew he was going to kill those men on the slightest pretext. And, knowing that, I still did not repeat my order that the VC were to be captured if at all possible. It was my secret and savage desire that the two men die. In my heart, I hoped Allen would find some excuse for killing them, and Allen had read my heart. He smiled and I smiled back, and we both knew in that moment what was going to happen. There was a silent communication between us, an unspoken understanding: blood was to be shed. There is no mystery about such unspoken communication. Two men who have shared the hardships and dangers of war come to know each other as intimately as two natural brothers who have lived together for years; one can read the other's heart without a word being said.

The patrol left, creeping off the outpost into the swallowing darkness. Not long afterward, I began to be teased by doubts. It was the other half of my double self, the calm and lucid half, warning that something awful was going to happen. The thought of recalling the patrol crossed my mind, but I could not bring myself to do it. I felt driven, in the grip of an inexorable power. Something had to be done.

And something was done. Allen called on the radio and said they had killed one of the Viet Cong and captured the other. They were coming in with the prisoner. Letting out a whoop, I called Neal on the field phone. He said he had monitored Allen's radio transmission. He congratulated us:

"That's good work your men did out there."

I was elated. Climbing out of the bunker, I excitedly told Coffell "They got both of 'em! Both of 'em! Yeeeah-hoo!" The night was hot and still. Off to the west, heat-lightning flashed like shellfire in the clouds that obscured the sky above the mountains. It was clear directly overhead, and I could see the fixed and lofty stars.

Waiting by the perimeter for the patrol to return, I heard a burst of rifle fire and the distinctive roar of Crowe's shotgun. Allen called on the radio again: the prisoner had whipped a branch in Crowe's face and tried to escape. They had killed him.

"All right, bring the body in. I want to search it," I said.

They came in shortly. The five men were winded from their swift withdrawal and a little more excited than such veterans should have been. Allen was particularly overwrought. He started laughing as soon as he was inside the perimeter wire. Perhaps it was the release from tension that made him laugh like that, tinny, mirthlessly. When he calmed down, he told me what had happened:

"We sneaked into the ville, like you told us, sir. Crowe guided us to the house where he'd talked to the informant. It was empty, so we went to the hooch where the VC lived. Me, Crowe, and Lonehill went inside. The other two stayed on the trail to guard our rear. It was dark in the house, so Crowe turned on his flashlight and there's the two Cong, sleepin' in their beds. Lonehill goes into the other room and this girl in there starts screamin'. 'Shut her up,' I said and Lonehill cracks her with his rifle barrel." Allen started to laugh again. So did Crowe and a few of the men who were listening. I was laughing, too. How funny. Old Lonehill hit her with his rifle. "So about then, one of the Cong jumps up in his bed and the broad starts screamin' again. Crowe went in and slapped her and told her to keep her damned mouth shut. Then he comes back into the room and pops the Cong sittin' up with his forty-five. The dude jumps up and runs— he was hit in the shoulder—and Crowe runs after him. He was runnin' around outside yellin' 'Troi Oi! Troi Oi!'" (Oh God) "and then Crowe greased him and he didn't do no more yellin'. The other dude made a break for the door, but Lonehill grabbed him. 'Okay, let's take him back,' I said, and we moved the hell out. We was right at the base of the hill when the gook whipped the branch in Crowe's face. Somebody said, 'He's makin' a break, grease the motherfucker,' and Lonehill greased him and Crowe blasted him with the shotgun. I mean, that dude was *dead*." Madly and hysterically, we all laughed again.

"Okay," I said, "where's the body?"

"Right outside the wire, sir."

The dead man was lying on his belly. The back of his head was blown out, and, in the beam of my flashlight, his brains were a shiny gray mass. Someone kicked the body over onto its back and said, "Oh, excuse me, Mr. Charles, I hope that didn't hurt," and we all doubled over with laughter. I beamed the flashlight on the corpse's face. His eyes were wide and glowing, like the eyes in a stuffed head. While Coffell held the flashlight, I searched the body. There was something about the dead man that troubled me. It was not the mutilation—I was used to that. It was his face. It was such a young face, and, while I searched him, I kept thinking, He's just a boy, just a boy. I could not understand why his youth bothered me; the VC's soldiers, like our own, were all young men.

Tearing off his bloodstained shirt, shredded, like his chest, by shotgun pellets, I looked for his papers. Someone quipped, "Hey, lieutenant, he'll catch cold." Everyone laughed again. I joined in, but I was not laughing as hard as before.

There were no documents in the boy's pockets, no cartridge belt around his waist. There was nothing that would have proved him to be a Viet Cong. That troubled me further. I stood up and, taking the flashlight from Coffell, held it on the boy's dead face.

"Did you find anything on the other one?" I asked Allen.

"No, sir."

"No documents or weapons?"

"No, sir. Nothing."

"How about the house? Did you find anything that looked like booby-trap gear in the house?"

"No, sir."

"And no forged papers or anything like that?"

"No, sir. We didn't find nothing."

The laughter had stopped. I turned to Crowe.

"Are you *sure* this was one of the two that kid pointed out?"

"Yes, sir," Crowe said, but he looked away from me.

"Tell me again why you shot him."

"Whipped a branch in my face, like Allen said." Crowe would not look at me. He looked at the ground. "He whipped a branch in my face and tried to make a break, so we wasted him."

The air seemed charged with guilt. I kept looking at the corpse, and a wave of horror rolled through me as I recognized the face. The sensation was like snapping out of a hypnotic trance. It was as jarring as suddenly awakening from a nightmare, except that I had awakened from one nightmare into another.

"Allen, is that how it happened?" I asked. "The prisoner tried to escape, right?"

"As far as I know, yes sir. Crowe shot him."

He was already covering himself. "Okay, if anyone asks you about this, you just say both these guys walked into your ambush. That's what you'll say,

and you stick to that, all of you. They walked into
your ambush and you killed one and captured the
other. Then the prisoner tried to escape, so you killed
him, too. Got that? You don't tell anybody that you
snatched him out of the village."

"Yes, sir," Allen said.

"Shove off and pass that on to the others. You too,
Crowe."

"Yes, sir," Crowe said, hanging his head like a
naughty child.

They walked off. I stayed for a while, looking at the
corpse. The wide, glowing, glassy eyes stared at me
in accusation. The dead boy's open mouth screamed
silently his innocence and our guilt. In the darkness
and confusion, out of fear, exhaustion, and the brutal
instincts acquired in the war, the marines had made a
mistake. An awful mistake. They had killed the wrong
man. No, not they; *we*. *We* had killed the wrong man.
That boy's innocent blood was on my hands as much
as it was on theirs. I had sent them out there. My
God, what have we done? I thought. I could think of
nothing else. My God, what have we done. Please
God, forgive us. What have we done?

Clicking off the flashlight, I told Coffell to get a
burial party together. I did not know what else to do
with the body of Crowe's informant, the boy named
Le Dung.

The typewriters in the quonset hut began to click
promptly at eight o'clock, when the legal clerks came
in to begin another routine day of typing up routine
reports. The red light on the electric coffee pot glowed
and the electric fans on the clerks' desks stirred the
warm, dense air. Having slept undisturbed for eight
hours, as they did every night, and breakfasted on ba-
con and eggs, as they did every morning except when
the division HQ mess served pancakes, the clerks were
happy, healthy-looking boys. They appeared slightly
bored by their dull work, but were content in the
knowledge that their rear-echelon jobs gave them what
their contemporaries in the line companies lacked: a
future.

Sitting in one corner of the hut with my defense counsel, Lieutenant Jim Rader, I looked at the clerks and wished I were one of them. How pleasant it would be to have a future again. A crowd of witnesses milled around outside: marines and Vietnamese villagers, the latter looking utterly bewildered by the courtroom drama in which they would soon play their assigned roles. One of the clerks muttered a curse as a fan blew some papers off his desk. The artificial gust blew against the wall behind him, rustling the pages of his short-timer's calendar. The calendar was graced by a pornographic drawing, beneath which the word *June* was flanked by the numbers *1966*. All the dates had been crossed off except today's, the 30th, the day on which Lance Corporal Crowe was to be tried on two counts of premeditated murder.

I was to appear as a witness for the prosecution. There was an absurdity in that, as I was to be tried on the same charges by the same prosecutor the following morning. But then, the fact that we had been charged in the first place was absurd. They had taught us to kill and had told us to kill, and now they were going to court-martial us for killing.

A bound sheaf of papers as thick as a small-town phone book and entitled "Investigating Officer's Report" sat on Rader's desk. It was the product of five months' labor on the part of various military lawyers, and the two top forms—DD457 and DD458— contained the charges against me: ". . . in that First Lieutenant Philip J. Caputo . . . did murder with premeditation Le Dung, a citizen of the Republic of Vietnam. In that First Lieutenant Philip J. Caputo . . . did murder with premeditation Le Du . . ." There was a third charge, resulting from my panicked attempt to deny that I had tried to cover up the killings: "In that First Lieutenant Philip J. Caputo . . . did subscribe under lawful oath a false statement in substance as follows: 'I did not tell them to stick by their statements,' which statements he did not then believe to be true."

There was a lot of other stuff—statements by witnesses, inquiry reports, and so forth—but one square on form DD457 was conspicuously blank. It was the square labeled EXPLANATORY OR EXTENUATING CIRCUMSTANCES ARE SUBMITTED HEREWITH. Early in the investigation, I wondered why the investigating officer had not submitted any explanatory or extenuating circumstances. Later, after I had time to think things over, I drew my own conclusion: the explanatory or extenuating circumstance was the war. The killings had occurred in war. They had occurred, moreover, in a war whose sole aim was to kill Viet Cong, a war in which those ordered to do the killing often could not distinguish the Viet Cong from the civilians, a war in which civilians in "free-fire zones" were killed every day by weapons far more horrible than pistols or shotguns. The deaths of Le Dung and Le Du could not be divorced from the nature and conduct of the war. They were an inevitable product of the war. As I had come to see it, America could not intervene in a people's war without killing some of the people. But to raise those points in explanation or extenuation would be to raise a host of ambiguous moral questions. It could even raise the question of the morality of American intervention in Vietnam; or, as one officer told me, "It would open a real can of worms." Therefore, the five men in the patrol and I were to be tried as common criminals, much as if we had murdered two people in the course of a bank robbery during peacetime. If we were found guilty, the Marine Corps' institutional conscience would be clear. Six criminals, who, of course, did not represent the majority of America's fine fighting sons, had been brought to justice. Case closed. If we were found innocent, the Marine Corps could say, "Justice has taken its course, and in a court-martial conducted according to the facts and the rules of evidence, no crime was found to have been committed." Case closed again. Either way, the military won.

"I was talking to your old skipper outside," Rader said. "He told me you seemed nervous."

"Well, how the hell do you expect me to feel? By tomorrow night, I could be on my way to Portsmouth for life." Portsmouth, the U.S. Naval prison, is a penal institution that was said to combine the worst aspects of Marine boot camp and a medieval dungeon. Nevertheless, a life sentence there was better than the alternative—execution by firing squad. That possibility had been hanging over our heads until only a few weeks before, when it was ruled that our case would be tried as noncapital. We were not to be shot if found guilty. A boon!

"Look, I don't want you thinking that way," Rader said. "I'm confident about what the outcome'll be. Even if you're convicted, we'll appeal. All the way up to the President if we have to."

"Terrific. Meanwhile I'll have brig guards playing the drums on my head with billy clubs. Christ, you've heard what it's like in that place. Can you imagine what they'll do to a busted officer?"

"I don't want you getting bitter. I want you to do well on that stand today. I can tell you that I admire you for the way you've borne up under all this. Don't mess it up now. Really, I would've cracked long ago."

"Well, I don't break, Jim. That's one thing I'm not going to do. I broke once and I'm never going to break again."

"Hell, when did you ever break?"

"That night. The night I sent those guys out there. I just cracked. I couldn't take it anymore. I was frustrated as hell and scared. If I hadn't broken, I would've never sent those guys out."

"Oh, that. We've been over that a dozen times. No drama, okay? This is the real world. We've been over that, over and over. You told them to capture those Vietnamese and to kill them if they had to. You didn't order an assassination. That's what you'll say on the stand and you'll say it because it's the truth."

Rader and I had argued the point before. We had argued it from the day that he was appointed my defense counsel. That had been in February, after several villagers from Giao-Tri lodged a complaint with their village chief, who went to the district chief, a Vietnamese Army colonel, who took the matter to the American military authorities in Danang. Two young men from Giao-Tri, both civilians, had been assassinated by a marine patrol. The investigation got under way. The battalion was meanwhile establishing new permanent positions forward of the old front line. The Viet Cong protested the intrusion into their territory with land mines, infiltrators, mortars, and snipers. My platoon lost several more men, including Jones, who was seriously wounded by a booby trap. The other two platoons suffered about sixteen casualties between them, and C Company became so short-handed that Neal had to make riflemen out of the mortar crews attached to the company, leaving no one to man the eighty-ones.

It was in this depressing atmosphere of steady losses that the five marines and I were called to battalion HQ to be questioned about what came to be known as "the incident at Giao-Tri."

Most of the particulars of that long and complicated inquiry have faded from memory. What remains most vividly is the mind-paralyzing terror that came over me when the investigating officer told me I was under suspicion of murder. *Murder.* The word exploded in my ears like a mortar shell. *Murder.* But they were Viet Cong, I told the IO, a hearty lawyer-colonel from the division legal section. At least one of them was. No, he said, they did not appear to be VC. That had been confirmed by the village police chief and the village chief. *Murder.* I knew we had done something wrong, but the idea of homicide had never occurred to me. Bewildered and frightened, I answered the colonel's questions as best as I could, but when he asked, "Did you tell your men to stick to their statements?" I blurted out "No!"

Accompanied by his reporter, a lance corporal who had tapped out my answers on a transcript machine, the colonel left a few minutes later with his papers, case books, and machine, all the paraphernalia from the tidy world of Division HQ, the world of laws, which are so easy to obey when you eat well, sleep well, and do not have to face the daily menace of death.

I was badly shaken afterward, so badly I thought I was going to break in two. It was not only the

specter of a murder charge that tormented me; it
was my own sense of guilt. Lying in a tent at HQ,
I saw that boy's eyes again, and the accusation in
their lifeless stare. Perhaps we had committed homicide without realizing it, in much the same way
McKenna had. Perhaps the war had awakened something evil in us, some dark, malicious power that
allowed us to kill without feeling. Well, I could drop
the "perhaps" in my own case. Something evil had
been in me that night. It was true that I had ordered
the patrol to capture the two men if at all possible,
but it was also true that I had wanted them dead.
There was murder in my heart, and, in some way,
through tone of voice, a gesture, or a stress on *kill*
rather than *capture*, I had transmitted my inner violence to the men. They saw in my overly aggressive
manner a sanction to vent their own brutal impulses.
I lay there remembering the euphoria we had felt
afterward, the way we had laughed, and then the
sudden awakening to guilt. And yet, I could not conceive of the act as one of premeditated murder. It
had not been committed in a vacuum. It was a direct
result of the war. The thing we had done was a result
of what the war had done to us.

At some point in this self-examination, I realized
I had lied to the investigating officer. Walking over
to the adjutant's tent, I called the colonel and said I
wanted to amend my statement and to exercise my
right to counsel. He returned to battalion HQ with
Rader, a tall redhead in his late twenties.

"Sir," I said, "that part in my statement where I
said that I didn't tell the men to stick by their statements? Well, that isn't true. I wasn't thinking straight.
I'd like it deleted and replaced with the truth."

Sorry, he said, that statement had been made under
oath. It could not be deleted. That was the law. If I
wished to say something else, fine, but the original
statement would remain in the record. The colonel
smiled, quite pleased with himself and the inexorable
logic of his precious law. He had me on another
charge. I made another statement.

Afterward, Rader and I had the first of our many

long interviews. He asked me to describe everything
that had happened that night.

"All right," I said, "but before I do, I want you to
read this. I wrote it while I was waiting for you and
the colonel to get here."

I handed him a turgid essay on front-line conditions. In a guerrilla war, it read, the line between
legitimate and illegitimate killing is blurred. The policies of free-fire zones, in which a soldier is permitted
to shoot at any human target, armed or unarmed,
and body counts further confuse the fighting man's
moral senses. My patrol had gone out thinking they
were going after enemy soldiers. As for me, I had
indeed been in an agitated state of mind and my
ability to make clear judgments had been faulty, but
I had been in Vietnam for eleven months. . . .

Rader crumpled up my literary ramblings and said,
"This is all irrelevant, Phil."

"Why? It seems relevant to me."

"It won't to a court-martial."

"But *why*? We didn't kill those guys in Los Angeles,
for Christ's sake."

Rader replied with a lecture on the facts of life. I
cannot remember exactly what he said, but it was
from him that I got the first indication that the war
could not be used to explain the killings, because it
raised too many embarrassing questions. We were
indeed going to be charged as if we had killed both
men on the streets of Los Angeles. The case was to
be tried strictly on the facts: who said what to whom;
what was done and who did it. A detective story. The
facts, Rader said, are what he wanted. He did not
want philosophy.

"Did you order your men to assassinate the two
Vietnamese?" he asked.

"No."

"Did you say they were to capture them, or to
shoot first and ask questions later?"

"No. They were supposed to capture them, kill
them if they had to. But the thing is, I must have
given them the impression that I wouldn't mind if

they just killed them. Jim, I wasn't right in the head that night . . ."

"Don't try temporary insanity. There's a legal definition for that, and unless you were bouncing off walls, you won't fit it."

"I'm not saying I was crazy. What I'm saying is that I was worn-out as hell. And scared. Goddamnit, I admit it. I was scared that one of those damned mines was going to get me if I didn't do something. You've got to realize what it's like out there, never knowing from one minute to the next if you're going to get blown sky-high."

"Look, a court-martial isn't going to care what it's like out there. You've got to realize that. This isn't a novel, so drop the dramatics. Nothing would've happened if those villagers hadn't complained. But they did and that started an investigation. Now the machine's in gear and it won't stop until it's run its course. Now, did anyone else hear you brief the patrol?"

"Yeah, Sergeant Coffell and the platoon sergeant were there."

"So, in other words, you gave orders to capture if possible, kill if necessary, or words to that effect. That's what you said, and there are two witnesses who'll corroborate you. Right?"

"That's what I said. I'm not sure if I completely meant it. I had this feeling that night . . . a sort of violent feeling . . ."

"Feelings aren't admissible evidence. I'm not worried about your psyche. The important thing is whether or not you ordered your men to commit an assassination."

"Damnit, Jim. It keeps coming back to the war. I wouldn't have sent those guys out there and they would never have done what they did if it hadn't been for this war. It's a stinking war and some of the stink rubs off on you after a while."

"Will you please drop that. If you ordered an assassination, tell me now. You can plead guilty and I'll try to get you a light sentence—say, ten to twenty in Portsmouth."

"I'll tell you this. I'll have a helluva time living with myself if those guys get convicted and I get off."

"Do you want to plead guilty to murder?"

"No."

"Why?"

"Because it wasn't murder. Whatever it was, it wasn't murder. And if it was murder, then half the Vietnamese killed in this war have been murdered."

"No. You don't want to plead guilty because you're innocent as charged. You did not order an assassination."

"All right. I'm innocent."

"So, what we have is this: you gave orders to a patrol to capture two Viet Cong suspects who were to be killed only if necessary. That's a lawful order in combat. And there are two NCOs who'll support you on that, right?"

"You're the boss. Whatever you say. Just get me out of this mess."

"Don't give me that 'you're the boss' routine. Are those the facts or aren't they?"

"Yes, those are the facts."

And so I learned about the wide gulf that divides the facts from the truth. Rader and I had a dozen similar conferences over the next five months. "Preparing testimony," it was called. With each session, my admiration for Rader's legal skills increased. He prepared my case with the hard-minded pragmatism of a battalion commander preparing an attack on an enemy-held hill. In time, he almost had me convinced that on the night of the killings, First Lieutenant Philip Caputo, in a lucid state of mind, issued a clear, legitimate order that was flagrantly disobeyed by the men under his command. I was fascinated by the testimony that was produced by our Socratic dialogues. Rader had it all written on yellow legal tablets, and I observed that not one word of it was perjured. There were qualifying phrases here and there—"to the best of my recollection," "if I recall correctly," "words to that effect"—but there wasn't a single lie in it. And yet it wasn't the truth. Conversely, the attorneys for the enlisted men had them convinced that they were all good, God-fearing soldiers who had been obeying orders, as all good soldiers must, orders issued by a vicious killer-officer. And that was neither a lie nor the truth. The prosecution had meanwhile marshaled facts to support its argument that five criminal marines, following the unlawful orders of their criminal platoon leader, had cold-bloodedly murdered two civilians whom they then tried to claim as confirmed Viet Cong to collect the reward their captain had offered for enemy dead, a reprehensible policy not at all in keeping with the traditions of the U.S. Marine Corps. And that was neither a lie nor the truth. None of this testimony, none of these "facts" amounted to the truth. The truth was a synthesis of all three points of view: the war in general and U.S. military policies in particular were ultimately to blame for the deaths of Le Du and Le Dung. That was the truth and it was that truth which the whole proceeding was designed to conceal.

Still, I was not without hope for an acquittal. Throughout the investigation, a number of officers told me: "What's happened to you could've happened to anybody in this war." In their eyes I was a victim of circumstances, a good officer unjustly charged. I had an above-average service record, and was normal to outward appearances. Those other officers saw in me a mirror image of themselves. I was one of them.

And the enlisted men were all good soldiers. There wasn't a mark on their records, not even for AWOL. Four of the five had been honorably wounded in combat. Two—Allen and Crowe—were family men. And yet, paradoxically, they had been accused of homicide. If the charges were proved, it would prove no one was guaranteed immunity against the moral bacteria spawned by the war. If such cruelty existed in ordinary men like us, then it logically existed in the others, and they would have to face the truth that they, too, harbored a capacity for evil. But no one wanted to make that recognition. No one wanted to confront his devil.

A verdict of innocent would solve the dilemma. It would prove no crime had been committed. It would prove what the others wanted to believe: that we were virtuous American youths, incapable of the act of which we had been accused. And if we were incapable of it, then they were too, which is what they wanted to believe themselves.

It was nine o'clock. Witnesses began to file into the neighboring hut, where the court-martial was being held. In our hut, the clerks continued to peck at their typewriters. Rader and I again went over my testimony. He told me how to behave on the stand: use a firm, but not strident, tone of voice; look at the six officers who were to be my judges when I answered questions; appear earnest and forthcoming.

I was called sometime in the late afternoon. Crowe, sitting at the defendant's table, looked very small. I confess I don't remember a word of what I said on the stand. I only recall sitting there for a long time under direct and cross-examination, looking at the six-man court as I had been instructed to do and parroting the testimony I had rehearsed a hundred times. I must have sounded like Jack Armstrong, all-American boy. Later, during a recess, I heard the prosecutor congratulating Rader. "Your client did very well on the stand today, Mister Rader." I felt pleased with myself. I was good for something. I was a good witness.

The trial dragged on to its conclusion. In my tent awaiting the verdict, I felt in limbo, neither a free man nor a prisoner. I could not help thinking about the consequences of a guilty verdict in my own case. I would go to jail for the rest of my life. Everything good I had done in my life would be rendered meaningless. It would count for nothing.

I already regarded myself as a casualty of the war, a moral casualty, and like all serious casualties, I felt detached from everything. I felt very much like a man who has lost a leg or an arm, and, knowing he will never have to fight again, loses all interest in the war that has wounded him. As his physical energies are bodily injuries, so were all of my emotional energies spent on maintaining my mental balance. I had not broken during the five-month ordeal. I would not break. No matter what they did to me, they could not make me break. All my inner reserves had been committed to that battle for emotional and mental survival. I had nothing left for other struggles. The war simply wasn't my show any longer. I had declared a truce between me and the Viet Cong, signed a personal armistice, and all I asked for now was a chance to live for myself on my terms. I had no argument with the Viet Cong. It wasn't the VC who were threatening to rob me of my liberty, but the United States government, in whose service I had enlisted. Well, I was through with that. I was finished with governments and their abstract causes, and I would never again allow myself to fall under the charms and spells of political witch doctors like John F. Kennedy. The important thing was to get through this insane predicament with some degree of dignity. I would not break. I would endure and accept whatever happened with grace. For enduring seemed to me an act of penance, an inadequate one to be sure, but I felt the need to atone in some way for the deaths I had caused.

Lying there, I remembered the South Vietnamese insurrection that had begun three months before and ended only in May. That insurrection, as much as my own situation, had awakened me to the senselessness of the war. The tragifarce began when General Thi, the commander of I Corps, was placed under arrest by the head of the Saigon government, Nguyen Cao Ky. Ky suspected him of plotting a coup. Thi's ARVN divisions in I Corps rallied to his support. There were demonstrations and riots in Danang, where Thi's headquarters were located. This prompted Ky to declare that Danang was in the hands of Communist rebels and to send his divisions to the city to "liberate it from the Viet Cong." Soon, South Vietnamese soldiers were fighting street battles with other South Vietnamese soldiers as the two mandarin warlords contended for power.

And while the South Vietnamese fought their intramural feud, we were left to fight the Viet Cong. In

April, with the insurrection in full swing, One-Three suffered heavy casualties in an operation in the Vu Gia Valley. Because of the investigation, I had been transferred from the battalion to regimental HQ, where I was assigned as an assistant operations officer. There, I saw the incompetent staff work that had turned the operation into a minor disaster. Part of the battalion was needlessly sent into a trap, and one company alone lost over one hundred of its one hundred and eighty men. Vietnamese civilians suffered too. I recalled seeing the smoke rising from a dozen bombed villages while our artillery pounded enemy positions in the hills and our planes darted through the smoke to drop more bombs. And I recalled seeing our own casualties at the division hospital. Captain Greer, the intelligence officer, and I were sent there from the field to interview the survivors and find out what had gone wrong. We knew what had gone wrong—the staff had fouled up—but we went along with the charade anyway. I can still see that charnel house, crammed with wounded, groaning men, their dressings encrusted in filth, the cots pushed one up against the other to make room for the new wounded coming in, the smell of blood, the stunned faces, one young platoon leader wrapped up like a mummy with plastic tubes inserted in his kidneys, and an eighteen-year-old private, blinded by shellfire, a bandage wrapped around his eyes as he groped down the aisle betwen the cots. "I can't find my rack," he called. "Can somebody help me find my rack?"

Meanwhile, the armies of Thi and Ky continued to spar in Danang. One morning in May, after I had been sent to division HQ, I led a convoy of marine riflemen into the city. They were part of a security detachment that was to guard American installations —not against the VC, but against the rebelling South Vietnamese troops. I returned to HQ in the afternoon. Division's command post was on Hill 327, which gave us a ringside seat. Looking to the west, we could see marines fighting the VC; to the east, the South Vietnamese Army fighting itself. Early that evening, I saw tracers flying over the city, heard the sound of machine-gun fire, and then, in utter disbelief, watched an ARVN fighter plane strafing an ARVN truck convoy. It was incredible, a tableau of the madness of the war. One of the plane's rockets fell wide of the mark, exploding near an American position and wounding three marines. The prop-driven Skyraider roared down again, firing its rockets and cannon once more into the convoy, packed with South Vietnamese soldiers. And I knew then that we could never win. With a government and an army like that in South Vietnam, we could never hope to win the war. To go on with the war would be folly—worse than folly: it would be a crime, murder on a mass scale.

The insurrection ended on May 25. General Walt sent a message to all Marine units in I Corps. In it, he said that the "rebellion" had been crushed and that we could "look forward to an era of good relations with our South Vietnamese comrades-in-arms."

The message shocked me. Even Lew Walt, my old hero, was blind to the truth. The war was to go on, senselessly on.

A few days later, my antiwar sentiments took an active form. The division HqCo commander ordered me to take part in a parade in honor of some visiting dignitary. I refused. He said I could not refuse to obey an order. I replied, yes, I could and would. I thought the whole thing was a mess, a folly and a crime, and I was not going to participate in some flag-waving sham. I was in no position to make such statements, he said. Oh yes I was. I was already up for the most serious crime in the book—one more charge made no difference to me. He could get somebody else to strut around to Sousa marches. Much to my surprise, I won.

It was then that I tried to do a bit of proselytizing among the clerks in the HqCo office. The war, I said, was unwinnable. It was being fought for a bunch of corrupt politicians in Saigon. Every American life lost was a life wasted. The United States should withdraw now, before more men died. The clerks, their patriotism unwavering, having never heard a shot fired in anger, looked at me in disbelief. I wasn't surprised.

This was 1966 and talk such as mine was regarded as borderline treason.

"Sir," said a lance corporal, "if we pulled out now, then all our efforts up to now would have been in vain."

"In other words, because we've already wasted thousands of lives, we should waste a few thousand more," I said. "Well, if you really believe that 'not in vain' crap, you should volunteer for a rifle company and go get yourself killed, because you deserve it."

Rader walked into the tent in the early evening. "Phil," he said, "they've come in with a verdict on Crowe. Not guilty on all counts."

I sat up and lit a cigarette, not sure what to think. "Well, I'm happy for him. He's got a wife and kids. But how does that make it look for us?"

"Well, I think it looks good. Just hang loose until tomorrow. You go up at oh-nine-hundred."

Curiously, I slept very well that night. Maybe it was my sense of fatalism. Worrying could do no good. Whatever was going to happen, I could do nothing about it. The next morning, I ate an enormous breakfast and managed a few quips about the condemned man's last meal. Then, long before I was due, I walked to the quonset hut, feeling much as I had before going into action: determined and resigned at the same time. I waited in the hut for about an hour, watching the same clerks sitting at the same desks typing the same reports. The red light on the coffee pot glowed and the fans whirred, rustling the pages of the calendar, which was now turned to July. The same crowd of witnesses milled around outside. Captain Neal was there. He looked worn and old. I went out and offered him a cigar. Smoking it, his eyes fixed on the ground, he shook his head and said, "We lost half the company. I hope they realize that. We'd lost half the company then."

At a quarter to nine, Rader called me back inside.

"Here's the situation. The general is thinking of dropping all charges against the rest of you because Crowe was acquitted. In your own case, you'd have to plead guilty to the third charge and accept a letter of reprimand from the general. What do you want to do?"

"You mean if I plead guilty to charge three, there's no court-martial?"

"Unless you want one."

"Of course I don't want one. Okay, I'm guilty."

"All right," Rader said ebulliently, "wait here. I'll let them know and get back to you."

I paced nervously for fifteen or twenty minutes. It looked as if my instincts had been right: the higher-ups wanted this case off their backs as much as I wanted it off mine. Wild thoughts filled my head. I would atone in some way to the families of Le Du and Le Dung. When the war was over, I would go back to Giao-Tri and . . . and what? I didn't know.

Rader returned grinning. "Congratulations," he said, pumping my hand. "The charges have been dropped. The general's going to put a letter of reprimand in your jacket, but hell, all that'll do is hurt your chances for promotion to captain. You're a free man. I also heard that the adjutant's cutting orders for you. You'll be going home in a week, ten days at most. It's all over."

We stood waiting in the sun at the edge of the runway. There were about a hundred and fifty of us, and we watched as a replacement draft filed off the big transport plane. They fell into formation and tried to ignore the dusty, tanned, ragged-looking men who jeered them. The replacements looked strangely young, far younger than we, and awkward and bewildered by this scorched land to which an indifferent government had sent them. I did not join in the mockery. I felt sorry for those children, knowing that they would all grow old in this land of endless dying. I pitied them, knowing that out of every ten, one would die, two more would be maimed for life, another two would be less seriously wounded and sent out to fight again, and all the rest would be wounded in other, more hidden ways.

The replacements were marched off toward the convoy that waited to carry them to their assigned units and their assigned fates. None of them looked at us. They marched away. Shouldering our seabags, we climbed up the ramp into the plane, the plane we had all dreamed about, the grand, mythological Freedom Bird. A joyous shout went up as the transport lurched off the runway and climbed into the placid sky. Below lay the rice paddies and the green, folded hills where we had lost our friends and our youth.

The plane banked and headed out over the China Sea, toward Okinawa, toward freedom from death's embrace. None of us was a hero. We would not return to cheering crowds, parades, and the pealing of great cathedral bells. We had done nothing more than endure. We had survived, and that was our only victory.

Epilogue

But the past is just the same—and War's a
    bloody game . . .
Have you forgotten yet? . . .
Look down and swear by the slain of the War
    that you'll never forget.

              —Siegfried Sassoon
              "Aftermath"

We were crouched in the second-floor corridor of the
Continental Palace Hotel, wondering if the North Vietnamese Army had finally invaded Saigon, hoping it
had not. The century-old walls trembled slightly from
the concussion of the seven-hundred-pound bombs
enemy planes were dropping on Tan Son Nhut airbase, five miles away. Every policeman and soldier in
the city seemed to be firing a rifle or machine gun.
The noise was deafening. Cringing in the hallway, we
had no way of knowing whether the shooting was
still directed at the planes or if a full-scale, street-to-street
battle for the capital had begun. Having spent the past
month observing the South Vietnamese Army losing
one battle after another, there was no doubt in our
minds that they would lose this one too. There was
considerable doubt about our own future. As we listened to the thud of bombs and the rattle of small-
arms fire, we asked each other unanswerable questions. Would there be enough time for an evacuation?
If not, how would we, American correspondents, be
treated by the Communist victors? In the final moments of chaos, would the South Vietnamese, feeling
betrayed by Washington, turn their weapons on every American they saw?

It was useless to speculate under the circumstances.
One of our more practical members suggested that we
forgo debating what might happen and find out what
was happening. After some hesitation, we left the shel-

ter of the corridor and walked downstairs to the lobby.
It was filled with frightened civilians and weeping
children who had been driven in off the streets by the
gunfire. The hotel's high, wooden door was now
barred, like the gate to a medieval castle. Four of us
opened it cautiously and went outside.

The small-arms fire was still heavy, but it seemed
aimed at the enemy jets that whined over the city,
heading with their bombs for the airbase. We saw no
green-clad soldiers in pith helmets—the enemy's distinctive headgear. There were quite a few policemen,
ARVN soldiers, and other newsmen running down the
streets. They were as confused as we. Together with
my colleague from the Chicago *Tribune*, Ron Yates,
I jogged over to the UPI offices, a block from the
hotel.

We found confusion there as well. One reporter was
melodramatically typing out a story while dressed in a
helmet and flak jacket. Teletype machines clacked ur-
gently. After reading the wire services' dispatches,
Yates and I decided that the final crisis, though near,
had not yet arrived. Enemy units were still a day's
fighting from the city. Assuming that the American
embassy would order an evacuation the following day,
Yates and I went back to the hotel to pack our gear.
It was dark by the time we finished. The air raid was
over. Through the window of my top-floor room, I
could see the flames of a burning fuel dump. Gekko
lizards clung to the room's white walls, the walls quaking from the secondary explosions set off by the
bombs, the lizards immobile in their reptilian indifference.

I dragged my gear down to Nick Proffitt's room,
which was two floors below. Proffitt, the correspondent
for *Newsweek*, had taken me in the week before when
an enemy rocket had devastated the top floors of the
nearby Metropole Hotel. Having survived one month
of the 1975 offensive in Vietnam, I had no intention
of being blown to bits in bed. Proffitt had kidded me
about my fear. I didn't mind. He could kid me all
he wanted. At thirty-three, with a wife and two children to support, I no longer felt the need to prove
anything to anyone.

Proffitt and I stayed up half the night, drinking the last of our beer, smoking the last of his dope, reminiscing about the past and speculating about tomorrow. Although we hoped the embassy would order an evacuation, we had our doubts. So far, it had refused to surrender its illusions that the ARVN could stop the North Vietnamese advance.

Like me, Proffitt was an "old" Indochina hand. He had been a correspondent in Vietnam in the late sixties and early seventies. When the final Communist offensive began, we were both in Beirut, based as Middle East correspondents for our respective publications. It was after reading about the fall of Danang in a dispatch coming over the newswire in my Beirut office that I had volunteered to go to Saigon. Reading the story resurrected long-buried memories of men and battalions, fire-fights and assaults, of nameless, numbered hills and joyless, rainy dawns on the line. Even after a decade's absence, I could clearly picture the part of Vietnam I knew best: the expanse of rice paddy and jungle west of Danang. It was as if a mental curtain had been raised, revealing a detailed battle map, with the dangerous places marked in grease pencil and the names of certain places underlined, names that meant something to me because men had died there. Hoi-Vuc, Binh Thai, Hill 270 and Charlie Ridge and Purple Heart Trail. It was difficult to accept the idea that they were now all in enemy hands.

I felt restless all that day and kept checking the teletype for the latest developments. It soon became clear that even ten years had not been long enough to break the emotional embrace in which the war held me. I *had* to go back, whatever the risks. I *had* to see the war end, even though it looked as if it was going to end in a defeat of the cause I had served as a soldier. I cannot explain this feeling. It just seemed I had a personal responsibility to be there at the end. So I sent a message to the *Tribune*'s home offices, offering to assist Yates—the paper's regular correspondent in the Far East—in covering the enemy's offensive. The editors said that was fine with them. The next morning I was on an Air France jet.

I landed at Tan Son Nhut on April 2, ten years and

one month after I had landed at Danang with the 9th
Expeditionary Brigade.

An accurate description of the final month of North
Vietnam's final campaign would require a book in it-
self. I am not even sure if what occurred could be called
a campaign; a migration, rather. The North Vietnamese
Army simply rolled over the countryside, driving on
Saigon. Except for a brief, hopeless stand made by a
single division at the provincial capital of Xuan Loc, the
ARVN offered no significant resistance. The South
Vietnamese Army broke into pieces. It dissolved.
There were terrible scenes of panicked soldiers beating
and trampling civilians as they fled from the advancing enemy. Late in the month, the atmosphere of dis-
integration became palpable. Not just an army, but
an entire country was crumbling, collapsing before our
eyes. The roads were jammed with refugees and routed
soldiers. Some of the columns were twenty miles long,
winding out of the hills and rubber plantations toward
the flat marshlands around Saigon. They stretched along
the roads for as far as we could see, processions that
seemed to have no beginning and no end. They
shambled in the rain and heat: barefoot civilians;
soldiers whose boots were rotting on their feet, some
still carrying their weapons and determined that their
little bands would stick together, most without weapons, broken men determined only to escape; lost children crying for their parents, parents for their children;
wounded men covered with dried blood and filthy battle
dressings, some walking, some lying in heaps in the
backs of ambulances; trucks, buses, herds of water
buffalo, and oxcarts creaking on wooden wheels. They
were packed densely and stretched down the roads,
solid, moving masses that rolled over barricades and
flowed past the hulks of burned-out tanks, past the
corpses and pieces of corpses rotting in the fields at
the roadsides. And from behind those retreating columns came the sound of bombs and shellfire, the guttural rumbling of the beast, war, devouring its victims.
There was so much human suffering in these scenes
that I could not respond to it. It was numbing.

Regardless of the outcome, I wanted to see it end. At the same time, a part of me did not want to see it end in a North Vietnamese victory. I kept thinking about Levy, about Sullivan, about all of the others, and something in me cried out against the waste of their lives. The war was lost, or very nearly lost. Those men had died for no reason. They had given their all for nothing.

I think these ambivalent feelings were typical of American veterans who, like me, were both opposed to the war and yet emotionally tied to it. After my discharge from the Marine Corps in mid-1967, I had drifted into the antiwar movement, though I was never passionately involved in it. I eventually joined the Vietnam Veterans Against the War, but my most explicit gesture of protest was made in 1970, when I mailed my campaign ribbons to President Nixon, together with a long and bitter letter explaining why I was opposed to American policies in Indochina. I thought, naïvely, that such a personal, individual act would have more effect than mass marches. About a month later, I received in the mail an envelope bearing the return address "The White House." It contained my medals and a curt note, written by some obscure functionary, which said that the Executive Branch of the United States government was not authorized to receive or hold military decorations; therefore, my ribbons were being returned to me. The writer concluded with the ominous phrase: "Your views about U.S. policies in South Vietnam have been noted and brought to the attention of the proper authorities." That episode sums up my career as an antiwar activist. My grand gesture of personal protest had been futile, as futile as the war itself. I seemed to have a penchant for lost causes.

Proffitt and I fell asleep in the early-morning hours. Lying on the floor behind the furniture with which I had barricaded the window, I was jarred awake when the North Vietnamese began shelling Tan Son Nhut and part of the city with rockets and 130-mm field guns. It was April 29. The bombardment went on for six hours.

Around ten-thirty, a reporter who had a citizens' band radio tuned to the American embassy's frequency announced, "They've just passed the word. That's it. It's one-hundred-percent evacuation. It's bye-bye everybody."

A hasty, undignified exit followed. Crowds of newsmen, embassy officials, Vietnamese civilians, and various other "evacuees" stumbled down the half-deserted streets toward the evacuation points. I passed a group of ARVN militiamen and smiled at them wanly. "You go home now?" one of them asked. "Americans di-di?"

"Yes," I said, feeling like a deserter, "Americans di-di."

Our motley column was eventually directed to a staging area across the street from a hospital. Columns of smoke were rising from the city's outskirts, and someone said that North Vietnamese troops had been spotted only two miles from where we were standing. We stood about, dripping sweat and listening to the steady thud of the incoming one-thirties. Finally, two olive-drab buses, led by a car with a flashing mars light, pulled up. We piled on board, some sixty or seventy crammed on each bus, the small convoy heading for Tan Son Nhut.

We were just passing through the airport's main gate as a South Vietnamese plane took off from the smoking, cratered runway. An old C-119 cargo plane, it had not climbed more than a few hundred feet when a spiraling fireball rose up behind it. There was a great boom as the anti-aircraft missile slammed into the C-119 and sent it crashing into the city. Our nervousness turned to fear, for we were to be evacuated by helicopter. Easy targets.

The buses stopped in front of a complex of buildings known as the Defense Attaché's Office. During the height of American involvement in the war, the complex had been called Pentagon East. It had served as Westmoreland's headquarters. The tennis courts nearby were to be the landing zone for the helicopters. We clambered off the buses, spurred on by a heavy shell that banged into the tarmac seventy-five yards away.

"Don't panic," someone said in a voice several octaves higher than normal.

Inside the building, we were lined up, divided into helicopter teams, and tagged. Every foot of every long corridor in the building was filled with Americans, Vietnamese refugees, newsmen from a dozen different countries, even a few old French plantation owners. The walls shook from the blasts of the shells hitting the runway. Small-arms fire crackled at the perimeter of the airbase. It was going to be a hot LZ. I hoped it would be my last one, and I tried not to think about those anti-aircraft missiles.

We sweated it out in there until the late afternoon, when the first of the Marine helicopters arrived. They were big CH-53s, each capable of holding as many people as a small airliner. "Okay, let's go!" yelled a Marine sergeant from the embassy guard. "Let's go. Drop all your luggage. No room for that. Move! Move! Move!" I dropped the valise I had lugged around all day and dashed out the door, running across the tennis courts toward the aircraft. Marine riflemen were crouched around the LZ, their weapons pointed toward the trees and rice paddies at the fringes of the airfield. Together with some sixty other people, half of them Vietnamese civilians and ARVN officers, I scrambled on board one of the CH-53s.

The helicopter lifted off, climbing rapidly. Within minutes, we were at six thousand feet, the wreckage of the South Vietnamese cargo plane burning far below. It was all so familiar: the deafening racket inside the helicopter; the door gunners crouched behind their machine guns, muzzles pointed down at the green and brown gridwork of the Mekong Delta through which flooded rivers spread like a network of blood vessels; and the expectant waiting—terrifying and yet exhilarating—as we looked for tracers or for the bright corkscrewing ball of a heat-seeking missile. One started to come up, but the lead helicopter in our flight diverted it with a decoy flare that simulated an aircraft engine's heat. We took some ground fire—fire from South Vietnamese soldiers who probably felt that the Americans had betrayed them.

My mind shot back a decade, to that day we had marched into Vietnam, swaggering, confident, and full of idealism. We had believed we were there for a high moral purpose. But somehow our idealism was lost, our morals corrupted, and the purpose forgotten.

We reached the coast about twenty minutes later. We were out of danger, out of range of the missiles, removed from all possibility of being among the last Americans to die in Vietnam. Relaxing their grip on the .50-caliber machine guns, the door gunners grinned and flashed the thumbs-up sign. Swooping out over the South China Sea, over the thousands of fishing junks jammed with refugees, the CH-53 touched down on the U.S.S. *Denver,* a helicopter assault ship that was part of the armada the Seventh Fleet had assembled for the evacuation. There was some applause as the aircraft settled down on the flight deck and as we filed out, a marine slapped me on the back and said, "Welcome home. Bet you're glad to be out of there." I was, of course. I asked him which outfit he was from. "Ninth MEB," he answered. The 9th Expeditionary Brigade, the same unit with which I had landed at Danang. But the men who belonged to it now seemed a good deal more cynical than we who had belonged to it ten years before. The marine looked at the faint blue line marking the Vietnamese coast and said, "Well, that's one country we don't have to give billions of dollars to anymore."

The evacuees were processed and sent down to the scorching mess deck for a meal. Most of us were giddy with relief, but one disconsolate diplomat from the American Embassy just sat and muttered to himself, "It's over. It's the end. It's the end of an era. It was a lousy way to have it end, but I guess it had to end some way." Exhausted and sweating, he just shook his head. "The end of an era." I supposed it was, but I was much too tired to reflect on the historical significance of the event in which I had just taken part: America had lost its first war.

The next day, April 30, the ship's captain announced that the Saigon government had surrendered to the North Vietnamese. We took the news quietly. It was over.